CRICKET'S
CHAMPION
COUNTIES

Lemmon. D

Cricket's
Champion counties

£ 14.95

CRICKET'S CHAMPION COUNTIES

David Lemmon examines the most successful teams in cricket's history.

17. FEB. 1992

BREEDON
BOOKS
SPORT

First published in Great Britain by
The Breedon Books Publishing Company Limited
44 Friar Gate, Derby DE1 1DA
1991

ISBN 0 907969 84 4

Printed and bound in Great Britain by The Bath Press Limited, Bath
and London.
Jacket printed by Arkle Print Ltd of Northampton.

Contents

Foreword

CRICKET, we are told, is a team game, yet the literature of the game invariably revolves around the deeds of the individual. There has long been a tendency to eulogise acts of personal heroism rather than acclaim the achievements of an eleven. This book is an attempt to balance that tendency.

There have been great men in cricket — Hammond, Tate, Freeman, Ames, Bailey, Gower — who have never been part of an outstanding county side. Equally, there have been lesser players who may have been denied individual glory, but who were integral parts of great sides. The Yorkshire team of the 1930s will ever be remembered through the names of Sellers, Bowes, Hutton, Verity, Leyland and Sutcliffe, but Barber, Turner, Fisher and Ellis Robinson, none of them Test players, were as vital to that Yorkshire side as any of their more noted contemporaries.

To qualify for consideration as one of cricket's great sides, a county should have dominated the game for some four to five years. There are stars that shone brightly and briefly, like Middlesex in the two immediate post-war periods, but the truly great sides attained a solidity, a sense of permanance, that lasted for several seasons. They were esteemed by their peers, and in the eyes of those who followed the game, they became the team against whom victory was most desirable because it was harder to come by. Until they won the Championship in 1979, Essex claimed that the greatest achievement in their long history was to beat Yorkshire at Huddersfield in 1935.

An examination of the outstanding teams from Hambledon until the present day reveals certain similarities in structure. There is a consistency in the batting, and, invariably, there is one batsman of considerable flair, a player rich in strokes. The attack has balance, the fielding is of the highest quality and the wicketkeeping top-class.

The men who have led the outstanding sides — Shuter, Hawke, Sellers, Surridge — are generally accepted as amongst the finest captains the game has known. One would not challenge this assessment with reference to the four men mentioned above, but one is always a little sceptical as to the way in which captains are evaluated. If a side wins, it is believed the captain must be good and vice-versa, but this is not always the case.

One thing that is apparent in examining the leading sides of each era is that their main strength lay in their bowling. This sounds a sacrilegious statement for a game in which it is the batsman who is consistently honoured and for whom, many would argue, the laws and conditions have been designed, but it is true. Arguably, only one county, Middlesex in 1947, have taken the Championship on the strength of their batting alone, and that side, with Robertson, Brown, Edrich and Compton, was one with abnormal batting strength allied to a remarkable rate of scoring. In every other case, a great side can point to a great bowling combination.

Lockwood, Lohmann and Richardson; Hirst, Rhodes and Haigh; Verity and Bowes; Lock, Laker, A.V.Bedser and Loader; these became legendary attacks, winners of titles, and when Stuart Surridge was confronted with the criticism that he did not really have a good batting side, his reply was short and simple: "We always scored enough." If you have bowlers who are capable of bowling sides out for under 150, then you only need batsmen capable of scoring 150. Massive scoring and drawn games were anathema to the ancients.

As we moved into the 1960s, a greater diversity of talent was needed to cope with the introduction of limited-overs cricket. Lancashire were the first to dominate in this field, to fathom its demands and tactics; and in recent years, the leading sides, Middlesex and Essex, have shown that it is both necessary and possible to be successful in all forms of cricket. A breed of one-day cricketers may have come into existence, but the wise and successful know that talent will dominate whatever the shape of the game and that a balanced side with potent bowling and fielding of high quality will most often come out on top.

David Lemmon
April 1991

Photographs have been supplied by The Hulton Picture Library, Adrian Murrell, The MCC Library and Popperfoto.

The Standard Bearers

Hambledon and The Good Old Kent Eleven

'THE Leicester youths having left the field of honour and retired to the *Bull Inn* to regale themselves after the fatigues of the day, to their utter astonishment a large body of colliers made their appearance in the market place, using every gesture that was hostile and alarming. The inhabitants of Hinckley became exceedingly alarmed and were obliged to have recourse to blows for their own defence. About 4 o'clock there seemed but one alternative: the Hinckley shopkeepers having shut their windows, a scene of bloodshed ensued scarcely to be credited in a country so entirely distinguished for acts of humanity.

'At length the colliers were worsted, and several left upon the field of action to all appearances in the most dangerous situations; the remainder were driven to the boundaries of their county. At present we have not heard of any lives being lost, though the weapons used in the contest were the most dangerous and alarming.'

This is not a report of soccer violence in the 1980s, but an account published in a Birmingham newspaper concerning events that occurred after a cricket match between Coventry and Leicester in 1787. Leicester had been bowled out for 13 in their first innings, ten less than Coventry, but they had eventually won by 45 'notches'.

The match had been played for a prize of 100 guineas, and the loss of money allied to the loss of local pride prompted the action of the miners from Bedworth and Nuneaton, many of whom were likely to have had bets on a game that Coventry had been favoured to win. So great had been the joy in Leicester that the team was met at the entrance to the town and the horses were taken from the shafts of the heroes' carriage so that it could be pulled in triumph through the town by the supporters. Some of the streets 'were illuminated for the occasion, and the evening was spent amidst the congratulations of their friends and the satisfaction of conquest'.

Winning was as important in the eighteenth century as it is today, although it was a time of pre-history as far as county cricket is concerned. Certainly Kent, initially, and Sussex and Surrey later, appear as dominant sides, but it is hardly likely that the sides they fielded were representative of the entire county. The Sussex side came mainly from Slindon, a village near Goodwood, and Surrey and Mitcham were practically synonymous. It was common for a town or village side to assume the name of a county, but the idea of a county championship lay more than a century in the future. Champions were the winners of local challenges; fervour was parochial.

Remarkably, the side that emerged from the second half of the eighteenth century as superior to all others came from a remote village in Hampshire. Hambledon, in spite of the B2150 and the adjacent vineyards, remains remote even by today's standards, yet it boasted the first great side in cricket history. 'So renowned a set were the men of Hambledon, that the whole country round would flock to see one of their trial matches.'

John Nyren, whose reminiscences give us such a vivid picture of Hambledon cricket at its high point, tells of the excitement aroused by one of the great matches.

'There was high feasting held on Broad-Halfpenny during the solemnity of one of our grand matches. Oh! it was a heart-stirring sight to witness the multitude forming a complete and dense circle round that noble green. Half the county would be present, and all their hearts with us — Little Hambledon, pitted against all England was a proud thought for the Hampshire men. Defeat was glory in such a struggle — victory, indeed, made us only a little lower than angels.'

John Nyren was the son of Richard Nyren, landlord of the *Bat and Ball Inn* and captain and secretary of the Hambledon Club for many years. By his own account, John Nyren was a sort of 'farmer's pony' to the side between 1776 and 1778 when he was 14, a position which helped him to learn the game. He asserted that no team in England could compare with the Hambledon men and gave details of the side that usually took the field when he was first associated with the club. Those details make an interesting study, for they give some indication of how the first team of champions was structured.

Richard Nyren was the heart and lungs of the side. He was a man of intelligence and integrity, whose knowledge of the game was highly respected. It seems that he was a natural leader, one whose authority was accepted without question. He played, of course, in the days when all bowling was under-arm, but he was considered quick left-arm. He also batted left-handed, had a sound defence and was capable of hitting the ball hard.

He was not as fast a bowler as Thomas Brett, 'beyond all comparison, the fastest as well as the straightest bowler that was ever known', but Brett did not have Richard Nyren's judgement of the game and, as a batsman, he was an intemperate hitter.

Brett and Richard Nyren were the main bowlers, with Barber and Hogsflesh the change bowlers. If not as quick as the first pair, Barber and Hogsflesh were sturdy and accurate medium pace, and John Nyren claimed that the quartet were 'tip-top men, and I think such another stud was not to be matched in the whole kingdom'. And this at a time when 'the bowling was all fast'.

After these four there was Lamborn, 'The Little Farmer'. The younger Nyren was quite amazed by Lamborn for 'he had the most extraordinary delivery I ever saw'. He was, to judge by Nyren's description, the original off-break bowler, and his 'deceitful and teasing style of delivering the ball' routed England on one occasion, the batsmen being unable to cope with 'that cursed twist of his'. Lamborn had little else to commend him as a cricketer. He was no batsman and no judge of the game, for he was not the brightest of men, but his bowling, which he practised assiduously, offered a somewhat eccentric dimension at a time when all was fast.

The wicketkeeper was Tom Sueter. He was reputed to have stumped many batsmen off the fast bowling of Brett and to let very little go past him. On top of this he was a forceful batsman, specialising in the cut. He was alert and adept at stealing the quick single. He was also noted as being one of the first batsmen to move down the wicket to drive, for it had been customary to play everything from the crease.

Another who was an excellent judge of a run was John Small, whom Nyren believed to have been 'the first who turned short hits to account'. As well as being one of the most accomplished batsmen of his day, he was an outstanding fielder at mid-wicket.

George Leer was also famed for his fielding, in the important eighteenth-century position of long stop, and he was a solidly consistent batsman. Edward Arburrow, known for some reason as Curry, was in the same mould as Leer, a solidly consistent batsman and a brilliant fielder in the deep. His fellow fielder in the deep was Peter Stewart, called Buck.

Buck was the wit of the side, eager in all that he did. He was a strong batsman, not in the same class as Sueter, but very useful.

The team was completed by Tom Taylor. Like Colin Bland of a later age, he was more noted for his fielding in the covers than for any other part of his game, but he was a most brilliant hitter, if somewhat impetuous.

There were, of course, other and more famous names that followed these into the Hambledon side, David Harris, George and William Beldham, Noah Mann, Richard Francis of Surrey, and James Aylward among them, but it is worth noting the structure of that Hambledon side of 1776-78 that John Nyren rememberred with such affection.

There was one class batsman, John Small, and three solid and consistent 'bread and butter' batsmen. There was a hitter who was a brilliant fielder, and, indeed, emphasis is put on the quality of the fielding of at least eight of the side. Sueter was considered the finest wicketkeeper of his day and had the added attraction of being a first-rate batsman.

Richard Nyren was a top all-rounder, with the bonus of being left-handed, and he was a thoughtful and revered captain. In attack, he was joined by one bowler reckoned to be exceptionally fast and two who above the average medium; and there was the off-spin of Lamborn.

Four pace bowlers, one of them left-arm, one exceptionally quick; a spinner; a wicketkeeper/batsman; five batsmen, one a class player, one a hitter and three of them dependable; the whole side good in the field — such was the structure of the first 'champions' side. It was not to differ very much 200 years later.

The County Championship was not formally recognised until 1890, but in the minds of the Press and in the minds of many who had offered patronage, it had been in existence for some years before then. Press and patron have had a greater influence on the game than many concerned with its administration would care to admit.

In the early years of the nineteenth century, most cricket matches were still between neighbouring towns and villages, for railway mania and a quicker, easier form of travel was yet to sweep the country. Inevitably, giants arose among the town and village clubs so that when Rochdale beat Manchester at Hulme in 1833 it was hailed as a great event. Rochdale had the assistance of E.Vincent of Sheffield so that they might meet Manchester on more even terms, and their victory meant that 'this was the first match lost by Manchester for several years, except that against Sheffield'.

Inter-county matches were very few and far between and were mainly in the south. Sussex, Surrey and Kent vied to be considered the strongest county, and passions often ran high among players and, particularly, among spectators, many of whom would have wagered large sums on the outcome of a match. When Sussex played England at Brighton in 1833 the supporters of the men from the south coast became so involved in the action that the gentlemen of the MCC declined to play against Sussex unless they were allowed to take their own umpires, 'considering the country umpires inexperienced'. This seems rather harsh on the Sussex umpires, for they were reported to have handled a difficult situation well, and 'England', some five or six professionals of repute supplemented by little known amateurs, were the victors.

In 1833, Sussex were deemed to be the strongest county and were challenged by no other side, but by the time Victoria came to the throne in 1837, the 'Good old Kent eleven' had come into the ascendancy. Their period of dominance was to last for most of the next 12 years, and there are those who would argue that the Kent team of the 1830s and 1840s was the finest county side that ever took the field.

It was a team that was great in every department of the game, and it was comprised of men who were honest, wise, steadfast and true and who were bound to each other by mutual affection and respect. It has not always been so among outstanding sides.

Kent excited passion and wonder among their countrymen, and when they played, first at Malling and then at Canterbury, the roads were choked from early morning by those eager to see the game. So great was their fame, so happy the feelings that they inspired that their deeds were celebrated in verse by W.J.Prowse.

And whatever was the issue of the frank and friendly fray,
(Aye, and often has his bowling turned the issue of the day),
Still the Kentish men fought bravely, never losing hope or heart,
Every man of the eleven glad and proud to play his part.

And with five such mighty cricketers, 'twas but natural to win,
As Felix, Wenman, Hillyer, Fuller Pilch, and Alfred Mynn.

Rarely can any county side have enjoyed the luxury of fielding
five men whom most considered to be the five best cricketers in
England.

Alfred Mynn was the greatest cricketer of his age, the finest to
adorn the game before the arrival of W.G.Grace. He was born at
Goudhurst in 1807, moved to Harrietsham when he was about
18 and played for Kent from 1834 to 1859. He was from a farming
family, and he was renowned for his stature and for his good looks.
He was a giant of a man, 6ft 1in tall, weighing 18 to 20st and
perfectly proportioned. He had massive hands and a presence, like
a great actor or ballet dancer, that made him instantly recognisable.
With his prowess and personality, he captured the imagination
of his generation. His immense strength and imposing stature was
complemented by a gentleness of spirit that was to inspire Prowse's
memorable epitaph —

Proudly, sadly we will name him — to forget him were a sin;
Lightly lie the turf upon thee, kind and manly Alfred Mynn!

He trained on beer and beef, and he took to bed with him each
night the family prayer-book and a tankard of bitter in case he
should wake thirsty.

He bowled fast round arm off a six-pace run and had practised
assiduously to attain an accuracy that was unapproached in his
time. His pace must have been frightening on the wickets on which
cricket was played in the mid-nineteenth century, and he would
pitch the ball on a perfect length on the leg stump for it to whip
across and hit the off. He was capable of turning the course of
any match with his bowling and with his batting. He was a
gloriously attacking player and, in 1836, he established a record
for the time by hitting 283 runs for twice out in two consecutive
matches.

Kent cricket had been in abeyance for five years before Mynn
first appeared for them in 1834 when Felix, too, was first seen
in the side. Felix's real name was Nicholas Wanostrocht. He was
a schoolmaster, an artist, a musician, an inventor of the bowling
machine and of tubular batting gloves, and the author of one of
the most famous of cricket books, *Felix on the Bat.*

Felix, in contrast to Alfred Mynn, was a small man, some 5ft 7in in height, and, in jest, Mynn would pick him up by the collar of his jacket and hold him suspended at full arm's length. Felix was a left-handed attacking batsman who could drive and cut with grace and power. He was an eager and outstanding fielder at point, a most important position in his day, and he was all that has ever been good in cricket. He played with a joy that infected all around him, and he never allowed his effort or his concentration to waver for a moment.

'He knew the whole science of the game, and he had a hand and eye such as no one e'er beat him at; and when he saw the ball was pretty safe to keep outside the off-stump, it was a beautiful thing to see him throw his right foot forward — for as you remember he was left-handed — and do a little bit of tip-toeing, with his bat over his shoulder; and if he did get the ball full, and it missed the watches, you heard her hit the palings on the off-side almost as soon as she left his bat.'

This tribute to Felix was paid by Fuller Pilch, who was brought from Norwich to West Malling in 1835 on a salary of £100 a year to manage a tavern and to look after the cricket ground. Seven years later, he moved to Canterbury where, for the next decade, he was the very spirit of the Kent eleven. He was the manager of affairs off the field, being responsible not only for the ground, but for the selection of the side and for spotting new talent. He was a generous and enthusiastic man, who encouraged many young players, and he imbued Kent cricket with the ideal that the public should be entertained and that players should be as active as a cat in the field.

Fuller Pilch was one of the greatest batsmen of his day and one of those men who appear from time to time in the history of the game to show that all is possible. He reached the summit just as round-arm bowling had replaced under-arm. The number of runs scored by batsmen had slumped dramatically, but Pilch showed that with the right technique all bowling could be mastered. He was essentially a forward player, and with his height — he stood over 6ft — and reach, he smothered the ball and placed it deftly through the field. He had a thunderous cover-drive, and he was an expert cutter of the ball.

If Pilch was the general off the field, Edward Gower Wenman was the general on it. Felix wrote of him, 'He had only to look and we moved, like the stars obeying the dictates of a great centre.'

Felix (Nicholas Wanostrocht), teacher, artist, musician, writer and a stalwart of the Good Old Kent XI. 'He knew the whole science of the game.'

Like Mynn, Pilch and Felix, Ned Wenman set standards of honesty and integrity which all in the team followed. He was a man who inspired confidence and respect. He was essentially a back player, sound in defence with a ferocious cut, but it was as a wicketkeeper that he was most admired.

He stood without pads or gloves, close to the wicket even to the fierce pace of Alfed Mynn from whose bowling he consistently pulled off the most remarkable stumpings. If there was no chance of a wicket, he was quite happy to allow the ball to pass through to Walter Mynn, Alfred's brother, at long-stop. This was a specialist position in the nineteenth century, and it was no sinecure, for the ball would often come through at a terrific pace. The injuries that long-stops sustained emphasises the quality of a wicketkeeper like Wenman who, with Box of Sussex, was paramount in his time. Wenman took some terrible batterings, but he was unflinching, and his judgement was considered without equal.

Wenman, whose family supplied seven men to the Kent side between 1807 and 1864, kept wicket to a variety of bowlers, for alongside the great pace of Alfred Mynn was the medium pace and subtle variations of William Hillyer. He could 'twist' the ball both ways, and he approached the wicket 'like a waiter carrying a lot of hot plates and anxious to set them down'. He was the perfect foil for Alfred Mynn and could bowl for long periods and with the accuracy and in the style that Wenman demanded. Like Walter Mynn, he was a fine defensive batsman, and he was also an excellent slip fielder, taking some splendid catches off Alfred Mynn's bowling.

Thomas Adams was another outstanding fielder who had the reputation of missing nothing in the deep field. He was not a batsman of top quality, but he was a most useful hitter and invaluable to the side.

For a brief time, too, Kent had the services of Edmund Hinkly, a left-arm bowler who made a sensational debut when he took 16 wickets for Kent against MCC at Lord's in 1848, including all ten in the second innings, but by then the great Kent side had begun to break up.

William Dorrinton and William Martingell, a Surrey man, were others who graced the side that was remembered as 'perfect sunshine on the cricket-field'. They were a band of brothers who were united by a common aim and who played the game with honesty and joy. They were well organised, well led and had among their number

Alfred Mynn, 'The Lion of Kent', a gentle giant who was acclaimed as the greatest cricketer in England before the arrival of W.G.Grace.

five cricketers who would have been outstanding in any age. In Alfred Mynn, they possessed one of the greatest all-rounders in cricket history. Most significantly, he was the demon bowler of his era. He was, too, an excellent fielder at short-slip, and his bowling was supported by the magnificent fielding of others. The good old Kent eleven were dynamic in the field, and they infected those who watched with their zest for the game.

Years later, at the *Saracen's Head* in Canterbury where he was host, Fuller Pilch told Fred Gale who wrote on the game as *Old Buffer* how the great days of Kent cricket came to an end.

'The fact was we all grew old together, and I often think some of us played a year or two too long; but then, the truth was, though I say it, the public liked the names of Mynn and Felix and Wenman and Hillyer, Adams, Dorrinton, Martingell — ay, and of Fuller Pilch too. And I think we kept the candle burning a little too long, till railways drew people away to take their pleasure somewhere else, and everyone was so busy that they didn't care for making a country holiday unless there was a lot of fiddling and dancing, and play-acting, and what not. They didn't come to hear a good old English song as they did then, so it has all drifted into committee cricket now, and our old backers are under the turf instead of on it.'

Pilch, like Mynn, Felix, Dorrinton, Hillyer and Martingell, became a member of William Clarke's All-England Eleven that toured the country and played against odds from 1846 onwards. This was the expanding time of travel and of cricket.

Sussex County Cricket Club had been established in 1839, although it was to be considerably reorganised 18 years later, and Nottinghamshire, also to be reorganised within 25 years, came into being in 1841. Surrey was founded in 1845. Within a few years, Surrey were to be recognised as the strongest side in England.

Amateurs and Professionals

Surrey, Nottinghamshire and W.G.Grace

SURREY County Cricket Club has enjoyed three golden periods in its history, and the first came some ten years after the formation of the club. In the three seasons, 1856, '57 and '58, the county side was beaten only once, and that by only three runs by Manchester at Eccles in September, 1857 when the Manchester side was strengthened by the inclusion of two redoubtable guest players, John Wisden and John Lillywhite. As Wisden took 12 for 70 in the match, and Lillywhite, bowling only in the second innings, had 4 for 29, their influence on the result is seen to have been considerable.

Most of Surrey's victories in this period were by substantial margins. Sussex, a very strong side, were thrashed by nine wickets at Hove in 1856, and the return game at The Oval saw Surrey triumphant by 240 runs. Kent were beaten by an innings, as were Sussex the following season, when even The North were humbled by the men from south of the Thames.

One of the factors that links this Surrey side with its great predecessors from Hambledon and Kent is the quality of leadership. Richard Nyren and Ned Wenman were singled out as mighty 'generals'. So, too, was Fred Miller. James Grundy, of Nottinghamshire and All England, was to say of Miller that he was worth 50 runs in the field to Surrey, and that at a time when 200 was an exceptional score for a side.

Miller led Surrey from 1851 to 1857. He was born within a few miles of The Oval and later lived in a house that overlooked the ground. He was not a man of gentle manner, and he did not suffer fools gladly. He played to win and those who played under him and those who played against him were soon aware of the fact. He was a leader who never asked anyone to do what he was not prepared to do himself. He was not intolerant, but he was a rigid disciplinarian, and he welded a group of highly talented, but disparate personalities into a combination that was near to being invincible.

His tactical grasp of the game was exceptional and his enthusiasm for it infectious. In the field he was inspirational; as a batsman he was courageous, ruggedly resolute and determined. His side accepted his judgement and authority without question. When he led, Surrey were supreme, and when he departed they began to fall into decline.

Miller had not played in the Surrey side which beat England at The Oval in 1852, although he was the county captain at the time, but that side already showed signs of greatness and within three years they were the mightiest in the land.

William Caffyn, Julius Cæsar, Tom Lockyer, Tom Sherman and William Martingell were in the Surrey side at the beginning of the decade, and all five were in the side which overwhelmed Sussex on the Royal Brunswick Ground, Hove, in June 1856. Martingell and Sherman were the opening bowlers and took 12 wickets between them in the match as Sussex were bowled out for 122 and 81.

Martingell was one of Surrey's first professionals. He was born in 1818 and played for Kent from 1841 until 1852, by which time he had also started to play for Surrey. He was tall, slim, strong, delivered the ball from a little below the shoulder and was recognised as being one of the best bowlers in England. So high was his reputation that Fuller Pilch had tempted him to Kent at a salary of £60 a year. Martingell was also a shoemaker and a gamekeeper.

Tom Sherman was from Mitcham, a great nursery for Surrey cricket, and had the reputation of being 'one of the fastest round-arm bowlers there has ever been'. He was also a fine fielder and an aggressive, if impetuous, batsman. The pair obviously offered a blend, for Martingell was able to turn the ball sharply from leg.

In looking at these champions of the early years of the game, it is interesting to note that each boasted a bowler of exceptional pace — Brett for Hambledon, Alfred Mynn for Kent and Sherman for Surrey. Each, too, claimed to have the outstanding wicketkeeper of the day. In Surrey's case, with Tom Lockyer, this is a claim that is not challenged. It was Lockyer who was the wicketkeeper when an England team first went on tour, to North America in 1859.

He was 'a tall, brawny man, with a pleasant smile on his honest countenance, with arms apparently covering most of the ground between short leg and short slip, such hands that the ball seemed bound to remain in them'. In the opinion of many, Tom Lockyer was the creator of modern wicketkeeping. It had been the custom, as we noted with Wenman, to allow fast deliveries on the leg side to go through to the long stop, but this was not Lockyer's style. He had remarkable agility and took catches and stumpings on the leg side which his teammates believed to be miraculous.

Lockyer was a brave, good-humoured and dedicated cricketer who must have taken some terrible batterings on the rough wickets of the day with the scant protection that he wore. He could also be a very fine hitter.

In the match at Hove in 1856, Surrey scored 148 to take a first-innings lead of 26. Burbidge's 41 was the highest score of a match in which no one else reached 30. No play had been possible on the first of the three days allotted to the game, so that when Surrey bowled out Sussex for 81 on the last afternoon, only 50 minutes remained for them to score the 57 runs that they needed to win. Chester was out with the score on six, but Lockyer was promoted to number three and hit 28 as he and Burbidge won the game for Surrey.

In the return match against Sussex at The Oval in July, Martingell and Sherman bowled unchanged in both innings as Sussex were out for 78 and 85. Surrey hit 297 in their second innings, one of the highest scores of the season, with Caffyn making 88 and Stephenson 57.

H.H.Stephenson had first played for Surrey in 1854. He was a first-rate batsman, a fine medium-pace off-break bowler and a very good wicketkeeper. He was an intelligent and popular man who was on that first England tour of North America in 1859 and was captain of the first England side to go to Australia in 1861-62. As a professional, he was never officially appointed captain of Surrey.

It shows the strength of the Surrey side that when they went to Tunbridge Wells to play Kent in August, Sherman, one of the heroes of the victory over Sussex at The Oval, did not bowl. This time it was Martingell and George Griffith who bowled unchanged in either innings and routed Kent, an ageing side, for 54 and 58 to give Surrey victory by an innings and 35 runs. Martingell had match figures of 10 for 67 and Griffith 9 for 35.

George Griffith was, in fact, making his debut for Surrey. He was a left-hand fast round-arm bowler who later also bowled slow under-arm. He was one of the most prodigious hitters in cricket history. At Hastings, in 1864, playing for the United XI, he hit the ball out of the ground four times in succession, and his left-handed batting inspired the line of verse: 'George Griffith gets a loose one, he will send it far away.'

Such was the talent at Miller's disposal that Giffith rarely batted above number eight in his early days and was not guaranteed a bowl. Miller was able to vary his attack to suit the needs of the occasion. When Kent were beaten at The Oval in June 1857, it was William Caffyn who did most of the bowling and took 11 for 53. Sherman and Martingell did not bowl in the second innings and Griffith very little in the first. William Mortlock who played for the county for 19 years and hit three first-class centuries was moved up and down the order to bat wherever Surrey wanted him. He was the most reliable of batsmen, 'Old Stonewall', and he went on the first three tours abroad by England teams, but in the Surrey side he hovered anywhere between number one and number nine in the batting order.

The professionals were, of course, the backbone of the Surrey side, and of the amateurs, only Miller, Burbidge and Lane appeared with any regularity. When six amateurs — and Lane and Fred Burbidge not among then — were fielded against Cambridgeshire at The Oval in 1857, Surrey had one of their narrowest of victories, by 36 runs. A week later, with nine professionals in the side, and Lane back, Surrey overwhelmed Sussex by nine wickets at Hove.

The following season was the pinnacle of achievement for this first great Surrey side. At the beginning of June, Sussex and Kent combined to challenge the champions at Hove. It seemed that Surrey had met their conquerors when Wisden and Stubberfield bowled them out for 38 in 37.2 four-ball overs. By the end of the first day, Kent and Sussex were 171 for 8, and they eventually made 204.

With his side 166 in arrears on the first innings, Miller chose to open the second innings himself. He made a typically gritty 31 and Surrey hopes began to revive. Caffyn made 81 and by the

The Surrey professional H.H.Stephenson, a talented all-rounder who captained the England side in Australia, 1861-2.

close of the second day, Surrey, 197 for 6, were 31 runs ahead with four wickets standing.

Another 52 were added on the final morning and the combined team were left with ample time in which to score 84 to win. Stephenson and Caffyn shared the bowling, although Martingell, Griffith and Sherman were all in the side. Within no time, Kent and Sussex were reduced to 16 for 5, and eventually they were bowled out for 59 to give Surrey victory by 24 runs. Caffyn took 5 for 18, Stephenson 4 for 36.

A predominantly amateur side beat Cambridgeshire at The Oval a week later, and a week after that, Nottinghamshire, the second strongest side in the country, made even stronger by the inclusion of guest player Diver, were beaten by nine wickets. Rain ruined the return match against Kent and Sussex, but Surrey held the upper hand, and then came the match against England.

Matches between Surrey and 'England' had been played long before the formation of the county club, but they had lapsed before being revived in 1848. The composition of the 'England' side was often dubious, but in July, 1858, the team that took the field was very strong indeed and arguably representative of the Rest of England. It was chosen by John Wisden and George Parr, captain of the Nottinghamshire side and manager of the All England XI, and it was captained by John Walker, co-founder and first joint-captain of Middlesex. One of Walker's six talented brothers, Vyell, a great all-rounder, was also in the side, and the third amateur was C.D.B.Marsham of Oxford University, who was considered the best amateur bowler of his day.

There were two Cambridgeshire players in the side, the much-travelled and highly talented all-rounder Alf Diver, and Robert Carpenter, approaching the maturity which was to earn him the reputation of being the finest batsman in England. Parr had brought with him three other Nottinghamshire players — fast bowler Jackson and all-rounders Grundy and Tinley. The side was completed by the formidable Kent bowler, Edgar Willsher.

The match began at The Oval at mid-day on Thursday, 22 July. England batted first and were quickly in trouble with Diver, Marsham, Parr and Tinley all back in the pavilion and only 13 scored. Wisden, who had opened, and Vyell Walker, brought about a brief recovery, but Stephenson dismissed them both and England were out for 62. Stephenson, 6 for 34, and Caffyn, 4 for 25, had bowled unchanged.

Miller opened with Charlton Lane, who was still up at Oxford where he won a blue for rowing as well as for cricket. He had been born in the parsonage which overlooked The Oval when it was still a market garden, and he was described as a 'model batsman' and an outstanding player of fast bowling. He entered the church and his talent as a cricketer was never fully realised. Against England in July, 1858, Lane did not last long. It was quite usual to open the attack with a fast bowler and a slow bowler, and Vyell Walker's slow under-arm proved too much for Lane, who was stumped by John Walker for four.

Miller and Stephenson added 40, and Surrey moved into the lead with only two wickets down. At the close, they were 185 for 5 with Lockyer 10 and Caffyn 74. This was one of Caffyn's great innings, and the next day he duly moved to 102 before being bowled by Jackson. This was one of only three centuries to be scored in the important matches of 1858, and the other two were hit for Cambridge University against Cambridge Town in May, a less significant fixture.

William Caffyn was one of Surrey's greatest cricketers. He was born in Reigate and had become a professional cricketer against the wishes of his father. He was a medium-pace bowler of quality, but it was as a stylish batsman that he was most valued. He was free and attractive with strong, flexible wrists and 'graceful to a degree'. He was neat, dapper and handsome and fielded brilliantly. He was one of those cricketers who was at his happiest when he had the ball or the bat in his hands. He played by the maxim 'get runs or get out', and he had a joy in the game that he transmitted to all who watched him. After the second of his two tours to Australia, 1863-64, he stayed behind to coach and he must take much credit for helping to raise the standard of the game in the Dominion. Arguably, when Caffyn departed, so did Surrey's greatness.

Possibly a little tired from his batting exertions, Caffyn bowled only ten overs when England batted again, needing 182 to avoid an innings defeat. This time it was the veteran Martingell who joined with Stephenson to bowl out the representative side for 154, so giving Surrey victory by an innings and 28 runs in two days. Heathfield Stephenson finished with match figures of 12 for 95. This was a momentous victory.

Caffyn recalled that he received the usual talent money and £13 that was collected for him to honour his innings. All the other

Surrey professionals were given a sovereign and Messrs Miller, Lane and Burbidge each received a prize bat. The Surrey club held a dinner to celebrate the occasion, and the historic victory is commemorated by a marble plaque in The Oval pavilion.

There are only two members of the side on whom we have not touched, Julius Cæsar and Fred Burbidge. Cæsar was one of a noted cricketing family from Godalming, and he was one of the first idols of The Oval crowd. He was a short, sturdy and steady batsman who excelled with shots to leg. He was a great wit and practical joker, but like many comedians he was temperamental and prone to depression when his form waned. Fred Burbidge was a courageous batsman and fielder and he was Miller's lieutenant. He succeeded Miller as captain in 1859, but he was not suited to the cares of leadership and, although there were to be future successes, in truth, the first golden age of Surrey cricket was at an end.

The young pretenders were already at hand. At The Oval in 1859, George Parr hit 130 and Nottinghamshire won by eight wickets, but Surrey were, as yet, far from being a spent force.

This was a time of considerable change and development in cricket. *Baily's Magazine* (of Sports and Pastimes) were thankful for to 'live in these new times' 'wherein men live, think, act, speak, write, and — above all — play at cricket with true and perfect freedom'. The magazine carefully studied the fortunes of Surrey of whom they were unashamed admirers and were gladdened that one advantage of 'the narrowing of success of Surrey' in 1860 had led to an 'increase of those 'best of all matches' — county matches' in 1861. Certainly, the popularity of county cricket was on the increase. In 1861, there were 12 inter-county matches; by 1864, the number had doubled, and it is from this year that we measure first-class cricket and the first 'unofficial' County Championship.

That the Championship was unofficial and was decided by the sporting Press is easy to understand as soon as we look at the discrepancies in the number of matches played by the eight counties. Surrey and Sussex played eight each, Cambridgeshire only three and two of those were against Yorkshire. Nor did any of the counties nourish any idea of winning a 'championship'. They played with a determination and desire to win each game, and that was reward in itself.

The matches between Surrey and Nottinghamshire were the highlight of the season. When the sides met at Trent Bridge in

July 1864, a low-scoring match reached its climax with Surrey, needing 62 to win, seemingly moving to an easy win at 40 for 1. Then six wickets fell for eight runs. 'Although the stumps ought (as previously agreed) to have been drawn at seven o'clock, still, in the true spirit of cricket, the game was continued (as settled by both sides) for 22 minutes longer to finish the match.' Surrey won by one wicket, but it should be noted that Nottinghamshire were without Parr and Alfred Shaw, two of their finest players.

Surrey ended up as 'champions'. The simple method devised by some of the Press was to deduct the number of losses from the number of wins and arrive at the following table:

	P	W	L	D	Pts
Surrey	8	6	-	2	6
Cambridgeshire	3	3	-	-	3
Sussex	8	5	2	1	3
Middlesex	4	3	1	-	2
Nottinghamshire	7	3	4	-	-1
Yorkshire	7	2	4	1	-2
Hampshire	4	-	4	-	-4
Kent	7	-	7	-	-7

The anomalies of the system are patently obvious, but anomalies were to plague the variety of methods devised for many years to come. Middlesex, in the first year of their existence, met only Hampshire and Sussex. Cambridgeshire had no properly constituted county club and their organisation was weak. Their match with Yorkshire on Parker's Piece was really arranged for the benefit of the leading professionals, and the match against Nottinghamshire was a last-minute arrangement and was played at Lord's. The significant factor about 1864 was that there was unanimity in deciding who was the leading county. It was not always to be so in the years that followed.

Of greater significance in 1864 was that in June, over-arm bowling was legalized at a meeting of MCC members in the tennis court at Lord's, at the end of the match between MCC and Oxford University. The debate regarding over-arm bowling had been raging for some time. In 1862, at The Oval, in the match between Surrey and England, Edgar Willsher had been no-balled by umpire John Lillywhite for raising the hand too high. Willsher had stormed off the field and play was brought to a halt as 5,000 bewildered spectators looked on. Peace was later restored, but some acrimony lingered among the professionals.

This was not the only cause for acrimony between them. The first tour of Australia, 1861-62, was arranged by a catering firm, Spiers and Pond, who, through their agent, offered terms to players during a North v South match at Birmingham in 1861. George Parr and most of the northern contingent rejected the terms; Stephenson and most of the Surrey players except Julius Cæsar accepted them. Stephenson came to lead the side by default.

The no-balling of Willsher and the breaking of ranks by the Surrey players over financial terms for the tour to Australia caused a rift between north and south which became wider in 1865 when Surrey beat Nottinghamshire at The Oval by one wicket. So incensed were the Nottinghamshire players at some of the umpiring decisions that had gone against them that there were angry exchanges after the game. The northern professionals had believed that the Surrey committee were behind the no-balling of Willsher three years earlier, and now they were convinced that they were again being unfairly treated. The breach was severe and Nottinghamshire and Yorkshire refused to play Surrey in 1866. There was a sharp rivalry between north and south, and the balance of power was now shifting to the north.

Nottinghamshire had long been heirs apparent to Surrey's crown, and the matches between the two counties were fiercely contested affairs. Nottinghamshire now held the upper hand and, although Middlesex were deemed the leading side by all authorities in 1866 and there were to be strong challenges from Yorkshire and Gloucestershire in the mid-1870s, Nottinghamshire virtually reigned supreme for the best part of 20 years. There seemed to be a bottomless reservoir of talent which meant that, by the end of the century, Nottinghamshire were even exporting quality players. More importantly, it meant that the side was being constantly replenished. Parr's side was to give way to Daft's side which, in turn, was succeeded by Alfred Shaw's side. All of them tasted success.

Nottinghamshire always seemed able to balance the need to bring on new players with advantages gained from fielding a settled side. Six players — Oscroft, Daft, Bignall, Biddulph, J.C.Shaw and A.Shaw — were in the Nottinghamshire side at the beginning of the period of supremacy in 1865, although Alfred Shaw played in only three matches and did not bowl a ball, and were still members

One of the greatest bowlers and captains in the history of cricket, Alfred Shaw of Nottinghamshire.

of the side that was to the fore seven years later. The side that Alfred Shaw led from 1883 to 1886 was virtually unchanged for four seasons.

Nottinghamshire differed from Surrey in that they were an all professional eleven, which could be one reason why there was, for a time, so much friction between Nottinghamshire and the Surrey committee. It was George Parr who brought the county to the forefront although, arguably, they would have been dominant much sooner had not William Clarke, nominally captain of the county from 1835 to 1855, turned his attention elsewhere. Clarke had formed the All England XI in 1846 and took with him into his eleven all the best Nottinghamshire cricketers so that for most of the next four years the county were not engaged in any matches.

The full potential of Nottinghamshire cricket did not begin to be realised until a reorganisation in 1859-60 allowed a committee to run the affairs of the club. George Parr had just succeeded Clarke as captain. Parr was not only a great cricketer, but a good organizer with a shrewd business sense. He took over from Clarke as manager of the All England XI in 1856, arranged matches against the rival United England XI and was a pioneer in leading teams to North America, 1859, and to Australia and New Zealand, 1863-64.

Parr was not a graceful batsman, but he was a mightily effective one, and by 1860 he was considered as the natural successor to Fuller Pilch as the best batsman in England. He may not have been graceful, but he was a most attractive and popular player because he was so aggressive, particularly strong on the leg side. A favourite leg-side target was the elm tree which stood at Trent Bridge until it was swept away in a gale in 1976. A branch from the tree, 'George Parr's tree', was placed on his coffin when he died in 1891.

He had a keen judgement, if an uncertain temperament, and he was among the first, if not the first, batsmen to allow the ball to pass outside the off stump without offering a stroke. He was a fine fielder with a mighty throw and in many ways he was a symbol of the final destruction of southern dominance which had started with Hambledon and passed on to Kent and Surrey. Not for nothing was George Parr known as 'The Lion of the North'. He led Nottinghamshire until 1870, by which time he had been in the game for 26 years.

Parr had several other veterans with him when he took over the Nottinghamshire side. John Jackson had been the leading fast bowler in the country, but by 1864 he was past his best, and he played his last game for the county in 1866. By that time, Robert Tinley had changed to his slow under-arm lob bowling and was to hold his place in the side until 1869 primarily as a middle-order batsman.

James Grundy was another veteran of many campaigns by the time that Nottinghamshire reached the ascendancy. He bowled briskly and moved the ball from the off to leg, always maintaining an impeccable length. He was also a very capable defensive batsman, a genial man who was a good judge of the game. In 1864, at the age of 40, he took 98 wickets in 18 first-class matches, but in his three remaining years with Nottinghamshire, he did not reach those heights again.

Grundy's decline afforded more opportunities to George Wootton who had come into the game later than most and played for Nottinghamshire until 1871. He was a left-hand round-arm bowler who had tremendous success at Lord's where he was on the groundstaff, and his most famous deeds were for MCC and the All England XI.

Nottinghamshire have always had a propensity for producing good bowlers and it is bowlers rather than batsmen who tend to win cups and titles for their sides, although there have been notable exceptions. The man who succeeded Jackson and Grundy as the spearhead of the Nottinghamshire attack was James Coupe Shaw, a left-hand fast round-arm bowler with the reputation for being the worst batsman in England. He played for the county from 1865 until 1875, so that his career coincides with the first ten years of their greatness. He took 44 wickets in his first season and headed the first-class averages, and in 1870, he captured 96 wickets in the season.

The generation of bowlers that succeeded J.C.Shaw, Wootton and Grundy was headed by Alfred Shaw, Fred Morley and Martin McIntyre. Martin McIntyre was a right-hand fast round-arm bowler who took 9 for 33 as Surrey were bowled out for 60 at The Oval in 1872, and Fred Morley, fast left-arm, was one of the great bowlers of the age. He played for Nottinghamshire from 1872 until 1883 and took more than 1,200 wickets in first-class cricket. Seven times he took 100 or more wickets in a season, and in 1878, he had 197 wickets at 12.11 runs each. He appeared in the first Test to be played in England, at The Oval, in 1880, and had match figures of 8 for 146 as England beat Australia by five wickets, and he went with Hon Ivo Bligh's team to Australia, 1882-83, and played in three Tests. Unfortunately, on the journey out, the ship was in collision with another, and Morley was seriously injured. He never fully recovered from this accident, played only one match for Nottinghamshire on his return to England in 1883 and died a year later.

The extent of his injury in the collision between the steamer *Peshawur* and the barque *Glenroy* off Colombo was not immediately recognised, and he played two or three matches in Australia before it was realised that he had a broken rib, a fact which must have hastened his death from congestion of the lungs. *Cricket,* the leading magazine of the time, considered that in the late 1870s and early 1880s 'no Eleven of England would have been considered thoroughly representative without the fast bowler who for some seasons rendered such efficient service to the Notts county team'.

In no way was the Nottinghamshire batting of the period inferior to the bowling. Charles Brampton, who was also a useful right-arm medium-pace round-arm bowler, was a most reliable batsman. His career ended in 1867, but he had helped establish the first flush of Nottinghamshire success. Tom Bignall's career lasted from 1863 until 1878, so that he spanned some of the great years of Nottinghamshire cricket. He was a powerful opening batsman and hit 97 against Surrey at Trent Bridge in 1867 to give his side victory while the rest of the Nottinghamshire batsmen were floundering against the spin of Southerton. The following season he hit 116 not out against Kent at Tonbridge and was given £5 in recognition of his century. His innings included three sixes, and as a six was only scored when the ball was hit out of the ground, his power is apparent.

His opening partner for several seasons was William Oscroft. Oscroft made a sensational start to his career when, playing for the Colts of England against MCC and Ground in 1864, he was opposed to Wootton and Grundy and hit 51 and 76 on a wicket of dubious character. Big scores were rare at the time and Oscroft was hailed as an outstanding batsman. He was an attractive, attacking batsman, strong on the leg side, and if he never quite fulfilled the promise of the sensational start at Lord's, he gave the county yeoman service for the next 18 years and led them in his last two seasons, 1881 and 1882, having succeeded Richard Daft as captain.

It is doubtful if any side has ever attained the highest honours without a batsman of outstanding quality. For Nottinghamshire, first there was Parr, and later there was Shrewsbury. Between them was Richard Daft. He played for the county from 1858 until 1880 and captained them from 1871 until the end of his career. In fact, 1880 was not quite the end of his career, for, in an emergency, he reappeared for Nottinghamshire against Surrey at The Oval in August, 1891, as an amateur. He was then in his 56th year and his son, Harry, was also in the Nottinghamshire side. The great days of the county had then faded, but the rivalry with Surrey was as sharp as ever and 45,000 people watched the three days of the game which Surrey won by an innings.

Richard Daft batted in the grand manner. He stood tall and upright at the crease, was quick on his feet and ever eager to drive. He had learned most of his cricket against fast bowling on wickets which would be despised today, and there was no better player of fast bowling in the 1870s. He was the master of the rising ball and contemptuous of the shooter. The statistical measure of his greatness can be seen from the fact that he headed the first-class batting averages in 1867; and in 1869, 1870, 1871 and 1873, he was second only to W.G.Grace.

By 1873, Daft had been joined in the Nottinghamshire side by Fred Wild and John Selby. Wild was a fine batsman who would probably have had a better record had he not been forced to keep wicket by the sudden death of Sam Biddulph in 1876. Biddulph had been a most reliable 'keeper for the county for 13 years. John Selby also found himself keeping wicket on occasions, notably in what is now recognised as the first Test match. James Lillywhite's party included only one wicketkeeper, Pooley of Surrey, and he was detained in New Zealand so that Selby opened the innings and kept wicket in the match against Australia at Melbourne.

Selby was a consistent batsman and hit four centuries in a career which lasted for 17 years and which covered the greatest days of Nottinghamshire cricket. He faded from the game in 1887 and he fell on hard times. He survived a criminal charge brought against him, but died following a stroke of paralysis when he was only 45.

The Nottinghamshire dominance had a temporary interruption in the 1870s when Gloucestershire were a power in the land, and at this time, the County Championship as we know it today was beginning to take shape.

In June 1873, following several months of discussion motivated by the Surrey club, a set of rules was drawn up to cover qualification to represent a county. They were as follows, and they were to stay in operation for many years:

1. No cricketer, whether amateur or professional, shall play for more than one county during the same season.
2. Every cricketer born in one county and residing in another shall be free to choose at the commencement of each season for which of those counties he will play, and shall, during that season, play for the one county only.
3. A cricketer shall be qualified to play for any county in which he is residing and has resided for the previous two years: or a cricketer may elect to play for the county in which his family home is, so long as it remains open to him as an occasional residence.
4. That, should any question arise as to the residential qualification, the same shall be left to the decision of the Committee of the Marylebone Club.

Some 30 years later, A.E.Knight, an articulate Leicestershire professional, wrote of these regulations that they gave 'a stability and firmness to the whole county cricket of the country'. That they were soon to be implemented can be seen from the story of William Midwinter and W.G.Grace.

Midwinter was a fine all-round cricketer who was born in Gloucestershire but was taken to Australia when he was nine, when his father went in search of gold. He impressed W.G. when he was in Australia in 1874, and Midwinter was in the Australian side that played in the first Test match, although the game was not sanctified by that name at the time. At the end of the Australian season, March 1877, Midwinter returned to England and became a regular member of the Gloucestershire side that were unequivocally 'champions' for the second season in succession. There was no argument that Midwinter was eligible to play for Gloucestershire, the county of his birth.

International matches had not yet taken on the importance that they were to gain later, and when the Australians arrived in England in 1878, no 'Tests' were in their programme. The party consisted of 11 players and there was the intention that Midwinter should bring the number up to 12. He played in the opening first-class match, at Trent Bridge, and was in the side that gained a sensational victory over MCC in under five and a half hours at Lord's. He appeared in three more matches for the Australians and was practising at Lord's prior to the game against Middlesex when W.G.Grace arrived. The great man insisted that Midwinter should be playing for his native Gloucestershire against Surrey at The Oval and bundled him into a carriage and drove across London.

The Australian manager, Conway, organized a posse to attempt to recapture the defector, and Grace and Midwinter were confronted outside The Oval. There was a heated argument and Grace called the Australians 'a damn lot of sneaks' for trying to bribe Midwinter to break his agreement to play for Gloucestershire.

The argument was continued in correspondence with the county asserting that Midwinter was a Gloucestershire man and had promised to play in all county matches. The Australians were accused of having attempted to induce him to break his commitment by offering him more money than the county could afford. Eventually Grace apologized for the strength of his language, but by then he had got his man and Midwinter played for Gloucestershire for six seasons. He also played for England and Victoria before returning permanently to Australia, saying that he was Australian to the core and again playing for his adopted country.

Midwinter's first game for Gloucestershire was against England at The Oval in July 1877. He was the only professional in a side which, the previous season, had been the leading county with an all amateur eleven. Grace's determination to acquire the services of Midwinter as a professional shows the importance that was now attached to county matches. It shows also how determined Grace was that Gloucestershire should remain the leading county. In 1877, their dominance was total. Uniquely, they owed their supremacy to one man — W.G.Grace. He and his two brothers, E.M. and G.F., filled three of the first five places in the batting order and did most of the bowling. It is worth looking at the record of Gloucestershire and of W.G.Grace in the two seasons, 1876, 1877.

1876

The Oval —	beat Surrey by 10 wickets (W.G.Grace 1 and did not bat; 5 for 68 and 3 for 64).
Hove —	beat Sussex by 131 runs (W.G.Grace 14 and 104; 0 for 26 and did not bowl).
Sheffield —	beat Yorkshire by 17 runs (W.G.Grace 19 and 57; 2 for 37 and 4 for 47).

Trent Bridge —   beat Nottinghamshire by 6 wickets (W.G.Grace 60 and 26; 1 for 31 and 5 for 52).

Clifton —   beat Nottinghamshire by 10 wickets (W.G.Grace 177 and did not bat; 1 for 69 and 8 for 69).

Clifton —   drew with Yorkshire —only two hours play possible on last day — (W.G.Grace 318 not out; 2 for 48).

Clifton —   drew with Sussex (W.G.Grace 78 and 7; 6 for 93).

Clifton —   drew with Surrey (W.G.Grace 29; 6 for 35 and 1 for 20).

1877

The Oval —   beat Surrey by 9 wickets (W.G.Grace 48 and did not bat; 4 for 60 and 5 for 42).

Hove —   beat Sussex by 84 runs (W.G.Grace 8 and 52; 4 for 35 and 7 for 46).

Sheffield —   drew with Yorkshire (W.G.Grace 9 and 84; 2 for 93 and 4 for 38).

Trent Bridge —   beat Nottinghamshire by an innings and 48 runs (W.G.Grace 3; 4 for 48 and 6 for 23).

Cheltenham —   beat Nottinghamshire by an innings and 45 runs (W.G.Grace 17; 9 for 55 and 8 for 34).

Clifton —   beat Yorkshire by 9 wickets (W.G.Grace 71 and did not bat; 5 for 31 and 4 for 88).

Clifton —   beat Sussex by 8 wickets (W.G.Grace 6 and 25 not out; 6 for 58 and 5 for 62).

Clifton —   beat Surrey by 10 wickets (W.G.Grace 4; 3 for 42 and 5 for 26).

The only match that Gloucestershire failed to win in 1877 was at Bramall Lane when Yorkshire, having led by 51 on the first innings, needed 139 to win. They finished on 121 for 9 with no accredited batsman left. This was Midwinter's first county match.

These two seasons saw Gloucestershire play 16 county matches, of which 12 were won and four drawn. In these 16 matches, W.G.Grace scored 1,217 runs, average 57.95, and took 125 wickets at 11.52 runs each. These are mighty figures in any age. In the 1870s, such a batting aggregate and average was phenomenal. No man in the history of the game has made as great a single-handed contribution to the success of his side as Grace made at this period. It should also be remembered that his feats outside county matches were equally prodigious.

Lancashire were another side to challenge Nottinghamshire's supremacy at this time, but, in truth, like Gloucestershire, they provided little more than a comma to interrupt the northern county's flow of success. Nottinghamshire contributed much to their own eclipse in 1881 and 1882, the first year being the year of the 'Nottinghamshire Schism'. This schism was, in fact, a strike by the Nottinghamshire professionals.

Alfred Shaw, Shrewsbury, Barnes, Morley, Selby, Scotton and Flowers refused to play for their county unless certain demands were met. Their grievance was really sparked by what they saw as preferential financial treatment given to the Australian sides who toured England. Shaw, the leader of the revolt, had long been an upholder of the professionals' rights, and he had refused to go to Australia with W.G.Grace's team in 1873 because the professionals were to be allowed only second-class travel facilities. Now he and his men demanded a formal contract of employment which would guarantee them an automatic benefit on completion of an agreed number of years service with a county, and they demanded the right to organize their own matches.

They received little support. James Lillywhite in his *Cricketers' Annual* saw their action as 'a deliberate combination against recognised administration'. Such anarchy was not to be tolerated, and the Nottinghamshire Committee dropped the seven offenders. The outcome was that a pattern of control in cricket was established which was to endure for another 80 years. Five of the 'strikers' were reinstated, 'after due submission', at the end of the 1881 season, but Shaw and Shrewsbury, judged as the prime movers in the conspiracy, were barred until 1882, when Nottinghamshire shared 'honours' with Lancashire.

The strike also placed the responsibility for the management of the club firmly in the hands of the Nottinghamshire Committee and sowed the seeds of the belief that an amateur captain was needed to control the professionals as he did in other clubs although the realisation of that ideal was still some years off. In 1883, Alfred Shaw, in his 41st year and veteran of many battles, was named as captain of Nottinghamshire.

In his early days, Alfred Shaw could be considered as an all-rounder, but he was to concentrate his efforts on his bowling and to allow his batting to lapse a little. Like Oscroft, he made his debut for the Colts of England against MCC and Ground in 1864 and, like Oscroft, he made a most significant impact, taking 13 wickets in the match. He was initially a quick bowler, but he slowed to medium pace with age and began to turn the ball far more. As a bowler, he had no equal in England in the 1870s, and his feats became legendary. In 1878, for Nottinghamshire against MCC at Lord's, he took 7 for 7 in 41.2 (four-ball) overs. He numbered W.G.Grace and Lord Harris among his victims, and the figures he returned in this match are indicative of his relentless accuracy. *Wisden* was to say of him that when it came to 'accuracy of pitch' he has never been surpassed. He could bowl for long periods without ever losing control, for, from the start of his career, he bowled with the easiest, most natural and economic of actions.

He always argued that it was not necessary to turn the ball prodigiously, that the most dangerous ball was the one that broke just enough to beat the bat. He insisted that the best of all methods was to bowl straight and to rely on variations of pace and flight and the batsman's impatient fallibilities. Grace said of him that he was 'one of the very few bowlers who could very quickly cause a batsman to make a mistake if he was too eager to hit. An impatient batsman might make two spanking hits in succession off him, but he would not make a third'.

In 1880, he took 177 first-class wickets at under nine runs apiece, and three years later, in his first season as captain of Nottinghamshire, when he was past his best, he took 67 wickets at 12.36 and was second in the national averages. It was not simply as a bowler that he was of value to the county, however, for his influence over the other Nottinghamshire professionals was immense, and his richness of experience and fine knowledge of the game made him an outstanding captain. Once he left Nottinghamshire the county's fortunes declined, and one of his team-mates was quoted as saying, 'We never went down the hill while we had Shaw with us.' In the four seasons in which he captained Nottinghamshire, the side were undisputed 'champions', and there are very few men in the history of the game who can claim a record equal to that.

It is worth considering the Nottinghamshire record during Shaw's period of captaincy. In county matches, it was —
1883 Played 12, won 4, lost 1, drawn 7.
1884 Played 10, won 9, drawn 1.
1885 Played 12, won 6, lost 1, drawn 5.
1886 Played 14, won 7, drawn 7.
That is a record which stands comparison with those of the leading

'The Champion' — W.G.Grace.

sides in any era, and it was accomplished by a side which remained virtually unchanged for all four seasons.

In four years, that side won 26 of the 48 county matches that they played and were beaten only twice, by Yorkshire at Trent Bridge in 1885, and by Lancashire at Trent Bridge in 1883, a match that was shrouded in controversy. The umpiring of Brownhill and Rigley caused much dissatisfaction and the match degenerated into a series of constant fatuous appeals. More significant were the objections raised to the action of the Lancashire bowler, Crossland. Nottinghamshire brought to the notice of MCC that, in their opinion, Crossland was not qualified to play for Lancashire as he still lived in his native county, Nottinghamshire. MCC accepted that Nottinghamshire were right to raise the matter, but they ruled that Crossland was qualified for Lancashire. The matter did not end there. At the Nottinghamshire AGM in January, 1884, the Nottinghamshire secretary, H.Bromley, included the following statement in his report:

'At a meeting held in the autumn your committee were appealed to by Lord Harris to support him in his protest against unfair bowling, and the committee feeling that the time had arrived when strong measures were necessary, decided not to play any counties having bowlers with deliveries open to suspicion. In accordance with this resolution your committee felt justified in declining to play Lancashire.'

Indeed, they did not play Lancashire again until 1886 when Nottinghamshire won by an innings at Trent Bridge and drew at Old Trafford.

As we have already said, the Nottinghamshire side during this period of triumph remained virtually unchanged for four years. Barnes, Flowers, Shrewsbury, Gunn, Selby, Scotton, W.Wright, Attewell and Sherwin were Shaw's regular teammates with C.W.Wright giving way to H.B.Daft or Shacklock by 1886. The strike of 1881 had had some beneficial effect in that it had given opportunities to young professionals on the Nottinghamshire staff, among them Dick Attewell, who was to develop into a medium-pace bowler and useful batsman good enough to play ten Tests for England against Australia. When the differences were resolved between the Nottinghamshire Committee and the dissident seven, Attewell could not longer hold a regular place in the side, but Morley's breakdown in health presented him with another opportunity, and from that point on he was an integral part of

Dour and dependable, William Scotton of Nottinghamshire.

the Nottinghamshire side, bowling with the same relentless accuracy that is associated with Alfred Shaw. Indeed, by 1886, he had taken over from Shaw as the county's leading bowler, sending down twice as many overs as his captain and taking 73 wickets in the 14 county matches.

Attewell and Shaw had highly capable support. Walter Wright may not have been a bowler in the top flight, but he was a very successful one. He was among the first bowlers to swing the ball and was able to disconcert the very best batsmen. He bowled left-arm and was to enjoy a second successful career with Kent after leaving Nottinghamshire at the end of the 1886 season.

The strength of the Nottinghamshire attack was its depth and variety. In Wilfred Flowers, another from the great nursery of Nottinghamshire cricket, Sutton-in-Ashfield, the county had an off-break bowler without equal in his day. On a wicket which gave the slightest assistance, Flowers was near to being unplayable, and he complemented his bowling with resolute batting and fine fielding. Flowers was the first professional cricketer, after the amateurs Grace and Studd, to accomplish the 'double' of 1,000 runs and 100 wickets in a season. In 1883, he scored 1,144 runs, average 24.86 and took 113 wickets at 14.95 wickets each in all matches. In a career that spanned 19 years, he hit 12,891 runs and took 1,187 wickets. He was in every respect the prototype for the hard-working county all-rounder who was to be an essential ingredient in every Championship-winning side in the twentieth century.

Flowers was not alone in bringing all-round strength to the Nottinghamshire side, for there was William Barnes of whom *Wisden* was to write, 'It may indeed be questioned whether Notts ever possessed a more valuable man, for over and above his splendid powers as a batsman he was for many seasons one of the best change bowlers in England.' He bowled medium pace and he batted with a rugged aggression. He was usually at number three in the order, ever adaptable to the needs of the moment if Shrewsbury or Scotton failed.

Such occasions were rare, for if the Nottinghamshire bowling was considered strong, then what word could one use to describe the batting. William Scotton was the excellent foil for the sparkling Barnes, who scarcely put a foot wrong on the 21 occasions he represented England. Barnes played with the zest of a man who loved cricket with all his heart and soul; Scotton batted often as if the cares of the world weighed upon him, but, in those four great years in the mid-1890s, there was no better professional left-handed batsman in England. He had a patience which could break the heart of any bowler and which could test the patience of the spectator. When, in 1886, he opened the innings for England against Australia at The Oval with W.G.Grace, he batted for 225 minutes for 34 and spent 67 minutes with his score on 24. His knock brought forth famous verse from *Punch* —

And the clock's slow hands go round,
And you still keep up your sticks.
But, oh, for the lift of a smiting hand,
And the sound of a swipe for six.
Block, block, block,
At the foot of thy wickets ah, do!
But one hour of Grace or Walter Read
Were worth a week of you!

What should also be remembered is that Scotton helped Grace to put on 170 for the first wicket, a record at the time, and England won by an innings to take the three-match series by three to nil. Scotton was Grace's opening partner in each of the Tests. He may not have shown in his play that he loved the game, as Barnes did, but it was all to him, and when, in 1893, at the age of 37, he took his own life, it was said to be as the result of having lost his place in the Nottinghamshire side some two seasons earlier.

Scotton's opening partner in the Nottinghamshire eleven was Arthur Shrewsbury. At Lord's, in the Second Test of that 1886 series, Shrewsbury hit 164, an England record which was to last only until the next Test when Grace hit 170. In essence, this symbolized the standing of the two men. There is no argument that W.G.Grace was the greatest batsman of his day — indeed of any day — but when, towards the end of his life he was asked by H.D.G.Leveson Gower to name the greatest batsman with whom he had been associated in the large span of his cricketing life, his reply was quick and decisive. 'Give me Arthur!' It is a statement that has passed into cricket folk lore.

Shrewsbury learned much from Richard Daft, on whom he modelled himself, adopting the same classical style. Like Scotton, he was the model of patience, but he had a richness of stroke play, a combination of power and delicacy and the effortless timing that is the heart of what we are pleased to call style. He was a great player on all wickets and his ability to watch the ball on to the bat and his mastery of back play made him supreme on a rain-affected or damaged wicket. He seemed impregnable in defence, and the story is told of how, in the days before there was a tea interval, if he were not out at lunch, he would tell Kirk, the Trent Bridge attendant, 'A cup of tea at half-past four, please,' and invariably Kirk would have to carry a cup out to him. There was a stillness in the man which attends only the very great.

At Lord's, in 1885, Nottinghamshire bowled out Middlesex for 128, but they lost six wickets in passing the home side's score. Shrewsbury had stood firm while wickets fell about him. At last he found a valuable partner in Attewell and the pair added 177.

Nottinghamshire finally made 415 and won by an innings. Shrewsbury carried his bat for 224, made in 470 minutes. It was the highest score to have been made in an important match at Lord's for 65 years. The following season, the season in which Shrewsbury played his great innings in the Test at Lord's, the closest that Nottinghamshire came to defeat was when they met Gloucestershire at Moreton-in-Marsh. Notts were bowled out for 124, and, inspired by Grace, Gloucestershire took a first-innings lead of 118. Batting again, Nottinghamshire lost Scotton at 32, but Shrewsbury and William Gunn put on 261, and the game was saved. Shrewsbury again carried his bat, finishing with 227 in 465 minutes. He was to make ten double centuries during the course of his career, an astonishing feat at that time.

Nottinghamshire were doubly blessed, for to accompany Arthur Shrewsbury they had William Gunn, another classicist, a fusion of power, grace and orthodoxy. Gunn was physically stronger than Shrewsbury, and he was always superbly fit, being an outstanding professional footballer with Notts County and England. He took longer to establish himself in the Nottinghamshire side than most, and he needed to curb his impetuosity a little before his potential was fully realised. He came to realise that there was no need for him to hit the ball in the air, and he matured into one of the most stylish and attractive batsmen the game has known. He stood to his full height, near to 6ft 3in, when at the crease, and he was an athlete whose every movement breathed grace. He was a batsman to emulate, playing with the bat perfectly straight and hitting through the off side with a power and beauty that is the loveliest sight in cricket.

Selby, H.B.Daft, son of the great Richard, fast bowler Frank Shaclock, the amateur Charles Wright, when available, and

Arthur Shrewsbury, the Nottinghamshire professional, whom Grace considered to be the finest batsman of his era.

wicketkeeper Mordecai Sherwin were others who served Nottinghamshire in these halcyon years. Sherwin was a strong, bulky man who had an immense appetite and capacity for work, and his strength left him almost undamaged compared with the other wicketkeepers of his time. He was the most cheerful of cricketers and kept wicket with a sense of showmanship that anticipated Godfrey Evans. He was appointed captain in succession to Alfred Shaw in 1887, but he held the post for only one more season, after which the amateur J.A.Dixon took over. Sherwin himself was to be discarded in 1893 much in the way that Shaw was discarded in 1886. Walter Wright, too, was to leave at the end of 1886 and, although what were arguably Shrewsbury, Attewell and Gunn's greatest days lay ahead, the greatest days of Nottinghamshire cricket ended with the departure of Alfred Shaw.

He coached in Sussex and played for them in 1894 and 1895, topping their bowling averages at the age of 51. At Nottingham, he had led a side that was balanced in structure, strong in self-belief, professional in attitude, tenacious in approach and had, in Shrewsbury, more than a spark of genius. Few sides have matched their impressive record over a four-year period, and when the supremacy of Nottinghamshire came to an end so did an important passage in the history of the game. Cricket was now on the eve of reorganizing in a way that would recognise the County Championship as being the premier competition and the title of County Champions as the most coveted prize in the game.

The Birth of the County Championship

John Shuter's Surrey

O N 10 December 1889, the annual meeting of the secretaries of the county clubs, for the purpose of arranging the programme for the following season, took place in the dining room at Lord's. Henry Perkins, secretary of MCC, chaired the meeting which was attended by representatives of all eight first-class counties and by representatives of 13 minor associations. While the secretaries were engaged in drawing up the fixture list after the main part of the business had been concluded, representatives from the eight first-class counties — Nottinghamshire, Surrey, Yorkshire, Kent, Sussex, Middlesex, Lancashire and Gloucestershire — adjourned to another room and held a private meeting to discuss the method by which the county championship should in future be decided.

Cricket, A Weekly Record of the Game reported: 'The meeting was, we understand, not quite unanimous, but a majority were in favour of ignoring drawn games altogether and settling the question of championship by wins and losses. As it was agreed to abide by the views of the majority, this decision was accepted as final.'

Subsequently, representatives of eight minor counties held a similar meeting and unanimously decided to apply the same rule to minor county cricket.

The significance of the meeting of the eight major counties was that it instigated the County Championship as an official competition.

The method of point-scoring (a constant source of debate in the century since), which was to last until 1909, was the one which some of the cricket Press had adopted since 1864, but there had never been a sense of unanimity. At different times various authorities had awarded accolades to different counties, and *Wisden Cricketers' Almanack* published no county table until 1888. From 1890 onwards there was to be no argument as to who were the official county champions.

There had been little argument since Nottinghamshire's domination was brought to an end after 1886, for Surrey had reasserted their claim to be considered the leading county and, although they could be bracketed with Lancashire and Nottinghamshire in 1889 and lapsed in 1893, they reigned supreme up to and including the 1895 season.

The first sign that Surrey were restored to their former glories came in 1887, when they twice defeated the hitherto all-conquering Nottinghamshire. The first match, at Trent Bridge, revealed the changing fortunes and attitudes of the two sides. With the departure of Shaw, a spark had gone out of Nottinghamshire cricket, and they seemed intent on a draw from the first ball of the match. On the other hand, Shuter, the Surrey captain, adopted methods which, although criticised in some quarters, were calculated only to try to win the match for his side.

At the time, a captain was forbidden to declare his side's innings closed. It was not until 1889 that a declaration was allowed on the last day of a match, and not until 1891 that a declaration was allowed any time after lunch on the second day. At Trent Bridge, on 1 June 1887, Shuter realised that the only chance his side, leading by more than 250 runs, had of victory was for his bowlers to have as long as possible to bowl at the strong and durable Nottinghamshire line-up. Accordingly, he ordered his later batsmen to throw their wickets away. Wood and Beaumont allowed themselves to be stumped, while Jones and Shuter himself knocked down their own wickets. Mordecai Sherwin and his side seemed unable to fathom Shuter's intentions and fell into the trap. Surrey won the match with 15 minutes to spare.

The return match at The Oval was played over the August Bank Holiday period. As the giants of nineteenth-century cricket, it was traditional for Surrey and Nottinghamshire to meet at this time, and only in recent years, when the August Bank Holiday has lost the joy and value it once possessed, has that tradition been violated.

John Shuter, Surrey's inspiring captain in the 1890s.

Nottinghamshire won the toss, batted first and led by 36 on the first innings. Eventually, Surrey had to make 205 to win on the last day. This was no easy task, but it was accomplished with four wickets in hand. 'There was a scene of excitement such as The Oval had not seen for a long time, cheers following cheers until the various members of the winning team had dispersed.'

If one wishes to know how important county cricket was to the people of the time, one only has to consider that 51,607 spectators paid for admission over the three days, and the attendance was said to be the highest ever known for a cricket match in England.

Nor did the interest in the matches betweeen these two great sides diminish over the years. Five years later, at The Oval in 1892, the paying attendance was 63,775. Nottinghamshire won the game by four wickets, but Surrey still went on to become champions.

They took the title in the first three years of the official championship, and, as Nottinghamshire had done a few years earlier, they fielded what was virtually an unchanged side throughout that period. It must have been somewhat galling to Nottinghamshire that two of their side, Bill Lockwood and John Sharpe, were Nottinghamshire exiles. Lockwood had been given a trial at Trent Bridge in 1886, but he accomplished little and the following year he accepted an engagement on the groundstaff at The Oval and qualified for Surrey. Similarly, Sharpe, fast medium-pace right-arm bowler, could not command a regular place in the strong Notts eleven and moved to Surrey, for whom he had immense success until 1893. So rich had been the talent at Trent Bridge that Nottinghamshire had also lost John Crossland, the very quick bowler with the doubtful action, and the redoubtable John Briggs to Lancashire, although it is fair to say that in Briggs' case, the player had lived and learned his cricket in Lancashire.

Sharpe's success with Surrey was quite brief, but it was significant. He took 102 wickets in 14 county matches in 1890 and 88 the following season, by which time Lockwood was turning his attention more to bowling. He had arrived at The Oval primarily as a batsman, but his fast bowling with a vicious off-break is for what he is now chiefly remembered. In three seasons, 1892-94, in all matches, he took 451 wickets. He headed the Surrey bowling averages in 1892, but he will always remain a shade behind two other Surrey men, Lohmann and Richardson.

Lockwood was not an easy man to handle, and his career certainly had its ups and downs, but Shuter, and later Key, were captains

An exile from Nottinghamshire, Bill Lockwood did yeoman work as a fast bowler for Surrey — a temperamental cricketer of immense talent.

capable of handling the strong-willed professionals that were the backbone of the Surrey side. In the history of the game, few sides have reached greatness without a captain of outstanding merit, and the Surrey side of the late 1880s and early 1890s is no exception. Indeed, it can be argued that Shuter ranks with Surridge, Robins, Hawke and Sellers as the greatest of county captains. He became captain of Surrey in 1882 and led them until the early months of 1894, when he decided that business commitments made it necessary for him to retire from first-class cricket. He was to write later, 'I think that I may look back on those years with some feeling of pride, and with the certain knowledge that they were some of the most enjoyable of my life.' No man had more justification for feeling proud of his achievement.

Surrey had always maintained the tradition that an amateur must lead the side, but John Shuter would have held his place in the Surrey eleven, or any other county eleven, on the strength of his batting alone. His greatest value, however, was the gift of leadership with which he had been blessed. It was a gift that set him apart from other men. He was cheerful, even-tempered, impartial and scrupulously fair. He had the warmth which could put men at ease, and he knew the strengths and weaknesses of those in his charge. He was ever encouraging, but he knew also when to be firm. His was no easy task, for he had command of a side of disparate and by no means easy characters, yet he fired them with his passion for the game and for Surrey.

He had an acute knowledge of the game, and his judgement was impeccable. Moreover, he captained from a single principle which the faint-hearted have never dared to follow, that in order to deserve to win a game, one must often be prepared to risk much. He played to win from the first ball that was bowled. A drawn game was poison to him and it is worth noting that, even in the four-year period of Nottinghamshire's supremacy, 1883-86, Surrey won 34 county matches to Nottinghamshire's 26.

Of course, Shuter had at his disposal a team of highly talented individuals. There was Maurice Read, representative of the new generation of professionals that was beginning to emerge. He was articulate, urbane, sober and thrifty, and, above all, he was a highly entertaining batsman. So was his namesake, the amateur Walter Read. He was one of those batsmen whose appearance sent a shiver of excitement through the crowd. He was essentially a front-foot player, a fine driver, but as time went on he became more and more obsessed with the pull, an obsession which often caused his downfall later in his career in the opinion of many judges.

Walter Read was a great favourite at The Oval, but none was more loved there than Bobby Abel, 'The Guv'nor'. He was the backbone of the Surrey batting. He was Surrey's leading run-scorer in county matches in 1890 and 1891, with 704 and 916 runs respectively, and from 1895 to 1902, eight consecutive seasons, he scored more than 2,000 runs each year. In 1892, he was overshadowed by Walter Read, who was at his dynamic best, blazing centuries against Sussex both home and away and against Gloucestershire at Clifton. Bobby Abel did not blaze. He stood under 5ft 5in, but he was in the first flight of batsmen, exceptionally strong in defence, patient, but with the ability to score freely all round the wicket. He was a happy cricketer and a born fighter. Surrey were to owe him much.

Kingsmill Key was the third amateur in the side. He was a most able batsman who had shone from his schooldays at Clifton College. He succeeded Shuter as captain and was successful although C.B.Fry considered this man of artistic leanings as 'quite the most silent and orginal captain ever'.

Increasingly we find in leading sides as we move into the twentieth century that core of honest, hard-working professional cricketers, the bread and butter players on whom the triumphs are really founded. The term brilliant is never attached to them, but it is their very reliability, the knowledge that with bat, ball or in the field, they will unfailingly contribute something that is of inestimable value that makes them the life-blood of a successful side. In Wood, Henderson and Brockwell, Surrey had three such players.

Robert Henderson was one of those 'bits and pieces' players whose contributions to Surrey's years of glory cannot be measured in statistics. Harry Wood was the bravest of wicketkeepers. He was smaller than Bobby Abel, and he stood up to the fastest bowlers of the day and never flinched from the terrible battering he took.

Bill Brockwell was a better cricketer than Wood or Henderson. He worked hard to become a respectable all-rounder and he blended well with the technically accomplished and precise Abel to make a fine opening batsman in his later years. Jephson, a future captain of the county, described him as 'the Admirable Crichton of the cricketing world', 'a bright, crisp player' who would force balls from middle and leg to the leg side boundary. There was to be one year, 1894, when he scored more runs and hit more centuries than any other batsman in England. Abel was second, and in their wake came such illustrious players as Gunn, Grace, Jackson, MacLaren and Fry. That was really the penultimate year of the second of the three golden periods in the history of Surrey, and by then their batting had been strengthened by the arrival of the great Tom Hayward.

Between 1887 and 1895, there were only two seasons, 1889 and 1893, when Surrey were not the leading county, and in the first phase of that magical and exciting period they were swept to the top by the genius of one of the greatest of all-rounders, George Lohmann. He was one whose talent was recognised when he was still young, and he was only 19 when he won a regular place in the Surrey side. Two years later, in 1886, he was an England player and took 12 for 104 when Australia were beaten by an innings at The Oval. The following winter he went to Australia with Shrewsbury's side and became the first bowler to take eight wickets in a Test match innings. Indeed, his 8 for 35 is still a record for an England bowler in a Test in Australia.

His feats for Surrey became legendary. He was a magnificent specimen of an athlete. He had fair hair and moustache, blue eyes set rather wide apart, and he had a lithe and supple frame with broad, strong shoulders. He was considered the 'perfect example of the Anglo-Saxon type'. Grace considered that, by the early 1890s, Lohmann had no superior as a bowler. He bowled well above medium-pace with a lovely action and he kept an impeccable length. Without any perceptive change of action, he could produce infinite variety. No bowler in England was more feared by batsmen.

To add to the genius of his bowling, he was a batsman who could turn any game with his quick-footed aggression and as a slip fielder he had no equal. In 1890, in county matches alone, he took 113 wickets at 12.66 runs each (in all matches he had 220 wickets) and averaged 29 with the bat. The following season he had 177 wickets in all matches, 132 at 10.87 in the county matches, and averaged 26.70 for Surrey with the bat. For seven seasons in succession up to 1892, he took more than 150 wickets each time. With such a spearhead the Surrey attack could sweep aside all opposition.

The saddest thing was that Lohmann's career was all too short. In the Championship year of 1892 there were signs that all was not well. His usual place in the batting order was number three,

'The Guv'nor' — Bobby Abel of Surrey.

but his 73 in the second innings of the opening match against Somerset was his only score of 50 in the season, and after a few matches he dropped down the order. He had some marvellous days with the ball, such as when he took 14 for 107 to bring about the defeat of Yorkshire at Headingley, but there were other occasions when he was less accurate than usual. In an ordinary bowler such days would have passed unnoticed; Lohmann was no ordinary bowler, and there was concern. The anxiety was proved to be justified when, in the autumn of 1892, it was learned that Lohmann was threatened with consumption. He was just past his 27th birthday and had been at the height of his powers. He was known affectionately as the 'Hope of Surrey', and the news that he must go south, to South Africa, for his health came as the greatest of shocks.

He was to return three years later, and there were to be some outstanding days, but he was never quite the same man again. He was also a man who knew his worth and drove a hard bargain. He was certainly not the easiest of men, but he was one of the very best of cricketers. His ability was always used to the full because his passion for the game was unquenchable. It was said of him that 'he loved not wisely but too well, crowding into 13 years more work than even his magnificent physique could stand'. He died in 1901 at the age of 56.

Remarkably for Surrey, as the genius of Lohmann was fading, another of the world's great bowlers first stepped out for the county. He was Tom Richardson, who made his debut for Surrey in 1892. Richardson, with the now formidable Lockwood, provided the south Londoners with a front-line attack which was to keep them at the top for a little longer. For Surrey, as for most other counties, fortunes have only been at their highest when they have had bowlers to whom one could apply the description 'great' without any fear of contradiction or of being accused of exaggeration.

In 1893, Surrey lapsed to fifth in the table with seven wins and eight defeats. It was a period of transition. Tom Hayward was just establishing himself and it was Richardson's first full season. He took 174 first-class wickets and returned some outstanding figures for the county, including 14 for 145 against Nottinghamshire. His action came in for criticism, however, as being illegal. He learned to straighten his arm and his action was never again suspect.

'His action moved one like music,' — Tom Richardson, one of the greatest of fast bowlers.

His record in first-class cricket over the next few seasons is worth considering —
1894 — 196 wickets at 10.32 runs each
1895 — 290 wickets at 14.37 runs each
1896 — 246 wickets at 16.32 runs each
1897 — 273 wickets at 14.45 runs each
1898 — 161 wickets at 19.54 runs each

Surrey's position in the table in these seasons was first, first, fourth, second and fourth.

As the figures above indicate, in the mid-1890s, Tom Richardson was a giant among bowlers. He became the first bowler to take 1,000 wickets in four consecutive seasons, and, in 1897, his nearest rival was exactly 100 wickets behind him. Sir Neville Cardus, whose judgements set the pattern of an era, wrote of him that he was 'the greatest cricketer who ever took to fast bowling'.

'His action moved one like music because it was so rhythmical. He ran to the wicket a long distance, and at the bowling crease his terminating leap made you catch breath. His break-back most cricketers of his day counted among the seven wonders of the game. He could pitch a ball outside the wicket on the hardest turf and hit the leg stump.'

He was a kind and gentle giant possessed of a fine physique and inexhaustible energy which passed unfettered into his fast bowling. Of him, *Wisden* said that he was 'perhaps the greatest of all fast bowlers'.

Richardson's rise and best years coincided with the final flourish of Surrey's greatness. Hobbs, Fender, Sandham, Strudwick and other great men were to come, but it was to be more than 50 years before The Oval was to see again a team that could compare with Shuter's men.

Although they were to take the title in 1899, and take it well, Surrey's success in 1895 really marked the end of the great days. It also marked the beginning of a new and broader system.

In April, 1894, a meeting of the captains of the nine first-class counties (Somerset had been elevated in 1891) decided to put before the annual meeting of MCC the following resolution:

That the matches played by the following four counties — Derbyshire, Warwickshire, Essex and Leicestershire — against the nine counties at present styled first-class, and also against one another and against the MCC, should be regarded as first-class matches, and the records of the players engaged in these matches shall be included in the list of first-class averages.

This was agreed and in October of the same year, MCC issued a circular which stated that, at the request of the counties, they would in future regulate the County Championship. Hampshire, too, had been reinstated as first-class so that 14 sides were to compete for the Championship in 1895. In effect, it was the beginning of the competition as we know it today. Worcestershire were to be added to the list in 1899, Northamptonshire in 1905, Glamorgan in 1921, and Durham will be admitted to the County Championship for 1992.

The first stipulation that MCC made was that each county must play a minimum of eight home and eight away matches. Derbyshire, Essex, Hampshire and Leicestershire were just able to meet this requirement. Surrey and Yorkshire played a full complement of county fixtures. The same point-scoring system was maintained — one point for a win, one deducted for a loss — but as counties played a different number of matches, the final order was worked out on a percentage basis, proportion of points gained to games completed. So the top of the County Championship in 1895 was as follows:

	P	W	D	L	Pts	%
Surrey	26	17	5	4	13	61.90
Lancashire	21	14	3	4	10	55.55

In effect, drawn and abandoned games were totally ignored, but the system was only effective while the proportion of drawn games was small — and the number of draws began to increase dramatically within the next 15 years.

Betwen 1896 and the outbreak of the World War One, seven different counties were to win the Championship. One of those counties was to take the title in eight of those years, five times within the space of seven seasons, and it is to them that we should now turn our attention — Yorkshire and their captain for 27 years, Lord Hawke.

The Flowering of the White Rose

Lord Hawke and Yorkshire

IT HAS not been uncommon in the past 50 or 60 years for a Yorkshireman to hustle his pregnant wife into a car and drive furiously across county borders so that the new child would be born in Yorkshire and so be eligible to represent that county at cricket. In contemplating this custom, we may feel that it is somewhat ironic that the man who infused Yorkshire cricket with a passionate dedication and pride and who was the most influential member of the county club for a period of 45 years, during which time 20 Championships were won, was himself born in Lincolnshire.

Hon Martin Bladen Hawke was born in Willingham Rectory, Gainsborough, in August 1860. He first played for Yorkshire in 1881, declined to take over the captaincy which was destined for him until he felt ready to take over, and happily served under the professional Tom Emmett for two years. Emmett, a talented all-rounder and a particularly fine medium-pace bowler, had at his disposal some equally talented cricketers. Indeed, Yorkshire had always had fine cricketers, but they had never achieved the fusion or the discipline that makes an outstanding side. Hawke, who was to become seventh Baron Hawke in 1887, was to change all that.

He was appointed captain of Yorkshire in 1883 and was to hold the position until 1910. No county captain has had a longer reign. It is indicative of the esteem in which he was held by his county that he was made captain of Yorkshire two years before he was appointed captain of Cambridge University.

Lord Hawke, the father of Yorkshire cricket.

Hawke was a batsman good enough to hold his place in any county side, but it is as a leader, a reformer and an administrator that he is best remembered. It is necessary first to consider the standing of the professional cricketer when Hawke joined Yorkshire.

The qualification restrictions imposed in 1873 had meant a loss of income for some players and, for the most part, professional cricketers were poorly paid. Evidence of a discontent with their lot is to be found in the Nottinghamshire players' schism of 1881 and in the 'strike' by five professionals at the Test match between England and Australia at The Oval in 1896. In a dispute over match fees, Abel, Hayward, Richardson, Gunn and Lohmann refused to play for England. The first three relented, but Gunn and Lohmann did not play. The professional's bargaining power was restricted because the rules bound him to one county; but within that county he was often idolised as a hero in a game in which interest was growing rapidly and at which attendances were large. That hero-worship had its attendant dangers, for several players were plied with drink, and a fondness for alcohol was a problem for many cricketers. Lockwood, the Surrey and England bowler, was only re-engaged for 1902 on the understanding that he signed the pledge, and Tom Richardson was among scores of others who had drink problems. Yorkshire were among the most intemperate of county sides, and with this intemperance had gone a lackadaisical approach to the game. Their many fine players had failed to achieve the results that their talent warranted.

Ephraim Lockwood was one of the best batsmen of the time, but as captain of Yorkshire he had a lack of self-control that was hardly likely to be conducive to success. He was not helped by the fact that he had under him some wilful personalities, whom he was neither willing nor able to command.

He was succeeded by Tom Emmett, a jovial man with a large nose and ready wit. He was a fine fast left-arm bowler and a great enthusiast who was much loved, but he achieved little as captain. It was said that he was too kind to run an opponent out. Moreover, he was so caught up in the game that he sometimes forgot that his was the responsibility for making decisions. He was even said to have muttered imprecations because he had been bowling too long and had not been taken off. The team he led was easy-going and undisciplined. Martin Hawke was to change all that.

Lord Hawke was Yorkshire's first amateur captain and he was

quick to recognise the difficulties that had existed under a professional skipper. He believed that the professional could be nagged by his fellows in the dressing-room, that he could be the butt for grumblers and that he could never exercise the same authority as an amateur. Hawke also perceived the grievances attendant on the system of talent money.

'The remuneration was a sovereign for a score of 50, and the same sum for six wickets. Sides suffered badly from a captain or a captain's chum being kept on to bowl too long in order to get his talent money.'

Hawke abandoned this system and awarded marks of his own. He would give more for 20 on a turning wicket than for 50 on a batsman's dream, and he rewarded good fielding, wicketkeeping, endeavour, enthusiasm and courage. He kept a meticulous record and at the end of the season his team gathered at Wighill Hall, there to be given the envelopes which contained their marks and their merit pay. He delighted in watching their faces as they opened their envelopes, and he was to write later: 'During all the seasons I allocated marks, I never had one grumble or remonstrance as to how I had doled out the rewards.'

This was but one of Hawke's many innovations, not accomplished overnight, but over a period of some years. He created the White Rose badge for the county. He abolished separate gates for the amateurs and professionals and he fought to establish winter pay. No man did more for the lot of the professional cricketer. In return he expected loyalty, self-discipline and total commitment to the cause of Yorkshire cricket. He was single-minded, determined and exerted a strength of discipline that had not been seen before in county cricket.

One of Hawke's first major acts was to dispense with the services of Edmund Peate, the greatest slow left-arm bowler of the age. In the summer of 1886, it had become evident that Peate was overweight and, after two games the following season, neither of them a first-class county match, his days with Yorkshire were ended. As *Wisden* was to remark in future years: 'He would have lasted longer if he had ordered his life more carefully.' Hawke was determined to rid his side of unruly and intemperate elements, and Peate was the first to go, but he was not the last.

Peate was the first in a long line of great slow left-arm bowlers associated with Yorkshire which stretches through Rhodes and Verity to Wardle. The second in the line was Robert Peel. In Test matches, Peel took 102 wickets at 16.81 runs each, and in all first-class matches he claimed 1,776 wickets at a slightly lower cost, yet he was to be dismissed from the Yorkshire eleven less than a year after taking six for 23 and helping to bowl out Australia for 44 at The Oval, so giving England a sensational victory. Indeed, in his last game for Yorkshire, he scored 40 and took five for 71 against Middlesex at Bramall Lane, Sheffield, in August 1897.

There are conflicting accounts about that last match at Bramall Lane, but there are some consistencies, too. Peel was idolised as a great all-rounder. The renowned Victorian actor, Henry Ainley, considered that the finest moment of his life was when he carried Peel's bag from the station to the ground. Such adulation and hospitality gave Peel a thirst which 'stretched from morning to evening'. In the fatal game at Bramall Lane he became very drunk and, despite the efforts of his colleagues to prevent him, he took the field with the effects of drink upon him still very apparent. Hawke told him to leave the field, but Peel replied cheerily that he was in fine form, turned away from the wicket and bowled in the direction of the sight-screen. There are versions of the story which suggest, too, that he urinated on the outfield. Hawke took him firmly by the arm and led him gently from the field and out of Yorkshire cricket. It was not an act that gave Hawke pleasure.

'It had to be done for the sake of discipline and for the good of cricket. Nothing ever gave me so much pain. I did not care for the fact that, by dispensing with our foremost all-rounder, we were losing the Championship. What hurt me was publicly censuring a valued comrade and a real good fellow. Peel thoroughly proved he was loyal, for he never bore me malice for my decision to dismiss him.'

Hawke's strength was that he had the courage to take such actions and to stand by them for the good of Yorkshire cricket. He loathed the waste of talent, and of another whose career was short and profligate, Joseph Merrett Preton, an exciting all-rounder, he wrote that he was 'an irresponsible individual, who, had he possessed the least self-restraint, might have become one of the finest cricketers Yorkshire ever produced.'

For Hawke, Yorkshire cricket was the most important thing in the world, and it was he who created the air of pride and invincibility which was to extend until World War Two and which others have been striving to recreate ever since. He immediately lifted the standard of the Yorkshire fielding and insisted upon a more professional approach to every game. Above all, he infused his men with the belief that there was something special, even superior, about being a Yorkshireman. There were occasions when Ted Wainwright was not released to play for England because Yorkshire needed him for a county match, and for the match against Australia at The Oval in August, 1890, Yorkshire refused to allow Peel and Ulyett to play for England as both were required for Yorkshire's match against Middlesex at Bradford. Stoddart also preferred to play for Middlesex in this match rather than for England, although neither Middlesex nor Yorkshire were real Championship contenders.

Hawke led Yorkshire to the title for the first time in 1893. They were second the following year, third in 1895 and Champions again in 1896. They finished fourth in 1897, the year of Peel's dismissal, but took the title again the following year. They were third in 1899, and then came the three great years.

They began at Bradford on 7 May 1900, in most sensational manner. Worcestershire were the visitors and, batting first, they were bowled out by Rhodes and Haigh for 43. Arnold scored 20, and no other batsman reached double figures. Rhodes had 4 for 16, Haigh 4 for 20. Fereday was run out, and Gethin, for some reason was absent. Yorkshire lost their first four wickets for 11 runs, but Ted Wainwright hit 34 and George Hirst 24, and they took a first-innings lead of 57. Worcestershire's second innings lasted only an hour. Rhodes was unplayable and took 7 for 20, while Haigh had 3 for 29. The pair bowled unchanged in each innings. Worcestershire were bowled out for 51, and Yorkshire were victors by an innings and five runs. The game was over by late afternoon on the first day. In three innings, neither side had made 100.

This win in one day heralded a whole string of successes for Yorkshire, who invariably had the better of affairs even when a match was drawn. Their cricket was always purposeful and victory was always their aim. They refused to accept that a match could not be won until the last ball was bowled. Against Gloucestershire, at Bradford in July, they suffered at the hands of Gilbert Jessop, who hit two ferocious centuries in the match. In the second innings, he scored 139 in 88 minutes and seven times hit Rhodes out of the ground for six, but Rhodes had him in the end and finished with 6 for 120 to add to his 8 for 72 in the first innings. Yorkshire won by 40 runs and never went on the defensive.

Even more remarkable was their victory over Essex at Harrogate at the beginning of August. Only two and half hours play were possible on the first day, when Yorkshire reached 159 for nine. They owed this score to Ted Wainwright, whom *Cricket* described as 'one of the few men who know how to make the best of things when the bowlers are getting the upper hand on a soft wicket'. No play at all was possible on the second day, so that when play began on the last day, the Saturday, there seemed no chance whatsoever of a result. Twelve more runs were added to the Yorkshire score before the final wicket fell, and then it was Essex's turn. They had no answer to Wilfred Rhodes — 'the most dangerous bowler in England on a tricky wicket' — and they were all out for 65. Rhodes opened the bowling and bowled unchanged to take 6 for 40.

There was still little time for Yorkshire to win the match, but they were 'fortunate in having men in the team who can put on runs very quickly'. Ernest Smith, Denton and Hirst were the men. They hit 42 for the loss of Smith in just over a quarter of an hour, and Hawke declared, setting Essex the task of scoring 149 to win in 110 minutes. In 65 minutes the match was over. Rhodes and Haigh bowled unchanged. Essex were out for 52, and Rhodes took eight for 28, 14 for 68 in the match.

It was the third time in the season in a county match that Rhodes had taken 14 wickets. In 26 Championship matches for Yorkshire, he took five wickets in an innings on 21 occasions. He became the first Yorkshire bowler to take 200 Championship wickets in a season, and his 206 wickets cost only 12.29 runs each. In all matches, he took 261 wickets at 13.81 runs each. Next on the list came Schofield Haigh with 163 wickets, 145 of them for Yorkshire in county games.

That Yorkshire owed a vast amount to these two is undeniable, but there were other factors. The batting was ever dependable, with Hirst, Tunnicliffe and Denton to the fore, and there was strength in depth. The fielding was dynamic, aggressive, always attacking, and the wicketkeeping of David Hunter, 40 years old, was as good as any in the land. The leadership was astute and strong.

In 1900, Yorkshire played 28 matches, of which 16 were won and 12 drawn. Under the system in operation, this gave them 100 per cent. Lancashire were second with 76.47.

They began the following season with eight Championship wins in succession. Drawn games against Surrey and Warwickshire were followed by seven more victories in succession. It seemed certain

Schofield Haigh, a prolific wicket-taker in the great Yorkshire side at the turn of
the century.

that the sequence would be extended to eight when Somerset came to Headingley in mid-July. Earlier in the season, Somerset had fought Yorkshire hard and had been beaten by one wicket, but when they were bowled out for 87 and Yorkshire had made 325 to take a first-innings lead of 238, it seemed that the result would be far from close this time. In fact, Yorkshire had struggled in the early part of their innings and were 55 for 5. The depth of the batting was always a trial for their opponents, however, and after Hirst and Hawke had righted matters, Haigh and Rhodes added 118 for the ninth wicket. Haigh hit 96 in an hour and three quarters.

Then a remarkable change came over the game. With exhilarating batting, Lionel Palairet and Braund began Somerset's second innings with a partnership of 222 in 140 minutes for the first wicket. Never before had the Yorkshire bowling been treated so savagely, and the White Rose's suffering was not over. Palairet went on to make 173, Phillips hit 122, and Sammy Woods and Hill also had a clout to take Somerset to 630 in their second innings. Yorkshire were bowled out for 113 to give Somerset victory by 279 runs. It was the most astonishing result of the season and it was the only reverse that Yorkshire suffered. By the time it happened, the Championship was almost certainly theirs.

Twenty wins, one loss and six draws gave them 90.47 per cent, way ahead of Middlesex in second place with 50 per cent. There was almost a weary sense of acceptance about their dominance, so far ahead were they of their comtemporaries. *Cricket* analysed the reasons for the Yorkshire triumph.

'The vast success of the Yorkshiremen was chiefly due to their famous pair of bowlers, Rhodes and Hirst, to their fine fielding, and to the ability of the tail to make runs on most occasions when runs were wanted. Hirst's famous swerve has become a household word in the land, and he often won a match for his side by disposing of some of the very best of his opponents in the first few overs.'

To have an opening bowler capable of making an early breakthrough in match after match is an asset that is vital to a side that aspires to greatness.

Of the batting, *Cricket* was less complimentary, but the writer still managed to pinpoint the essential quality which made the side so dominant.

'Yorkshire cannot be said to have had a great batting team as far as individuals are concerned, but it was a team in which every

George Hirst, the heart of Yorkshire cricket and one of the greatest all-rounders the game has known.

single man was as likely to make 50 as not under any imaginable circumstances, and, therefore, the batting was exceedingly strong on the whole.'

In fact, Mitchell, Hirst, J.T.Brown senior and Tunnicliffe all passed a 1,000 runs in county matches, and Denton hit 967. Twelve of the 13 players who played eight or more innings averaged more than 20, and the 13th, Hunter, averaged 14.60. As Stuart Surridge was to remark of his Surrey side more than 50 years later, when it was put to him that his team were not prolific scorers: 'We always made enough'.

All pointed to the strength of the Yorkshire bowling, with Rhodes taking 196 wickets at 13.59 and Hirst 135 at 16.75 runs apiece. They were ably supported by Haigh, who had less work than he had had in the previous season, and by J.T.Brown senior. What should not be forgotten is the quality of support that they were given by the Yorkshire fieldsmen.

John Tunnicliffe was one of the great slip fielders and in 1901, he took 62 catches in county matches. C.B.Fry said, 'Yards of him wrapped up in the slips — alert to unfold — to shoot out an unerringly prehensile hand followed by an unerring eye.' Lord Hawke considered that Tunnicliffe 'possessed an insidious, instinctive type of knowledge of where to place himself on every type of wicket, and then Ted Wainwright would measure his distance from him with outstretched arms, as invaluable ally at second slip'. Hawke was adamant that in Yorkshire's halcyon days: 'All my bowlers relied on the almost infallible power of Tunnicliffe and Wainwright to hold anything within their reach.'

In 1902, Tunnicliffe no longer had Ted Wainwright alongside him at slip, and his number of catches dropped to 32, but then this was the year when Schofield Haigh reasserted himself as a leading strike bowler and relied less on the close catchers than Hirst and Rhodes. Haigh's figures in 1902 were astounding. He captured 123 wickets at 11.99 runs each, and 82 per cent of his wickets came without the help of a fielder. He clean bowled 91 batsmen and had ten leg-before, a remarkable achievement.

Haigh's phenomenal bowling failed to earn him an England cap in 1902, although, like T.L.Taylor, he was named in 12 selected for a Test and omitted on the morning of the match. Yorkshire did lose Jackson, Rhodes and Hirst to the England side, and Mitchell, like Wainwright, had gone, having settled in South Africa. He was was to captain that country in Test cricket although he

Arguably cricket has seen no better slow left-arm spinner than Wilfred Rhodes, nor a man who served the game more nobly. He completed the 'double' on 16 occasions, a record that is likely to stand for ever.

had already played for England against them. Mitchell had been the leading batsmen in 1901, but the Yorkshire side of this golden period always seemed to have a quality replacement ready and waiting. Irving Washington won a regular place as Mitchell was not available and shone in a side where once again every man in the eleven contributed valuable scores.

There was an early-season defeat, a surprise, at the hands of Somerset. The game was played on a sticky wicket at Bramall Lane. Somerset made 106 and 86 and bowled out Yorkshire for 74 and 84. It was to be the only Championship defeat in a wet summer in which 11 matches were drawn. Yorkshire again pulled away from the rest of the field and won their third Championship in succession with ease.

It was in this year, 1902, that Yorkshire's great side of the early part of the twentieth century reached the pinnacle of their achievements. Not only did they take the title for the third year running, but they also became the only county to overcome one of the very best of Australian touring sides, and they were also providers of the two men who brought about England's solitary Test victory.

The Australians arrived at Headingley having just narrowly escaped defeat in a soggy first Test at Edgbaston, where they had been tormented by Hirst and Rhodes. There was immense interest in the meeting between the Australians and the champion county, and excitement and joy was increaed by the news that the Boer War was at an end. There was a holiday, festival, celebratory spirit in the air, and 33,705 people, a record for a cricket match in England, crowded into the ground on the first day with thousands more locked outside. Overnight rain meant that the pitch was soft and the start was delayed. The Australians fielded the side that had played in the first Test. Yorkshire were at full strength.

Play began 70 minutes late, and Trumper and Duff opened the Australian innings on a pitch that was drying under the sun and would become increasingly more difficult. Trumper was a batsman whose ability mocked the difficulty of any surface, but at 31, Duff was bowled by Hirst's swerver. The lunch interval had to be extended by a quarter of an hour. The crowd had swarmed onto the field during the break in a state of patriotic fervour and the police had the greatest of problems in coaxing them back behind the boundary ropes.

When play resumed, Australian wickets began to tumble. The

wicket was becoming spiteful, and the Yorkshire fielding was electric. Clem Hill was taken in the slips, and Syd Gregory was caught by Jackson off Hirst. Washington dived to his left to take a one-handed catch low to the ground to account for Joe Darling, the Australian skipper, and Noble was a Tunnicliffe victim in the slips. Trumper was seventh man out, having scored 38 out of 76. His was to prove to be the highest score of the match.

The Australians were eventually bowled out at 4.45pm for 131. Hirst and Jackson had four wickets apiece. So delighted were the spectators by the success of the Yorkshire bowlers that they again swarmed onto the pitch, and it took a half an hour for the police to clear the ground. There were those who believed that Yorkshire should not have been allowed to begin their first innings, for the crowd could not be contained behind the boundary ropes, but there was only an hour of play left, and Brown and Tunnicliffe came out to open the innings.

It was not an easy time, and both openers and Taylor were out before the close which came with Yorkshire on 48. The following morning conditions were even worse. There was rain in the early hours and now the pitch was steaming under the sun. Every run had to be fought for, and once more there was a huge, excited crowd. Yorkshire were bowled out before lunch for 107, and, in the circumstances, a lead of 24 seemed immense.

There was time for only three overs before lunch. George Hirst bowled the first. Duff could make nothing of the first three deliveries, but the fourth was the ball that swerved into the batsman viciously, 'like a good throw in from mid-off'. Duff turned it to leg, where Jackson got a hand to it, juggled with the ball for a moment and then clasped it firmly. Clem Hill played out the over.

Stanley Jackson bowled the second over with his medium-pace right-arm. Trumper took three runs off the over to bring him down to face Hirst. Trumper leg-glanced the third ball for four, but he was completely beaten by the next delivery and his stumps were wrecked. Lunch was taken with the Australians 7 for two.

There were hints of a revival in the tense period after the restart, but in the sixth over of the innings, Hill was splendidly stumped by Hunter off Jackson. Seven balls later, Hirst bowled Darling, and the tourists were 14 for four.

There was to be no respite. The score moved to 20 before Hirst bowled Noble and Armstrong with successive deliveries, and Jackson finished the innings with a sensational over in which he took the wickets of Hopkins, Kelly, Jones and Howell in the space of five deliveries. The Australians were all out for 23, the lowest score that they have made against a county. The bowling figures of the two Yorkshiremen were:

| Hirst | 7 | - | 4 | - | 9 | - | 5 |
| Jackson | 7 | - | 1 | - | 12 | - | 5 |

Yorkshire needed 48 to win on a wicket that was now at its most vicious. Brown and Tunnicliffe gave their side an encouraging start with a stand of 19, but the going was slow and both openers and Denton were out with 25 scored. Jackson, too, was soon out and, although Taylor batted tenaciously for 11, he was one of five batsmen out with the score on 41. At this point Washington joined Hirst, who did not score but defended defiantly. Washington had made five when he on-drove Noble beautifully to the boundary to give the game to Yorkshire.

This was a famous victory and there were scenes of great rejoicing. Washington's on-drive has passed into Yorkshire legend. His career was brief, but for this shot he will always be remembered. In Lord Hawke's mark system, one wonders what value was placed on his nine not out as opposed to a 50 on a benign wicket.

Matches against the tourists have lost currency in recent years, but in 1902, victory over the Australians was an event of national importance, and in many ways it was the culmination of Yorkshire's great period. In the three seasons, 1900-02, their Championship record was among the most formidable in history. They played 80 matches, of which 49 were won, 29 drawn and only two lost. It should be emphasised that the 11 draws in 1902 were primarily due to a very wet season, and Yorkshire were robbed of victory on several occasions by yet another downpour.

More than anything Yorkshire's success depended upon the strength of their bowling. Only Hirst and Tunnicliffe managed 1,000 runs each season between 1900 and 1902. In the same period, Rhodes took 542 Championship wickets, Haigh 317 and Hirst 237. Another important factor was that Hawke was able to keep a stable side for nearly the whole of the period.

John Thomas Brown and John Tunnicliffe were one of the greatest opening partnerships in the history of county cricket. The only pairs to rival them being their successors Holmes and Sutcliffe and the Surrey pair Hobbs and Sandham. Brown followed the

J.T.Brown of Yorkshire, one of county cricket's finest opening batsmen.

Hawke maxim of dedication to the game in that the night that he decided to become tee-total and concentrate his energies on scoring runs, he poured all the beer in his house down the kitchen sink. Immensely popular, he could never quite rid himself of his yearning for tobacco and he died of a heart condition brought on by acute asthma in 1904, when he was only 35.

He and Tunnicliffe were a perfect blend. 'Long John' Tunnicliffe of Pudsey was the most disciplined of cricketers and was content, in his later days, to offer the rock-like solidity while J.T.Brown chased runs more eagerly. In 1898, at Chesterfield, the pair hit 554 in five hours to establish a world record for the first wicket which lasted until 1932 when it was beaten by two other Yorkshiremen. Brown hit 300, Tunnicliffe 243. A year earlier, they had scored 378 against Sussex when Brown went on to make 311. Tunnicliffe's share was 147.

Tunnicliffe curbed his natural instincts for the good of Yorkshire. He absorbed Lord Hawke's White Rose fervour, and he looked with contempt on a cosmopolitan side like Middlesex, whom he considered to be a 'bunch of foreigners'. A batsman who was a fine judge of a run, Tunnicliffe was, as we have mentioned, an outstanding slip fielder.

After Tunnicliffe and Brown came David Denton, who provided the risk and the flair that people are unwilling to associate with Yorkshire. He was an uncertain starter and was known as 'lucky' for the number of times he was said to have been dropped, but he was a glorious leg-side hitter and a magnificent fielder.

Frank Mitchell was one of those sportsmen blessed with ability in every direction. Captain of Cambridge and a batsman of brilliance since his days as a schoolboy, he played rugby for England, but he felt lured to South Africa where he served in the Boer War.

An off-side player of classical style, he was the county's leading batsman in 1901 and considered to be one of the finest in the country, but he emigrated to South Africa at the end of the season and was lost to Yorkshire.

Mitchell was one of only three amateurs, apart from Lord Hawke, who could hope to command a regular place in the Yorkshire side at this time on their ability. There were those among southern counties who would omit a professional and play an amateur much inferior in accomplishment, but this was not the Yorkshire policy. Cricket was a game to be won.

The other two amateurs who would always be chosen when

John Tunnicliffe, J.T.Brown's partner in Yorkshire's legendary opening pair.

available were Hon F.S.Jackson and Tom Taylor. Taylor was another schoolboy batting prodigy, who shone at Cambridge and performed with elegant consistency for Yorkshire. He was on the fringe of the England side and was considered by most good judges to be a wicketkeeper of the highest quality. Indeed, there were those who believed that he should have displaced David Hunter in this position whenever he was available for the Yorkshire side. He was a fighting cricketer in the best Yorkshire tradition, and he was to give the county splendid service as an administrator.

Sir Stanley Jackson must rank above Taylor and Mitchell. Indeed, he ranks above most men who have played the game. He could have been created by John Buchan, Ridger Haggard or P.C.Wren, but he was essentially a man of the Golden Age. As a batsman he was a genius on any wicket, and as a bowler he bowled quickish off-breaks which, as we have noted, could destroy any batsman in the world. Cricket was a hobby, not an occupation. His career was in business and politics — an MP, Financial Secretary to the War Office, Privy Councillor and one-time Governor of Bengal where he survived an assassination attempt. He served in the Boer War and was invalided home with enteric fever in June 1900. He was persuaded to play for the Gentlemen at Scarborough, although he had not taken up a bat in two years and was still convalescing and very weak. He hit 134 and 42 against a Players' attack that included Haigh, Hirst and Rhodes. Then he returned to the Boer War and could not play for Yorkshire until 1902. What the man would have achieved on the cricket field, had he given himself fully to the game, one can only conjecture.

Ernest Smith was another fine amateur all-rounder who assisted the county occasionally during the years when the Championship was won three times in succession, but, like Ted Wainwright, he was by that time drawing towards the end of his career.

Ted Wainwright was one of the great characters of Yorkshire cricketer, and he was later immortalised by Neville Cardus, who served as assistant coach to Wainwright at Shrewsbury where the Yorkshire off-break bowler and defiantly successful batsman was employed after he retired in 1902. 'Find out the batsman's poorest stroke and spin the ball against its direction,' was Wainwright's maxim, and there were times, particularly in the 1890s, when he was unplayable. But it is as a cricketer in every aspect of the game, batting, bowling and fielding, that Ted Wainwright is remembered.

Sir Stanley Jackson, a man of so many talents that cricket could have only a fraction of his time.

He provided whatever Yorkshire needed when it was needed, and such men are the life blood of a county side.

Irving Washington won a regular place when Wainwright was in his last season. Illness destined that it was to be Washington's last season, too. He was the first left-handed batsman to be chosen for the county on the strength of his batting alone. He was strong in technique, rich in shots and elegant in execution. He was to be sadly missed. Like Lees Whitehead, the all-rounder who was almost a permanent 12th man, he gave invaluable service.

Faithful service was a necessary ingredient of Yorkshire cricket, and David Hunter, an eminently reliable wicketkeeper for 21 years, was very much the true and faithful servant, a fact which Hawke recognised. He was the only one of the leading members of the Yorkshire side not to gain representative honours, but he was highly respected. In the closing years of his career, he often captained the side in Hawke's absence.

The achievements of Schofield Haigh in this golden age of Yorkshire cricket we have already noted, and his career, 1895 to 1913, saw him part of eight title-winning sides. Not only was he a lethal medium-pace bowler with deceptive quicker and slower deliveries, he was, for 18 years, 'the sunshine of the Yorkshire eleven'.

He had a round, pleasant, whimsical face, but he was anything but a pleasant prospect for a batsman who had no indication of what was coming next from what C.B.Fry described as Haigh's 'long quick and very elastic swing which gives the ball a rather low level flight'. It was not only batsmen who feared Haigh, for he posed the greatest problems for a wicketkeeper, giving no signal nor indication whatsoever for what was coming next.

By sheer perseverance, Haigh made himself into a useful batsman who was capable of scoring 1,000 runs in 1904 and giving able support to Hirst and Rhodes as an all-rounder. Haigh never quite realised at Test level what he achieved at county level where he had few equals. With Hirst and Rhodes, he formed a lethal trio of bowlers, a trio which must rank alongside Richardson, Lohmann and Lockwood and Lock, Laker and Alec Bedser of Surrey as supreme in the history of county cricket.

Haigh's idol was his colleague George Hirst, and it is said that he feared Hirst's disapproval above all else, just as he respected his judgement. 'In a county match, if I had one man to play for me to save my life pre-war, it would have been George Hirst,' wrote Sir Home Gordon in 1939. He was lion-hearted, good-tempered, and his prowess as a county all-rounder has never been surpassed. He always felt more at home with his fellow Yorkshiremen than he did in a Test match. He bowled fast left-arm and 'swerved' the ball prodigiously, as a batsman could defend or hit as the occasion demanded, and as a fielder had no peer at mid-off. He was all that was good in county cricket in its best years with its finest side. He is the only man in the history of the game to have scored 2,000 runs and taken 200 wickets in the same season, and there are many who believe that he is the greatest all-rounder the game has known. In Yorkshire, they will only say that the greatest all-rounder batted right and bowled left and he came from Kirkheaton. That grim little village on top of a hill near Huddersfield produced Wilfred Rhodes as well as George Hirst.

During the course of a career which spanned 32 years, Rhodes was the slow left-arm bowler supreme, the only bowler to capture more than 4,000 wickets in a career; an opening batsman with Jack Hobbs through a victorious Ashes series, sharing a record partnership of 323 at Melbourne where he scored 179; a lower-order batsman of durable qualities; a sure, safe and vigorous fielder; and a master judge of the game. Ironically, had Hawke not dismissed Peel, it is likely that Rhodes, the epitome of Yorkshire cricket, would never have represented his native county.

He left Yorkshire and went as professional to Scotland. Warwickshire were very interested in acquiring his services, but before they could arrange a trial, Peel had been dismissed by Yorkshire. Rhodes and another left-arm bowler Albert Cordingley were called for trial. Cordingley played in the first match of the 1898 season, took 0 for 24, and was replaced by Rhodes for the next match. A year later, the all-rounder from Kirkheaton was taking seven wickets in his debut Test for England.

He took 126 wickets in county matches in his first season, and 129 in his second. In 1900, he took 206 and no man was more vital to the Yorkshire cause in those years of glory, for the slow left-arm spinner was ever the hub of the attack when the White Rose was in bloom.

These, then, were Hawke's men. He chose them and fused them into a combination which dominated English cricket, and his influence was to extend far beyond the time when he surrendered the captaincy in 1910. Arguably, the only other side that could rival Yorkshire for consistency in the Edwardian period was Kent.

At the beginning of the century they fielded a predominantly amateur side, but by 1906, although the nucleus of the side was still amateur, they had a professional contingent which turned them into a Championship-winning side for the first time.

J.R.Mason, the former captain and an astute man as well as a fine cricketer, R.N.R.Blaker, a cultured batsman, and C.J.Burrup, another fine amateur batsman, were still occasionally available, but it was the consistent scoring of the professionals, Humphreys and James Seymour, that gave the side a necessary stability to balance its rather aristocratic flamboyance.

The arrival of Frank Woolley in 1906 gave the Kent team a spark of genius. He was to be arguably the greatest left-handed batsman England has known and, in those early years of his career, a very good left-arm bowler. Indeed, he was an all-rounder of the highest quality.

K.L.Hutchings, a brilliantly attacking amateur batsman from Tonbridge; Hardinge, a most dependable batsman; Huish, a very fine wicketkeeper in the Kent tradition; Hubble, a good middle-order batsman who took to wicketkeeping after the war; Fairservice, a medium-pace off-break bowler; and, briefly, D.W.Carr, a leg-break bowler of mature years; all these played an integral part in the Kent successes of the years just before World War One, but the real diamonds of the side were the bowlers Fielder and Blythe.

Arthur Fielder was a fast bowler of splendid physique and stamina and honest endeavour. He had a high action and was strong and powerful, and his ability to swing the ball away brought him many wickets caught behind by Huish or in the slips by Woolley, Hutchings or Seymour. He was an admirable foil for the slow left-arm spin of Frank Woolley and of 'Charlie' Blythe.

Blythe was an artist with the artist's sensitivity and movement. He had an alert mind, a love of his art and he was tuned to perfection, like the violin he played as his hobby, and with devotion. On a turning wicket he was unplayable and on a placid wicket he could deceive the best with changes of pace and flight. He was the spirit of Kent cricket in the Golden Age which ended with what was then known as the Great War.

Colin Blythe died with the age he had graced, as did his team-mate K.L.Hutchings. Hutchings died at Ginchy in 1916, blown up by a shell, and Blythe fell at Passchendaele a year later. Kent cricket was to take many years to recover the heights that they had known, and by then cricket had become a very different game.

The Wars of the Roses

The County Championship in the 1920s

T HE decision to play two-day matches in the County
Championship when first-class cricket resumed after World
War One was a total disaster and was quickly abandoned.
In 1920, the tried and trusted formula of three-day matches was
reinstated, and the competition excited widespread interest, just
as it was to do in the years immediately following World War
Two.

The similarity in these two post-war eras does not end there,
for both provided what are best described as romantic interludes
before the giants of the game reasserted themselves. Neither the
Middlesex sides of 1920 and 1921, nor the Middlesex side of 1947,
were great teams, for they lacked strength in bowling, but their
successes have somehow become redolent of lost youth and 'blue
remembered hills'.

Following the ill-starred experiment of 1919, the 1920 programme
was considered to be the first real season after the carnage of war
and it was tinged with the drama that 'Plum' Warner, the Middlesex
captain, an influential and revered figure in the game at the time,
had announced that it was to be his last season. When, on 27
July, at Leyton, Essex beat Middlesex by four runs, the team from
Lord's stood ninth out of 16 in the Championship table and there
seemed no prospect of them taking the title, even though Yorkshire,
Surrey and Kent, early pacemakers, were showing signs of decline.
The cricket world became captivated by what happened in the
closing weeks of the season.

From Leyton, Middlesex went to Hove where they beat Sussex
with ease. The game against Kent at Canterbury was a different

proposition. If not the side that they had been before the war, Kent were still a good side with the young 'Tich' Freeman making his mark as a leg-break bowler of exceptional talent. Kent led by five runs on the first innings, and when Freeman took six for 36 to help dismiss Middlesex for 127 in their second innings, a Kent victory appeared to be inevitable. Bickmore hit 51, and, needing but 123 to win, Kent reached 90 for 5 with Woolley, the master, yet to bat. But Jack Hearne bowled Woolley first ball and the complexion of the game changed. Hearne went on to take 8 for 26, one of the finest performances of this great all-rounders career, and Middlesex snatched victory by five runs.

Hearne followed this with 178 at The Oval where the mighty Surrey were overwhelmed by an innings. Nottinghamshire were beaten by nine wickets at Lord's and, at Bradford, after trailing by 64 runs on the first innings, Middlesex won an astonishing victory over Yorkshire by four runs. When Somerset were beaten by seven wickets at Lord's, Middlesex moved to the top of the table and only three matches remained.

The Middlesex lead was marginal. They had 72.94 per cent to Lancashire's 72.50 and Yorkshire's 72.38, but, importantly, they were in front. Comfortable wins over Warwickshire and Kent did nothing to ease the position, for when Surrey came to Lord's for the last match of the season, Middlesex had to win to secure the Championship.

Excitement was intensified by the news that, at Old Trafford, Lancashire had beaten Worcestershire and would take the title if Middlesex failed to beat Surrey at Lord's. The game attracted enormous interest and close to 65,000 people saw the three days of cricket, such was the power of the County Championship in those days immediately following World War One.

Initially, little went right for Middlesex and they trailed by 73 runs on the first innings, a considerable deficit. But Lee and Skeet began the Middlesex second innings with a stand of 208. This gave Warner and his men the chance that they wanted, and they plundered quick runs. At 3.40pm, Warner declared and left Surrey three hours in which to score 244. This was a most reasonable declaration in an age when 20 overs in an hour was a common minimum and when brisk scoring was the norm.

The match turned in Middlesex's favour when the great Jack Hobbs was caught at slip, at the second attempt, off the bowling of Nigel Haig. The hero from then on was Greville Stevens, a leg-break bowler and attacking batsman who should have been the golden boy of English cricket in that post-war period, but who could never give enough time to the game after leaving university. He took 5 for 61, and at 6.20pm, he bowled Strudwick with his googly to give Middlesex victory by 55 runs and the Championship by 77 per cent to 74.61 per cent. The achievement was all the more remarkable in that it had been brought about by Middlesex winning their last nine matches of the season.

Warner's retirement, the winning sequence in the closing weeks of the season and the dramatic climax at Lord's conspired to make this a year memorable in the history of the County Championship. They have tended, too, to overshadow the equally remarkable achievements of the following season when Middlesex retained the title.

Frank Mann succeeded Warner as captain and led the county to victory in the first eight Championship matches of the 1921 season. Of the next 11 matches, three were drawn, two were lost and six were won, and Middlesex once again arrived at the last match of the season, against Surrey at Lord's, needing victory to

Middlesex, 1920. Back row (left to right): Lee, H.K.Longman, Durston, N.Haig, G.T.S.Stevens, C.H.L.Skeet. Front row: J.W.Hearne, F.T.Mann, P.F.Warner (captain), Murrell, Hendren.

secure the title. The fixture was of even greater moment than the one the previous year, for, in 1921, if Surrey won the match, they would be champions.

Fender's side dominated the early stages of the match, with huge crowds again in attendance. Surrey made 269 and bowled out Middlesex for 132. Without Hobbs, who was ill for most of the season, the Surrey batting was a little suspect, and they were bowled out on the second afternoon for 184. In the quarter of an hour left before the close, Twining and Lee made 19. So Middlesex began the last day with all their wickets intact and needing another 303 runs to win.

Lee was out at 48, and Jack Hearne joined R.H.Twining just after midday. They were not separated until 5.20pm, by which time they had added 229 in four hours and ten minutes. Both batsmen were dismissed, as was Bruce, but Hendren and Mann took Middlesex to victory and the title, Hendren hitting the winning six at five minutes past six.

If this Middlesex triumph has become somewhat obscured by time, it is because a reality had intruded rather sharply into the romantic complacency of English cricket. Some weeks after Warner's success at Lord's in 1920, an England side under J.W.H.T.Douglas had set sail for Australia, where they had lost all five Test matches, an unprecedented humiliation. Nor did the sorrows end there, for Warwick Armstrong brought his side to England in 1921 and won the first three Tests with disdainful ease before, seemingly bored, they drew the last two.

When Mann led Middlesex to victory in their first eight Championship matches of 1921, the innings wins over Nottinghamshire and Yorkshire at Lord's were punctuated by a defeat inside two days at the hands of the touring Australians. This tended to put English cricket into perspective, and Sydney Pardon of *Wisden* wrote the epitaph of the 1921 season — 'there has never been a season so disheartening'.

There was a such a ruthless, professional efficiency and approach to the game by the Australians that the English county game and its standards were put under close scrutiny. It was now that the legend grew that English cricket was only strong when Yorkshire was strong, for perhaps only Yorkshire could produce that quality of iron determination and total dedication that the Australians had shown.

Yorkshire had taken the doubtful Championship of 1920, and

they were now to emulate Nottinghamshire's record of the 1880s by winning the Championship four years in succession, 1922-25. Indeed, with their close rivals from across the Pennines, they were to dominate English cricket from 1922 until the outbreak of World War Two in 1939.

By 1922, the only survivor of the great Yorkshire side of the pre-war years was Wilfred Rhodes, yet the side already had a scent of experience and that supreme self-confidence that is associated with only the greatest of sides. In 1922, Geoffrey Wilson succeeded David Burton as captain of Yorkshire. He was an old Harrovian who had won his blue at Cambridge in 1919. He was to lead Yorkshire for three seasons, and they were to take the title in each of those three seasons, a remarkable record. He was an adequate batsman, career average 16.22 and with one century to his name, but a brilliant fielder and, under his leadership, Yorkshire were to develop that oppressive hostility in the field that was to be so characteristic of their play in the years between the wars. It was a characteristic which was to place their opponents at a psychological disadvantage.

Nottinghamshire gave Yorkshire a fierce struggle for the Championship in 1922. Yorkshire won eight and drew two of their first ten matches before Nottinghamshire beat them by an innings at Sheffield. What is most marked is the colossal gap between Yorkshire and the majority of their opponents. They were bowled out for 112 in the opening match of the season at Northampton, but they still won by ten wickets. In the second match, at Cardiff, they hit 404 for two and bowled out Glamorgan for 78 and 68 to win by tea on the second day. The pattern was continued over and over again, and no side reached 200 in their second innings against Yorkshire throughout the season.

Yorkshire won the return match with Nottinghamshire, and the only other reverse that they suffered in 1922 was when they were surprisingly beaten by Hampshire at Bradford. Rain prevented any play on the first day, and when Yorkshire batted on the Monday, they were bowled out by Kennedy and Boyes inside two hours for 56. Lord Tennyson decided to open the Hampshire innings himself, and he hit at everything, making 51 out of 64 and helping his side to a first-innings lead of 57. It was an advantage they never lost, and Hampshire went on to win by five wickets in spite of the fact that Waddington had match figures of 11 for 69.

It was only the points system that allowed Nottinghamshire to finish so close to Yorkshire, for there could be little argument as to the merit of the records of both sides.

Yorkshire P29 W19, L2, D8

Nottinghamshire P26, W17, L5, D4

The points system gave Yorkshire 73.79 per cent to Nottinghamshire's 71.53, but the following season, 1923, their margin of superiority over their rivals had increased to 17.80. The only defeat that Yorkshire suffered in 1923, when they won 25 of their 31 matches, was at the hands of Nottinghamshire at Headingley when they lost by three runs.

It is a judgement on the temper of the time that Nottinghamshire were strongly criticised for scoring only 112 runs in 200 minutes on the first day, but the excitement of the close was ample compensation. With five wickets standing, Yorkshire needed 29 runs to win and looked to have the game safe, but when the eighth wicket fell they were still 21 runs short. Macaulay made a brave effort and hit 17, but Sam Staples dismissed Waddington and Dolphin in one over and won the game.

It is significant that we have dwelt on Yorkshire's lone defeat, for victory over Yorkshire at that period, and indeed in many of the years between the wars, was an event that caused a considerable stir. They were beaten three times in 1923, Wilson's last year as captain, but once again took the title with ease.

One of the defeats was at the hands of Middlesex at Lord's, and it was Middlesex who finished second in the table, but it was not the defeat at Lord's which caused concern but the drawn match at Sheffield at the beginning of July. Wilson won the toss and, wrongly as it transpired, asked Middlesex to bat first. They made 358, and Yorkshire replied with 334 so that the game petered to a draw on the last day. It was not a happy match. The Sheffield crowd barracked the Middlesex side throughout and the umpires, Reeves and Butt, reported to MCC that the behaviour of some of the Yorkshire eleven, most notably Waddington, had ignited the crowd's temper.

It was alleged that Waddington's 'attitude towards decisions incited barracking'. Middlesex's reaction was to make a public statement to the effect that they would not play Yorkshire in 1925, but, following an MCC enquiry and a written apology from Waddington, they retracted and fixtures between the counties continued as normal.

There were suggestions in the Press a month after the incidents at Sheffield that all was not well in relations between Yorkshire and Surrey, and although comment on this issue subsided, it was apparent that Yorkshire's sense of aggression and lust for victory and the attitude that it engendered was disturbing more than one county. At the end of the season Geoffrey Wilson stood down as captain.

It is easy to lay blame on Wilson for his laxity, but one should not forget that he was a captain with vision who advocated brighter cricket and who fired his side with the will and dedication to win. He led Yorkshire for three seasons and they won the title in each of those three seasons. There are very few captains who can boast such a proud record.

Yorkshire were concerned about their tarnished reputation, however, and the man brought in to restore order was Major Arthur William Lupton. He had first played for Yorkshire in 1908, but he did not become regularly associated with the county until he took over the captaincy in 1925 at the age of 46. He never hit a half-century in first-class cricket and his medium pace bowling, highly successful in minor cricket in his youth, was to play no part in the Yorkshire attack when he was skipper. Lupton inherited a highly talented and successful side, yet this presented him with no easy task, for it was expected of him that he should both keep the side at the top of the cricket world and restore their reputation. With firm, but understanding discipline and wise leadership, which derived much from the advice of his senior players, he achieved both his tasks. In 1925, Yorkshire went through the season unbeaten, winning 21 of their 32 matches and claiming the Championship for the fourth year in succession by a considerable margin. Indeed, although Yorkshire did not win the title in 1926, they were again unbeaten. Their record in the five seasons between 1922 and 1926 was 95 victories and only six defeats in 154 matches. This was an astonishing record, and what is equally astonishing is the fact that the four consecutive Championships were won with what was practically an unchanged eleven.

Norman Kilner, the younger brother of Roy, played occasionally in 1922 and 1923 but joined Warwickshire in 1926; and Rockley Wilson, then in his mid-40s, also played occasionally in 1922 and 1923, the last seasons of his broken, happy, somewhat eccentric career, but, for the most part, the same ten professionals took the field for each match over a period of four years.

It has been said that soundness was the main principal of the

Yorkshire batting, but this accepts the cliché of the Yorkshire character with which we have become imbued and does scant justice to a side of multiple talents and distinct personalities.

Herbert Sutcliffe was a regal cricketer. He was always immaculate in dress, and his black hair was brushed and combed and never out of place. He was, more than any other batsman of his time, imperturbable. Nothing upset him; nothing destroyed his equanimity. He simply did not believe that a bowler was capable of getting him out, and he had the technique and determination to score runs even on the worst of wickets. The more adverse the conditions, the more determined he became, for he relished a fight, but to paint a picture of Sutcliffe as a dour fighter on crumbling wickets is to give only half a picture. He was equally adept at scoring runs quickly in search of a target or in quest of a declaration. It is appropriate to the man's neatness that his career was compounded into the years between the wars and that he scored at least 1,000 runs in each of those seasons. With Jack Hobbs he formed the greatest opening partnership that Test cricket has ever known, and with Percy Holmes he constituted an opening partnership in county cricket that has not been bettered.

If Sutcliffe was something of a dandy in appearance, Holmes, in contrast to the accepted image of a Yorkshireman, was something of a dandy with the bat. He had a flourish, a dash and a sparkle, but he did not treat the Yorkshire cause with levity. Robertson-Glasgow wrote of him in *More Cricket Prints* that he 'batted with a sort of volatile precision entirely his own'. He was a master of the square cut and the hook, and his running between the wickets with Sutcliffe became legendary. They shared 69 century partnerships for Yorkshire's first wicket, and the only blight on Holmes' career was that it coincided with that of Jack Hobbs so that he was to play only seven times for England.

That was seven times more than Edgar Oldroyd, one of the best number-three batsmen that county cricket was known. Len Hutton considered him to be one of the finest batsmen he ever saw on a turning wicket and said that he learned much from him. It was Oldroyd's rock-like defence and infinite patience that made him such a great player in adversity, but he was strongly influenced by Geoffrey Wilson's demands as captain, and in that great period at the beginning of the 1920s he became a pugnacious batsman, capable and eager to attack the bowling. When he hit his highest score, 194 against Worcestershire in 1923, the runs came in under

Herbert Sutcliffe and Percy Holmes of Yorkshire, the most successful opening pair in county cricket.

four and a half hours. Small, tough and witty, Oldroyd was an outstanding fielder in an outstanding fielding side.

His rival in wit in the Yorkshire side was Maurice Leyland. A very powerful, broad-chested, clear eyed, shortish man, Maurice Leyland was not an elegant left-hander. Indeed, when chosen for the 1928-29 tour ahead of Woolley, he was called a 'village green swiper', but that was a jaundiced view. He was one of the great left-handed batsmen in the history of the game for whom cricket was a joy to be taken seriously. He had an array of powerful shots and breathed defiance in his every gesture. He was born to cricket, drank it from the elders of the side and later passed on its wisdom to the next generation.

He was, for many of his county, 'the man of which Yorkshire dreams are made'.

After Leyland came the all-rounders. Wilfred Rhodes was 45 in 1922, but he still managed to complete the 'double' of 1,000 runs and 100 wickets as he did in 1923, 1924 and 1926, when he was recalled to the England side for his slow left-arm bowling and played a significance part in recapturing the Ashes. And there was Roy Kilner — left-handed batsman of grace and sparkle, an ebullient fielder and a slow left-arm bowler who captured 469 wickets in the Championship in Yorkshire's four title years.

Kilner was a man of great charm, an eccentric genius who enjoyed life to the full. It was he who said of the matches between Yorkshire and Lancashire, 'We say good morning and after that the only thing we say is 'How's That?' ' He mocks the description of Yorkshire dourness, for he was controlled by his impish genius, but no man was ever more critical of his own feelings.

Emmott Robinson did not make his debut for Yorkshire until 1919, by which time he was 36, and he played until 1931. He was a medium-pace bowler, a good cover point and a batsman good enough to reach a 1,000 runs in a season twice and hit seven centuries in his career. He was hungry for the game and a sage in judgement. Lupton turned to him for advice, as he did to Rhodes, and it was Robinson who was watching his colleagues bat at The Oval while talking to Neville Cardus and, suddenly seeing a ball jump, said in an aside to Lupton, 'Call 'em, Major, call 'em in!'

Robinson has been immortalised by Cardus, for whom he epitomised all that was good, honest and true about the game and about Yorkshire. He was always passionately concerned about cricket for every minute that he was on the field, and for most

Maurice Leyland, powerful, broad-chested and the epitome of Yorkshire's strength.

of the time off it. When Waddington was stumped in a Roses match, so conceding first-innings points to Lancashire, he remarked, 'I'd 'a died first before they stumped me.' He was saying no more than the truth.

The fire of the Yorkshire attack in those bounty years was provided by two men of ferocious dedication, George Macaulay and Abram Waddington. They were men of dynamic personality and brooding menace. The sight of a Harlequin cap or a gentleman from Middlesex convinced them that the Civil War was still in progress.

In the four Championship seasons, Macaulay took 604 wickets in the Championship matches alone, and they were achieved with astonishing economy —

1922 120 at 13.31
1923 149 at 13.34
1924 159 at 11.73
1925 176 at 15.21

His appetite for wickets and for success was insatiable.

He arrived at Headingley as a fast bowler, but George Hirst turned him into a medium-pace spin bowler. What he never lost was his fire and an antagonism for the batsmen that bordered on the fanatical. He was one of the most hostile bowlers that the game has known. He wanted a wicket every ball, and 604 wickets at 13.46 in the four Championship seasons suggests that he came close to achieving that aim. He could bat, as three centuries for Yorkshire would testify, and he was a good fielder. He played his cricket with a white-hot passion as did Waddington.

Waddington was a left-arm fast-medium pace bowler who, like Hirst, could swing the ball prodigiously. He had a beautiful, rhythmical action which was almost in contrast to his aggressive approach to the game, an aggression which, as we have seen, could, and did, land him in trouble.

Keeping wicket to Waddington, Macaulay, Rhodes, Robinson and Kilner was no easy task, but Arthur Dolphin's quick brain, keen eyesight and courage made the job look simple, and he had the tenacity that was such an important ingredient in the Yorkshire character.

It is right that we have analysed, in turn, the men who served under Wilson and Lupton, but in treating them singly we have done them an injustice. Their bowling was a unit that had variety and accuracy, and their fielding was tigerish. Runs were not cheaply made against Yorkshire; they were hard earned. Above all, every man was second in his own estimation. Yorkshire was first.

It was no myth that England were strong when Yorkshire cricket was strong. When, amidst the greatest possible excitement, the Ashes were regained at The Oval in 1926, two of the major contributors to England's famous victory were Herbert Sutcliffe and Wilfred Rhodes. Sutcliffe hit 76 and 161, and in the second innings he and Hobbs put on 172 on a sticky wicket. Rhodes took 2 for 35 and 4 for 44. The young England captain, Percy Chapman, took Rhodes off in the second innings in order to let Geary and Stevens bowl and have a chance of getting a wicket so that everyone could share in the triumph. This was not something that Rhodes could understand. Whatever the state of the game, Yorkshire would have bowled to dismiss their opponents as quickly and as cheaply as possible.

Yorkshire understood the ruthless and vigorous approach that Armstrong's Australians had shown in 1921, and in their county matches they adopted a style that was not dissimilar. This attitude was neither fully comprehended nor fully appreciated by many of the southern counties for whom playing with a sole dedication to winning had a taint of something faintly bad mannered about it. Lancashire and Nottinghamshire had no doubts about Yorkshire's attitude to cricket and to the County Championship, and they admired it. The pendulum was now to swing in their direction.

Nottinghamshire, in fact, were destined to be the perpetual bridesmaids for the second half of the 1920s, although, under the positive, strong and uncompromising leadership of A.W.Carr, they did take the title in 1929, but from 1926 to 1930, Lancashire were Champions four times and runners-up once.

Lancashire had been challenging strongly for the Championship since cricket had resumed after the war, and they were strongly ambitious. This ambition was heightened by the success that Yorkshire had enjoyed, and there was wealth in Lancashire that was anxious for the Red Rose to topple its greatest rivals.

The Lancashire leagues had come into existence in the closing years of the nineteenth century, and clubs had begun to engage professionals from the start of this century. The first professionals were retired county players whose job it was to tend the ground, coach and perform on a Saturday afternoon only when strictly necessary. After the war, the calibre and the role of the professional began to change, and clubs jostled to acquire the services of the best possible players. The cotton trade was enjoying a period of boom, and wealthy business men were prepared to subsidise clubs who attracted leading players.

There was great consternation when it was rumoured towards the end of the 1921 season that McDonald, 'the best fast bowler on our wickets that Australia has ever sent us', was to remain in England as he had been engaged as professional on a three-year contract by the Nelson club. The rumour proved well founded, and the fast bowler who, with Gregory, had formed one of the most lethal opening attacks in Test history, albeit for a very short period, began his career with Nelson in the Lancashire League at the beginning of the 1922 season. He was in his 31st year.

County clubs had imported players from Australia and elsewhere since the turn of the century although the occasions were few, but professional importations had disappeared after World War One. In Lancashire there was amibition, however, and the county began to cast its net wide in the search for talent. It was discovered that Alfred Hall, a left-arm fast medium bowler who played Test cricket for South Africa, had been born in Bolton and was therefore qualified for Lancashire. Hall appeared in nine matches for the county in 1923 and 1924, but he failed to impress and returned to South Africa, for whom his record of 40 wickets at 22.15 in seven Tests was considerably better than his record for Lancashire.

The search had not ended with Hall, for Lancashire also pursued Frank O'Keefe, a most gifted young batsman who had enjoyed two outstanding seasons with New South Wales. O'Keefe agreed to come to England and to play for Church in the Lancashire League while qualifying by residence for the county. He was due to take his place in the county side in June 1923, but, tragically, he died of peritonitis in the spring of that year.

By this time, McDonald was qualified to play for Lancashire under the residential qualification, but there was no indication in the Press in the spring of 1924 that there were any plans for him to assist the county. Quite the reverse in fact, for *The Daily News* stated that although it had been rumoured at one time that McDonald was qualifying to play for Lancashire, he had said emphatically that he had no desire to play county cricket. He either changed his mind very quickly or Lancashire kept their secret well, for at the end of May 1924, days after he had fulfilled the two

Ted McDonald, the Australian fast bowler who helped Lancashire to three successive County Championship titles, 1926-8.

years' residential qualification, he played for Lancashire against Kent at Old Trafford and took six for 73.

In 1924, he was still under contract to Nelson and could assist Lancashire only in midweek matches, but the following year he was a regular in county cricket, taking 186 wickets in the Championship and 205 in all first-class matches. The golden age of Lancashire cricket was about to begin.

Every effort had been made to get together a match-winning side, and what Lancashire had done in acquiring the services of McDonald was to anticipate what would happen more than forty years later, but they had shown more wisdom than several counties were to do in the 1960s and 1970s when some overseas players were enrolled who were no more than average cricketers. What Lancashire did in signing McDonald was to enlist the services of a bowler who they believed would win them the Championship. In effect, they were the first county who attempted to buy success, and the move was far from popular in some quarters.

E.H.D.Sewell, one of the most forthright writers of the period, condemned the action totally. 'Had one of the lesser and struggling counties contained a rich patron who, wishing to see his county XI sometimes in the first three, placed his cheque book at the county club's disposal, there might have been some excuse; but, for any very large and wealthy county to descend to such methods was, and always will be, an unpardonable offence against the high and dignified example which any and all of the 'Big Six' county clubs are expected to set to the others.'

Sewell went on to say that no other county club would ever be able to do what Lancashire had done, which shows that he was no fortune-teller. His views may have been excessive, but he was not alone in holding them. What he also ignores is that crowds of people flocked to see McDonald and Lancashire, and that the county made a big profit on the 1926 season.

There were, of course, other factors in Lancashire's sudden transformation into a Championship-winning side in 1926 as well as the bowling of McDonald. Not the least of them was the captaincy of Leonard Green. It was unthinkable in the 1920s that a professional should captain a county side, and when Lancashire found themselves leaderless in 1919, they appointed an Old Etonian, Myles Kenyon, as captain. He had never before played first-class cricket, but he led the side from 1919 to 1922, when he gave way to John Sharp. A soccer international, Sharp had played three Tests for England in 1909, when he had been a professional. He turned amateur after the war, but his best days were behind him and he was 44 when he was called upon to captain Lancashire. Like Kenyon, he commanded a talented side, but he could not fuse them into the stuff of which champions are made.

One does not know whether the Lancashire committee had discerned the qualities of cricket leadership that they were looking for in Leonard Green. Certainly, he had the pedigree, having risen to the rank of lieutenant-colonel during the war, and he was a fine all-round sportsman and a batsman good enough to score two first-class hundreds. It also transpired that he had the ability to turn a side of individual talents into a winning team. He had a strength of character and personality, and that blessed gift of being able to get the best from those under him. He had charm and read men well. He captained Lancashire for three years, and they won the title in each of those three seasons. It is a proud record. It was Leonard Green who took Lancashire into their golden age.

They were never to dominate as Yorkshire had done, but to win the Championship four times in four years was an achievement that places them among the great sides. The debt that they owed to one man, Edgar Arthur McDonald, was incalcuable.

In 1926, Lancashire began the season indifferently. The first three matches were drawn, and at Whitsun, Yorkshire beat them by an innings at Bradford. Lancashire won four of their next six county matches, but when they gave a dreadful batting display at Ashby-de-la-Zouch and lost to lowly Leicestershire, there were those who felt that they would finish in the bottom half of the Championship. Adding substance to this belief was the fact that Cecil Parkin, one of the leading wicket-takers in the country since the war, had severed his connection with the county after the 14th match of the season and gone into league cricket. In 1924, Parkin had been at the centre of a controversy over a newspaper article which attacked the England captain, Arthur Gilligan. Parkin's 'ghost' had said that Parkin refused to play for England again after being given little bowling to do in the Edgbaston Test against South Africa. Parkin denied he had said this, but his reputation never recovered.

The loss of Parkin in mid-season, and the poor form shown by the batsmen in particular, suggested that Lancashire had no hope of taking the title, but the embarrassment of the defeat at Ashby-de-la-Zouch gave the side the shock it needed. Ernest Tyldesley ran into a rich vein of form and, like Harry Makepeace, finished the season with more than 2,000 Championship runs to his credit.

Ernest Tyldesley has become the most under-rated batsman in cricket history. He hit 102 centuries, four of them in successive innings in 1926, and was, according to Neville Cardus, one of the most accomplished batsmen ever to play for Lancashire and one of the three greatest professional batsmen in the history of the game, yet he rarely commanded a regular place in the England side and posterity has treated him shabbily.

Harry Makepeace was reaching the veteran stage in 1926. He celebrated his 44th birthday ten days before Lancashire claimed the title. He was an opening batsman with a solid defence and he gave his life to Lancashire cricket and to Everton football.

The third of the authentic batsmen in the side was the stylish left-hander Charlie Hallows, who, in 1928, was to accomplish the most remarkable feat of scoring a 1,000 runs *in* May. Tall, slim and handsome, Hallows was the Sutcliffe of the Lancashire side, and he and Makepeace invariably gave their side the best of starts.

Iddon, Sibbles and the rather inelegant Watson provided the rest of the batting, while leg-spinner Richard Tyldesley, a regular wicket-taker who played seven times for England, was the main support for McDonald. Dick Tyldesley was a man of some bulk who relied more on variations of pace and flight than on any great amount of spin. Frank Sibbles bowled medium-pace off-breaks, but, in 1926, he was quite expensive and had not yet fulfilled the promise that he had shown in the previous season.

As we have said, the side found a new steeliness after the defeat by Leicestershire, and nine of Lancashire's last 11 matches were won. In the two drawn games, they claimed first-innings points, one of them was the August Bank Holiday match against Yorkshire at Old Trafford.

Green won the toss, and Lancashire batted on the Saturday. Makepeace and Ernest Tyldesley hit centuries and they closed at 297 for two. On the Bank Holiday Monday, the biggest crowd that had ever witnessed a single day's cricket in England, 38,000, saw the struggle of the giants. In all, 75,000 people saw the three days' play in which Lancashire made 509 for nine declared, and Yorkshire made 352.

Despite this welcome first-innings success, Lancashire were behind Yorkshire, who remained unbeaten throughout the season, with only ten days of the Championship remaining. But sides were

Ernest Tyldesley, one of the most accomplished batsmen ever to play for Lancashire and the scorer of 102 first-class centuries.

forcing draws against Yorkshire while Lancashire were winning. Yorkshire's concession of first-innings points to Surrey at The Oval proved crucial, and on 28 August, Lancashire arrived at Old Trafford knowing that victory would give them the title. Their opponents were Nottinghamshire, who batted first with Gunn and Whysall putting on 120 for the first wicket, and Whysall and Carr 98 for the third, so that the visitors passed 200 with eight wickets standing. Inevitably, McDonald brought Lancashire back into the game, and the last six Nottinghamshire wickets went down for 60 runs.

Facing a total of 292, Lancashire were 73 for two before, in three and a quarter hours, Makepeace and Ernest Tyldesley put on 279. Both batsmen hit centuries, and Lancashire took a first-innings lead of 162. On the Monday evening, in the space of 50 minutes, Nottinghamshire lost four wickets for 46 runs and rain during the night made their position hopeless. They were bowled out for 199, and McDonald added to his 5 for 93 in the first innings with 6 for 80 in the second innings. Lancashire won the match by ten wickets and took the Championship.

The part that McDonald played in this success cannot be over-emphasised. He bowled 1,074.5 overs in the Championship and took 163 wickets at 19.04 runs each. In the closing weeks of the season, when it was essential that Lancashire won their matches if they were to take the title, he took 29 wickets in three matches. Cardus, writing in *Wisden,* knew to whom Lancashire owed their triumph. 'It was McDonald, more than any other player in the eleven who won the matches at the season's end.'

He was 'rarely as fast as he was in 1921. None the less, he was faster than the average English fast bowler. His temperament seemed to thrive on any situation which gave his side a sporting chance; he won more than one game against time in a manner that did credit both to his imagination and opportunism. He is a bowler of varying moods — and varying paces. But, at a pinch, he can achieve true greatness, both of technique and temperament.'

What is strange about McDonald's success, and indeed Lancashire's, is that he was not particularly well supported in the field. Duckworth was a brilliant, although inconsistent wicketkeeper, but Lancashire were not renowned as a great fielding side, nor did they hold all their catches. This was notably the case in 1927 when they again took the title.

There is a vast difference between fighting to win a

The portly leg-spinner Richard Tyldesley was the main support for McDonald in the Lancashire attack of the late 1920s.

Championship for the first time in 22 years, as Lancashire were doing in 1926, and struggling to hold on to it as they were the following year. The first is permeated by a gaiety and excitement; the second is characterised by a what-we-have-we-hold attitude and by the less friendly attitude of one's opponents. Everyone is happy when Cinderella goes to the ball; few people want her to be there every night.

Generally, critics found Lancashire's cricket less attractive in 1927 than it had been the previous season, and the nature of their ultimate success was quite astonishing. They won seven of their first ten matches, but appalling weather devastated cricket towards the end of June and through July and August, so that only four of the last 22 fixtures in Lancashire's programme could be brought to a definite result.

The weather deemed that it was not a happy season for English cricket, but it was noted that Lancashire's approach lacked the exhilaration that it had had the previous year. Nevertheless, they moved to the top of the table at the beginning of June and stayed there for seven weeks before being deposed by Nottinghamshire. Lancashire regained the lead early in August and looked set to hold the title until disaster befell them on 26 August.

They travelled to Eastbourne and, for no apparent reason, were bowled out by Tate and Browne for 99 and 76. Sussex scored 371 and won by an innings. Nottinghamshire moved above Lancashire and now seemed certain to win the Championship.

On the day that Lancashire lost to Sussex, their only defeat of the season, Nottinghamshire beat Glamorgan at Trent Bridge. They followed this with a nine-wicket win over Derbyshire at Ilkeston, while Lancashire completed their programme by drawing at Leicester.

Nottinghamshire now stood top of the table and had only to avoid defeat in their last match, against Glamorgan at Swansea. This seemed to suggest no difficulty for Glamorgan had not won a match all season. Nottinghamshire batted first on a rain-affected pitch on the Wednesday, and, thanks to Gunn and Paynton, they made 233, their last seven wickets falling for 90.

Bates and Bell opened the Glamorgan innings and shared a partnership of 158 which, at the time, was a record opening stand for the county. The next four batsmen managed only eight between them, but the tail wagged strongly, and Glamorgan took a first-innings lead of 142. Mercer dismissed Gunn and Walker before the close of play on Thursday evening and, on the last day, Nottinghamshire were caught on a wicket that was drying under a hot sun after early-morning rain. They lost their last eight wickets to Mercer and Ryan for 38 runs, to be all out for 61 and lose by an innings and 81 runs.

The defeat reduced Nottinghamshire's percentage to 67.85. Lancashire had finished on 68.75 and were Champions again.

It was natural that, in a wet summer, McDonald should take fewer wickets, but he still managed 143 in the Championship matches alone. He was poorly supported in the field, and when the ground was soft he bowled off-breaks around the wicket so dependant on him were Lancashire for their success. Once more he bowled well over 1,000 overs.

Although Ernest Tyldesley did not enjoy the triumphs of the previous season, Watson scored more runs and Hallows was magnificent, but it was McDonald who was the Lancashire match-winner. He remained the most feared bowler in the country, and, shades of things to come, at times he 'pitched very short and when he did so, much exception was, in some quarters, taken to his methods'.

In 1928, Lancashire took the Championship for the third time in succession and with a record that booked no argument. They were unbeaten in 30 matches, of which 15 were won. The batting was now more stable than it had ever been. Hallows enjoyed his *annus mirabilis*; Watson was his opening partner in 12 three-figured partnerships, four of them over 200; Ernest Tyldesley and Makepeace were at their best; and Iddon's talent had begun to flower. Yet the pursuit of the crown was taking its toll of Lancashire cricket, and of cricket in general as *Wisden* was to comment:

'A finely equipped side, working skilfully for and thoroughly deserving the honour which rewarded their efforts, Lancashire in achieving their object pursued desperately stern methods. The early batsmen, even when well set, rarely made any attempt to force the game, and this example being followed by most of the other members of the team, play, while correct and effective, was apt at times to become rather tedious. Lancashire, it is true, scored no more slowly than several of the other counties, but there was so often a machine-like regularity of pace observed, whatever the situation, as to raise the question whether, if batsmen have always to keep in mind the gathering of points, success in the Championship may not be purchased at too dear a price.'

The cricket world, at least in the south where the amateur ideal still dominated, was not yet ready for a relentless attitude in the pursuit of trophies. *Wisden,* however subtle in expression, was critical of such an attitude: 'If the plan of action which now obtains with Lancashire enabled them last year to retain the Championship, and to carry it off again this season, the desirability of adopting lighter-hearted methods — however the matter may present itself to the actual players and the average spectator — will scarcely be obvious to those with whom the winning of the Championship is everything in county cricket.'

For the early part of the season, Lancashire had trailed behind Kent, for whom Woolley was in fine form with the bat and for whom 'Tich' Freeman provided almost a one-man attack. Then, in the last days of July and the first days of August, Kent lost three matches in succession, one of them to Lancashire, and Lancashire went to the top of the table and stayed there for the rest of the season.

Kent's last hope of toppling the leaders came in mid-August when they visited Old Trafford. Ashdown and Hardinge went early, but Woolley was at his most fluent and reached 151 out of 248 in just over three hours. Les Ames had given him admirable support, but the last six wickets went down to McDonald and Sibbles for 15 runs, and Kent were all out for 277.

In 70 minutes on the Wednesday evening, Watson and Hallows hit 98. They took their partnership to 155 on the second day, and Hallows and Ernest Tyldesley then added 207. Rain interrupted play several times on the Thursday, but Lancashire had reached 391 for two by the close. They batted on for an hour on the last morning and declared at 478 for five. Kent lost their first five second-innings wickets for 95 runs, and the last five went down for a mere 18 runs.

McDonald had taken 7 for 101 in the first innings. He bowled unchanged in the second and took 8 for 53 as Kent were out for 113. Cardus singled this out as one of the great achievements.

'He, of course, won the match; on the flawless wicket every other bowler who took part in the game was helpless. Lockwood could not let us have seen a greater attack. Bowling of McDonald's skill and dreadful beautiful energy ennobles the game; the spark of it belongs to life immortal and it kindles imagination's fires in all men who look on. When McDonald ran to the wicket yesterday

Old Trafford held its breath; you could have heard a pin drop. The greatest bowler of our day!'

It is hard to argue with Cardus' assertion. It was once more the deadly bowling of McDonald that brought the Championship to Lancashire. 'Considering the amount of work he was called upon to perform and the pace he generally maintained, McDonald kept up his form splendidly, and time and again accomplished a performance which should have — and often did — put Lancashire well on the road to victory.' He bowled 1,173 overs and took 178 wickets at 19.34 runs each in Championship matches. Richard Tyldesley, Iddon and Hopwood, the next three leading wicket-takers, claimed 174 wickets between them. There was, indeed, a terrible beauty in McDonald's bowling.

Lancashire lost their crown in 1929, to Arthur Carr's Nottinghamshire, with Larwood and Voce. Under the new scoring system in which counties each played 28 matches, Lancashire finished in joint second place, ten points behind the leaders. Most people felt that they had slipped to second place because of a decline in McDonald who took *only* 140 wickets in the Championship.

The Championship returned to Old Trafford in 1930. Gloucestershire were beaten by three points, although they won five more matches than Lancashire, who won ten and drew 18 of their 28 matches. It was a wet summer, but times and priorities were undergoing significant changes. In 1930, Bradman and the Test series drew people's attention away from the County Championship and interest in the destination of the crown lessened considerably.

In 1919, 1920, 1922, 1923 and 1927, there were no Test matches played in England. The County Championship reigned supreme and all interest was focussed upon it. From 1928, when three Tests were played against West Indies, until the present day, there has been at least one Test series in England every season, often sapping the leading counties of their best players and drawing the interest of the public away from the domestic competitions. It was in 1930 that there was the first sign of that trend.

Richard Tyldesley was Lancashire's leading wicket-taker in 1930, with 121 Championship wickets; McDonald had 104. He was still a force, but not quite the bowler he had been. He made 1931 his last season in county cricket, and he appeared in only 14 matches before returning to the League. He was now nearly 40.

McDonald began his career with Lancashire with a half-season in 1924 and finished it with a half-season in 1931. In the six full seasons in which he played for the county, they won the Championship four times, were second once and third once. They have won the title outright upon seven occasions — and four of them were with McDonald in the side. In those four Championship seasons, he took 588 Championship wickets at 20.50 runs each.

More than any other man, McDonald was responsible for the first golden age of Lancashire cricket. Arguably, he was the first man who was bought by a county in order to win prizes at cricket. He did not fail those who had trust in him.

Lancashire had superseded Yorkshire as the dominant county in English cricket; now, with the departure of McDonald, and the start of a new decade, they were to bow the knee again to the old enemy.

The Yorkshire of
Brian Sellers

Ferocity, Power and Total Dominance

LORD Hawke died in 1938. He had been captain of the Yorkshire Club from 1883 until 1910, when he was 50, and was president from 1898 until his death. In reality, he controlled the club for most of that period and, contrary to the Blimpish image with which he has been encrusted because of one remark half-quoted out of context, he did a vast amount to modernise the game. His greatest love was Yorkshire cricket and he established a tradition and a standard which those who have followed him, particularly in recent years, have found increasingly difficult to maintain. As a captain, Hawke had led Yorkshire to their ascendancy, and in the six years immediately before his death he was to look down proudly as president upon a Yorkshire side which many would consider to be one of the greatest county sides, if not the greatest, that English cricket has ever known.

In the nine seasons between 1931 and the outbreak of World War Two in 1939, Yorkshire won the title seven times. In 1934, they were fifth, their lowest position since 1911, but this was the year of the visit of the Australians and heavy calls were made on Yorkshire for the Test series; and in 1936, they finished third. This was the year that Derbyshire, with Copson, A.V.Pope and Mitchell an excellent attack, and Worthington and Townsend shining with the bat, took the title on a percentage basis. Yorkshire were beaten only twice in 30 matches. The rest of the decade belonged to the White Rose.

From the side that had dominated county cricket in the early part of the 1920s, Holmes, Leyland, Macaulay and Sutcliffe remained. Oldroyd and Emmott Robinson played their last first-class cricket in the Championship season of 1931. Wilfred Rhodes had retired in 1930, at the age of 53, and, tragically, Roy Kilner had died of enteric fever shortly before the beginning of the 1928 season. He was 37 and much missed.

Since the title had been won in 1925, there had been a period of transition which had involved three different captains. Lupton had resigned at the end of the 1927 season and Sir William Worsley, father of the Duchess of Kent, led the side in 1928 and 1929. It is apparent that Yorkshire were having problems in finding a suitable amateur captain, for Herbert Sutcliffe, touring in South Africa, was offered the leadership without his professional status being affected, but he tactfully declined the job, saying that he would be willing to play under any captain elected. This led to the committee turning to Worsley, to whom they gave unanimous backing.

Worsley took over the side at a most difficult period. Roy Kilner died weeks before he began his period of leadership, and Dolphin had just retired. New men had to be blooded. The emphasis was on caution and containment as players found their way so that, in 1928, although Yorkshire went through the season unbeaten, they won only eight matches and finished no higher than fourth in the table. Worsley stood down at the end of the season, although he was later to return as committee member and was president of the club in 1961.

It was not just the dourness or lack of imagination and the comparative lack of success that had become Yorkshire's problem, but there was also a resurgence of the laxity that had dogged Wilson's last season. The county looked for a saviour, and they turned to Alan Theodore Barber. He was 25 years old and had captained Oxford University in 1929.

A.T.Barber was a most gifted and versatile sportsman. He captained Oxford at both cricket and soccer and was also in the university golf side. He was probably the first Yorkshire skipper since Lord Hawke was at his best to be worth his place in the county side as a player. *Wisden* was to write of him after his death: 'In all his games he was a fine competitor: the more critical the situation, the better he played, and it was this determination, combined with a wonderful vitality and zest for life, which enabled him to instil into a side of tough Yorkshire professionals a discipline which had been lacking under some of his recent predecessors and yet to win at the same time, not only their respect, but also their affection.'

Herbert Sutcliffe had no doubts about Barber. In his book *For England and Yorkshire,* published in 1935, he wrote: 'I shall always have the keenest admiration for the manner in which he tackled his job when he joined Yorkshire in 1930. When he was compelled to leave county cricket at the end of the season he was sorry, but his regret was no greater than that of the members of the Yorkshire side, for they knew they had lost a first-class captain; indeed, they felt they had lost the lead of a man who, had he been able to devote himself to county cricket, would have qualified in a very definite fashion for the captaincy of England. Barber had method in every move he made, he had personality, he earned the respect and comradeship of every member of the side. A great captain was A.T.Barber — one of those rare men with the power of inspiring confidence.'

Barber reigned for only one season, yet his impact on Yorkshire cricket was significant, and it would be unjust to speak of what was achieved between 1931 and 1939 without mentioning the part he played in making possible those triumphs.

He was succeeded by Frank Greenwood, and Greenwood inherited a side that was ripe for success, even if the bowling was neither as dominating nor as varied as it had been under Wilson and Lupton. Greenwood relied heavily on Sutcliffe and other senior professionals, but there was a sense of adventure in him which, on one historic occasion, got him into trouble.

The weather at the end of May and the beginning of June 1931, was wretched. During this period, Yorkshire played three matches in which a ball could not be bowled for seven out of eight days. The second of these matches was against Gloucestershire at Bramall Lane, Sheffield, and there was no play possible on the first two days. Gloucestershire were led by Beverley Lyon, a man to whom cricket was fun and a draw anathema. As Alan Gibson wrote of him: 'He had no funeral. He bequeathed his body to the Royal College of Surgeons — still looking for a positive end to the match.' Lyon suggested to Greenwood, an enterprising and keen captain, that both sides should declare their first innings closed on four, so leaving the destination of the 15 Championship points to the second innings. If the match was drawn, the sides would then share the points for a draw on the first innings.

Greenwood was a little hesitant in accepting the plan and sought the advice of Sutcliffe who 'realised at once it was a magnificent idea, and, without any delay, gave it my support'. Sutcliffe did caution that the captains should not reveal their plan in advance as there was sure to be controversy and that they should study the rule books carefully. Greenwood slept on the advice, but when he arrived at Bramall Lane on the Friday morning, he told Lyon that he would agree to the plan.

Greenwood won the toss and asked Gloucestershire to bat first. Sinfield and Dipper opened. Robinson bowled the first ball, and it was allowed to go through for four byes. Gloucestershire declared. Holmes and Wood opened for Yorkshire. Hammond bowled a ball that was allowed to go through for four byes, and Yorkshire declared. Now the game began in earnest.

Sinfield and Barnett gave Gloucestershire a good start, but the later batsmen fared badly against the bowling of Hedley Verity, and the visitors were dismissed for 171.

Yorkshire had two and a half hours in which to make 172. Holmes was soon out, but Sutcliffe and Leyland batted freely. Goddard then began to turn the ball as sharply as Verity had done, and the game was over at 5.40pm with Gloucestershire winners by 47 runs. It was Yorkshire's only defeat of the season and their first defeat at the hands of Gloucestershire since cricket had resumed after World War One.

Significantly, the day's play had begun with only a handful of spectators, but as news spread through Sheffield that the captains had conjured a match of meaning, the crowd grew appreciably. Sutcliffe remarked, 'Had it been possible to make an overnight declaration of intention, there would have been a tremendous crowd at Bramall Lane that day.' However pleased the paying customers, the authorities were not amused.

Greenwood repeated the plan when similar circumstances arose in the match against Northampton at Bradford. This time his collaborator was Vallance Jupp, one of the best off-spinners in the country. Jupp chose to bat first when he won the toss and after the one-ball four-bye declarations, Northamptonshire were bowled out on a *glue pot* for 86. Verity returned the staggering figures of 7 for 62 in 16.5 overs, staggering in that the other three bowlers used conceded only 22 runs in their 25 overs. Verity's 'expensiveness' is testimony to the aggressive, attacking fields that he and Greenwood were prepared to use.

*Brian Sellers, captain of Yorkshire. County cricket has seen
none better.*

Sutcliffe hit 62, and Yorkshire won by five wickets. The whole game was completed in four and a quarter hours.

Forfeitures of innings and freak declarations have become an accepted part of the game today, but following Greenwood's second use of the Lyon plan, authorities acted and the laws were amended to prevent any further repetition of what had happened at Sheffield and Bradford.

Greenwood was the elected captain of Yorkshire for the 1932 season, but he was able to lead the side in only six Championship matches and Yorkshire suffered their only two defeats in these matches. His deputy was Brian Sellers, son of Arthur Sellers, chairman of the Yorkshire selectors and a fine amateur batsman for the county at the turn of the century.

Brian Sellers had not appeared in first-class cricket before leading Yorkshire to victory over Oxford University at the beginning of May 1932. He was to lead them to 17 more victories that season and not taste defeat in 25 matches. The heir to Hawke's crown had arrived.

Sellers was 25 years old and his cricketing experience was limited to captaining St Peter's School, York, and his home town, Keighley, in the Bradford League. He inherited a strong Yorkshire side with the strength in depth that is so necessary to maintain success, but his post was no sinecure. 'His first victory,' wrote Robertson-Glasgow more than a decade later, 'which did not receive the notice of print, was the greatest, the showing that he was to be captain in fact as well as in name. The medicine was bitter to some; they swallowed it, and felt better. He stood no nonsense and was liked.

Brian Sellers hit four centuries, averaged 23.04 with the bat and took nine expensive wickets during the course of his career. It is not a record that would earn him a prominent place in the history of the game as a player, yet ten years after his death passions rage at the mention of his name and there are those who aver that cricket has known no greater leader. He could talk to the professionals he captained in their own language, and he never minced his words. If they were first sceptical of his ability, his fielding soon convinced them that here was a man to be followed and admired, and they became a unit deeply attached to the man.

Willie Watson, who played under Sellers, recalled how he cowered in the dressing-room while Sellers castigated the great Len Hutton for arriving less than one hour before the start of a game. Names and reputations meant nothing to Sellers. All were part of the

Master batsman Len Hutton, Yorkshire and England.

Yorkshire team and treated the same. 'Sellers was ruthless, as, indeed, all skippers must be ruthless. He believed in discipline, but he subjected himself to the same discipline. On the field he intended Yorkshire not only to be the best cricket team but also the best disciplined, and I believe he was right in thinking that those two qualities are one and the same thing. You cannot be the best team unless you are the best disciplined.'

He insisted on smartness in dress, and he would roar at any man who put his hands in his pockets or who sat down on the field. He expected every man in his team to concentrate on every ball in the field and on their skipper in between deliveries. He was a master tactician who could analyse the strengths and weaknesses of any opponent within seconds. He played cricket sternly but fairly, and under him Yorkshire straddled the cricket world like a Colossus. 'He liked anything that helped towards making the Yorkshire team the happiest, smartest and most efficient in county cricket. He disliked everything that would interfere with that ambition'.

It is worth noting that the only man whose record as a county captain is on a par with Sellers', Stuart Surridge, maintains that it was from the Yorkshireman that he learned the greatest lesson. 'He told me you get nothing for coming second.'

There was a ferocity and power in Sellers' fielding with which he infused the rest of his side. They terrified the opposition, and it almost seemed that Yorkshire won their victories in the 1930s by mesmerising their opponents. Sellers fielded close to the wicket in the company of Arthur Mitchell, Turner and, later, Norman Yardley. They took spectacular catches off the face of the bat without the least sign of the spectacular. Another member of the close-to-the-wicket posse was Ellis Robinson, the off-spinner who won a fairly regular place in the side in 1937.

Robinson worked himself hard as befits a great enthusiast, and if his bowling and zestful batting were inconsistent, he could hit lustily and turned the ball an exceptional amount to the end of his career, with Somerset, in 1952. As a fielder he was consistently brilliant as a member of the vulture-like posse. Once, at slip, he took a stunning low catch to his right, turning a somersault after his dive but still clutching the ball. He was rebuked by Arthur Mitchell with the words, 'Get up, thy's makin' an exhibition of thyself!' It was Mitchell, too, who rebuked a young fielder who stopped a ball with his boot — 'We catch 'em in this team'.

Arthur Mitchell had made his debut for Yorkshire as early as 1922, but he did not become a regular until the late 1920s. 'Ticker' Mitchell, so called because he never stopped nattering, was a solid, dependable, often dour batsman, often opening the innings; as a slip fielder, he had no superior. He was plain and honest in all he did, and he wanted nothing showy or fancy. He was a wonderful corrective for younger players who threatened to get too excited by instant success and its attendant fame.

Mitchell played six times for England; Cyril Turner never did, but Turner was the type of cricketer that Mitchell and Yorkshire appreciated. He was a left-handed batsman and a useful right-arm medium pace bowler, but at short leg he was outstanding. He took breathtaking catches with a phlegmatic air, and then settled down for the next ball. Mitchell was to become coach after his retirement, and Turner was scorer for a while during which time he introduced a pace bowler named Freddie Trueman to the county.

Norman Yardley was not able to play regularly until 1937, by which time he was in the third of his four years in the Cambridge eleven. He captained not only Cambridge and Yorkshire but also England. He was a man of great charm and kindness, an elegant batsman, a useful medium-pace bowler and a brilliant and courageous fielder. With Sellers, Mitchell, Yardley, Turner and Robinson clustered round the bat, no wonder opponents felt intimidated. How much Bowes and Verity owed to them cannot be calculated.

George Macaulay was very much part of the Yorkshire attack until 1933, yet it is the names of Bill Bowes and Hedley Verity that dominate the 1930s. Bowes was on the MCC groundstaff before he was taken into the Yorkshire side in 1929. His rise was meteoric, and, although not as fast as his contemporaries, Larwood, Allen, Farnes and Copson, he was at the forefront of new-ball bowlers. He was on the body-line tour of Australia, 1932-33, but he had bowled leg-theory before that tour, particularly on the passive wickets at The Oval, and he maintained until the end of his life that he, like Larwood, was able to bowl it because he was accurate enough, a quality he did not ascribe to 'Gubby' Allen. Bowes was the one member of the great Yorkshire side of the 1930s who was a poor fielder, but he was hidden and tolerated not just because of his ability as a bowler, but because of his character as a Yorkshireman. He toiled relentlessly for the side and sent down a number of overs which bowlers of today of half his pace would think so excessive that they would disappear for two or three weeks with an undiagnosed muscle complaint.

Bowes was taken prisoner-of-war at Tobruk in 1942, and although he returned to first-class cricket for a couple of seasons after the war, and played in a Test match, he was neither fit enough nor young enough to continue as a pace bowler. He became a fine journalist, was liked by all and remained a rich Yorkshire character. When entertained for lunch by Yorkshire Television in a pub a few years before his death in 1987, he was asked what he would like to eat, and replied 'Duck'. Then he looked at the blackboard on which the menu was written and said, 'Duck, five pounds! No bloody fear. I'll have steak and kidney pie.'

Like Bowes, Hedley Verity took a commission in the war, but he was not to survive. Leading his men into action at Catania, Sicily, in 1943, he was struck by a bullet and died in hospital later. Rarely can a death have been so mourned. Incredibly, the career of this great left-arm spin bowler lasted for only nine years, but in that time he took 1,558 wickets at 13.71 runs each for Yorkshire alone — that is an average of 173 wickets a season.

He first played in 1930, when he was 25, and he did not earn a regular place until 1931, by which time Rhodes had retired in the knowledge that his natural successor had arrived. Verity's impact on the game and on Yorkshire cricket was every bit as immediate as Rhodes' had been. He took 188 wickets in the season, including all ten in the match against Warwickshire — four in one over — at Headingley in mid-May.

There were sceptics who believed that Verity could not maintain the standard he had shown in 1931, but he quickly proved them wrong. In 1932, he finished second in the national bowling averages behind Harold Larwood. Both took 162 wickets, Larwood at 12.86 each, Verity at 13.88. Only Bowes, 190, Goddard, 170, and the tireless 'Tich' Freeman, 253, took more wickets. This was the season when Verity stamped his name indelibly in the record books.

Yorkshire were playing Nottinghamshire at Headingley and the visitors hit 234 on the first day. Yorkshire were struggling at 163 for nine in reply when a violent thunderstorm burst over the ground on the Monday afternoon. Sellers declared before play resumed on the Tuesday when more rain was looming. J.L.Carr, the novelist and then a schoolboy, was present at the match, but 'left the Headingley ground fearing rain and thus condemned him to a life of bitter remorse'.

Keeton and Shipston scored 38 before lunch, but after the interval the ball began to turn viciously on the drying surface. The ten wickets went down for a further 27 runs, all ten of them to Verity. He sent back Walker, Harris and Gunn to perform the hat-trick. He followed this by dismissing Arthur Staples and Larwood with the last two balls of his next over, and brought the innings to a close by disposing of Sam Staples and Voce with the third and fourth balls of the following over. In the last 16 balls he bowled, he took seven wickets for three runs. His ten wickets for ten runs remains a record, and one feels that it will never be equalled. Perhaps one should consider the scorecard to note how important a part fielding and catching meant to Verity and Yorkshire.

Keeton W.W. c Macaulay b Verity 21
Shipston F.W. c Wood b Verity 21
Walker W. c Macaulay b Verity 11
A.W.Carr (capt) c Barber b Verity 0
Staples A. c Macaulay b Verity 7
Harris C.B. c Holmes b Verity 0
Gunn G.V. lbw b Verity 0
Lilley B. not out 3
Larwood H. c Sutcliffe b Verity 0
Voce W. c Holmes b Verity 0
Staples S.J. st Wood b Verity 0
Extras (B 3, NB 1) 4
Total 67

	O	M	R	W
Bowes	5	0	19	0
Macaulay	23	9	34	0
Verity	19.4	16	10	10

Yorkshire won the match by ten wickets, Holmes and Sutcliffe hitting 139 in 90 minutes before the rain returned.

Only a month before this, Holmes (224), and Sutcliffe (313), had established a world-record opening partnership of 555 against Essex at Leyton. On the same pitch, with no deterioration in the weather, Essex were bowled out for 78 and 164. Verity took 5 for 8 and 5 for 45.

This quiet, unassuming, modest man of great dignity played his last game for Yorkshire at Hove at the beginning of September,

1939. Sussex were bowled out for 33 in their second innings. Yorkshire won the match and the title, and Verity's career ended with an analysis of 7 for 9 in six overs, one of which was a maiden.

He died in July 1943, and, with the war still in progress, his grave was located by his teammate Frank Smailes, who had a tombstone erected. Smailes made his debut in 1932, but it was not until 1934, by which time Macaulay had retired, that he established a regular place in the side. He was one of those marvellous bits and pieces cricketers who are the substance of any side that aspires to honours. He bowled medium-pace with considerable hostility, and he later developed as an off-break bowler. He batted left-handed and was capable of resolute defence or violent attack. He took all ten wickets against Derbyshire in 1939 and he was in the England 13 for the Third Test against Australia at Old Trafford in 1938, but the match was abandoned without a ball being bowled and Smailes never learned whether or not he would have played. He said later that he was determined to survive the war in order to win the Test cap that was owed him. He fought all through the Mediterranean campaign and won that England cap against India in 1947, but by then he was past his best.

This splendid attack of Bowes, Verity, Smailes and Robinson was most capably supported in the field and behind the stumps where the stocky, nimble Arthur Wood, a man of great wit, was the driving force. He was first chosen for England at the age of 40, as a late replacement, and after being notified on the eve of the game, he had to take a taxi from Nottingham to The Oval, after first waiting for his cricket gear to arrive from Scarborough.

Percy Holmes retired in 1933, but Sutcliffe, Leyland and Mitchell remained until 1939, and they were joined in the batting line-up by Len Hutton, one of the most stylish and technically accomplished batsmen ever to have graced the game. His honours and achievements were to become legion, but one that is often overlooked is that, in 1939, he took 37 Championship wickets at 18.40 runs each with his leg-breaks and googlies, a frivolity in which Yorkshire did not usually indulge.

To support this nucleus of great players there were Barber, Turner, Fisher and, briefly, Arthur Rhodes, bread and butter players who provided the strength in depth that was so necessary. Yet while it is right that we should identify the individuals in the Yorkshire side of the 1930s, their success was founded on their unity as a team driven by the discipline and dedication of Arthur Sellers.

Hedley Verity, whose career was condensed into ten seasons, but whose slow left-arm bowling brought him 1,558 wickets for Yorkshire alone, and an average of 173 wickets per season in first-class cricket.

Although they lost the title to Lancashire in 1934 and to Derbyshire in 1936, they towered above all other sides for a decade. Cricket was measured by what one achieved against Yorkshire, and the ambitions of many counties became limited. This was the era in which Northamptonshire went from May 1935 until May 1939, without a Championship victory and in which Yorkshire could afford to export batsmen of the calibre of Dennis Brookes, the hero of Northamptonshire's victory over Leicestershire in 1939, and Arnold Dyson of Glamorgan.

Before they became a winning side in 1979, Essex boasted that their greatest achievement in their history was victory over Yorkshire at Huddersfield in 1935. Nichols and Read bowled Yorkshire out for 31 and 99, and, with Nichols hitting 146, Essex won by an innings and 114 runs. The victory is still commemorated by a framed scorecard in the pavilion at Chelmsford.

The one county to threaten Yorkshire's supremacy towards the end of the 1930s was Middlesex. In 1937, 1938 and 1939 they were runners-up, and in the first of those seasons, Robins, the Middlesex captain, challenged Sellers to a deciding match at The Oval, the receipts to go to charity. Hutton hit 121, Verity took 2 for 51 and 8 for 43, and Yorkshire won by an innings, although it should be said in defence of Middlesex that they fielded a weakened side.

The rivalry between the two sides continued unabated. At Lord's, in July 1938, Yorkshire suffered one of their two defeats of the season and, in the process, on a spiteful pitch, lost Hutton, Leyland and Gibb with injured fingers. But the pre-eminence of Yorkshire was unquestioned, and when England beat Australia at The Oval in August 1938, by an innings and 579 runs, there were five Yorkshire players in the side — Hutton, who hit 364; Leyland 187; Wood 53 and three catches; Bowes, 7 for 74; and Verity 2 for 30. Three other Yorkshire players, Smailes, Yardley and Paul Gibb, the wicketkeeper and opening batsman, were all named in sides during the series, and Gibb would certainly have played at Old Trafford as he was the only 'keeper in the party. He, like Yardley, was still at Cambridge.

These were, indeed, the years of Yorkshire supremacy.

Surrey and
Stuart Surridge

Dynamism, Balance, Vision and Genius

BRIAN Sellers led Yorkshire to the Championship for the sixth time in eight seasons in 1946. Middlesex won the same number of matches, 16, but were 12 points adrift in second place. There was a sense of unreality about the 1946 season. It was more the end of an old era than the beginning of a new one. It was almost as if we tried to pretend that nothing had happened, that six years of war had been nothing more than a minor irritant in the flow of first-class cricket and that Wally Hammond, now 43 years old, would be as good as ever. It was, perhaps, important to believe that all was as it had been.

Yorkshire helped to maintain that dream. They remained unbeaten until their penultimate Championship match of the season, and they seemed as invincible as ever. Bowes, Coxon, Robinson and Smailes could muster more than 300 wickets between them in the Championship, and Arthur Booth, a slow left-arm bowler, took 111 wickets at 11.61 runs each in all first-class matches and was top of the national averages.

Booth had been brought in to succeed the late Hedley Verity, but that 1946 season was to be his one full season in county cricket, for he was then 41. He had been given a brief trial in 1931, but was not seen again until 1945 when he played in some of the first-class friendlies that were arranged. After his successes of 1946, he played only four times in 1947 and then vanished again into league cricket. Leyland, Barber and Turner retired at the end of the 1946 season, and Yorkshire's golden period was at an end. The following season was Brian Sellers's last as captain.

As we indicated earlier, a pattern emerged in cricket after World War Two similar to the one that had been apparent in the early 1920s. Middlesex were once more cast in the romantic lead.

The only captain who had been able to match Sellers in tenacity and tactical flair in the late 1930s was Walter Robins. Like Sellers, he was not an easy man, and he could be a ruthless, even insensitive, disciplinarian, but Mike Murray, the present Middlesex chairman who played under him, has said, 'I would have died for that man on the cricket field.' And he is not alone in holding Robins in such esteem. Robins was a year older than Sellers, having been born in 1906.

So much has been written about the Middlesex side of the period immediately after the war that it seems almost sacrilegious to imply that they were not a great side. They were second in 1946, third in 1948 when the Test series against the Australians ravaged them severely, won the title in 1947, shared it in 1949 and then passed into an oblivion which was to last for the best part of another 30 years.

The great year was, of course, 1947 when their gaiety and their whole dynamic approach to the game seemed to symbolise the country's rebirth or reawakening after years of war and austerity. The season will long be remembered for the batting records of Denis Compton and Bill Edrich. In all matches, Compton hit 18 centuries, scored 3,816 runs and averaged 90.85, records which are unlikely ever to be broken. Edrich hit 12 centuries and scored 3,539 runs, average 80.43.

The Middlesex run-getting was not restricted to Edrich and Compton, for in Jack Robertson and Syd Brown, they had two exciting and consistent openers. In Championship matches, the first four batsmen in the Middlesex side hit 8,213 runs between them and, vitally and breathtakingly, they scored them at a rate of close to 80 runs an hour.

It was not just the amount of runs that Robertson, Brown, Edrich and Compton scored, nor the number of matches that were won, but the way in which the runs came and the way in which matches were won which captured the public imagination.

Typical of the type of cricket that Middlesex played was seen in the match against Surrey at The Oval at the beginning of August. Watched by a vast crowd, Middlesex hit 537 for two on the Saturday, only Brown (98) failing to score a century. Surrey replied with 334, which was not enough to save them from having to follow-

Denis Compton, the golden boy of Middlesex and England in the immediate post-war period. No batsman had given greater pleasure.

on, and Middlesex won by an innings by one o'clock on the last day. Even more exhilarating was the match against Leicestershire at Leicester three weeks earlier. The home side hit 409, but Middlesex replied with 637 for four declared. Edrich and Compton shared a stand of 277 in 131 minutes. Eventually, Middlesex needed 66 to win in 27 minutes. Compton and Edrich opened, with Robertson and Brown padded up behind the sight-screen, waiting to run in should a wicket fall. It did not. The Middlesex 'twins' won the match with four minutes to spare.

The amount of runs scored and the speed with which they were scored were integral to Robins' positive approach to the game. It was also the only way in which Middlesex could possibly have won the title, for their bowling resources were limited in the extreme. They had one fast-medium bowler, Laurie Gray, who was an honest worker, a very useful county bowler who had been with Middlesex since 1934 and, at the age of 32, one who was ever willing to take on a mountain of work. He had no adequate new-ball partner. Mostly Edrich, with his tearaway style, would take one end, but, on occasions, wicketkeeper Leslie Compton would take off his pads to bowl medium-pace, not with great success. There were other times when left-arm spinner Jack Young would open the attack. He, with veteran leg-spinner Jim Sims, was the main 'strike' bowler. Denis Compton, too, was a consistent wicket-taker with his slow left-arm variations, and, remarkably, in the most important match of the season, one of the heroes was a reserve, Harry Sharp, who gave a fine all-round performance.

The match was against Gloucestershire at Cheltenham, and, in effect, the Championship depended upon the result. Middlesex were without Denis Compton and Jack Robertson, and Edrich had an injury which prevented him from bowling. The veteran off-spinner Tom Goddard took seven wickets and Middlesex were bowled out for 180, but Young and Sims gave their side the edge, taking all ten Gloucestershire wickets between them and bowling the home side out for 153. Goddard followed his seven first-innings wickets with eight in the second, and Gloucestershire needed 169 to win. They did not get them. Jack Young took 5 for 27, and Harry Sharp, who had hit an invaluable 14 not out and 46, took 3 for 39 with his off-breaks. They were the only three wickets he took in the season. Middlesex won by 68 runs, and the game, watched by a capacity crowd, was all over in two days. Ten days later, Middlesex took the title.

Bill Edrich, whose name will ever be linked with that of Denis Compton. In 1947, both batsmen exceeded 3,000 runs, and Middlesex won the Championship.

This was a joyous and memorable summer, but, scintillating as was the cricket played by Middlesex, they cannot truly be remembered as one of the great sides in cricket history. Despite the honest efforts of Young, Sims, Gray and the rest, they did not really have an attack that was capable of keeping them at the top for any length of time, and they will remain as something of a curiosity in cricket history — the one side to have taken the title on strength of batting alone.

Although Middlesex were deposed, the age of romance continued with Glamorgan taking the title for the first time in their history in 1948. They had not entered the Championship until 1921 and for many years in the period between the wars had struggled at the bottom of the table. They had been kept alive by the enthusiasm and energies of a dedicated group of men, one of whom was the honorary secretary, J.C.Clay. Clay had played for Glamorgan in their first season in first-class cricket, had led the side from 1924 to 1927, jointly in 1929, and again in 1946 after which he had given way to the outspoken and uncompromising Wilf Wooller, a man with a zest for winning.

Clay, who was in his 51st year in 1948, had reduced his pace from medium to bowl off-spinners. He took 10 for 66 as Surrey were beaten by an innings at Cardiff in mid-August, and Glamorgan then travelled to Bournemouth to play Hampshire knowing that victory would give them the title. They made 315, and Muncer and Clay bowled out Hampshire for 84. Following-on, Hampshire were out for 116. Clay took six for 48, and his sixth wicket, C.J.Knott leg-before, won the match and the title. The umpire was Dai Davies, a Glamorgan stalwart of the 1930s. Knott was hit on the pads right in front of the stumps, and Clay and all the fielders appealed, and as he lifted his finger, Davies said excitedly, 'That's out and we've won the Championship!' That was the stuff of legend, but a professional reality lurked at hand.

Surrey were only four points behind Glamorgan in 1948, and two years later they shared the title with Lancashire. They had had captaincy problems shortly after the war and for one season were led by N.H.Bennett, a club cricketer. He was succeeded by the dashing Errol Holmes, who had been captain in the years immediately before the war and had to be persuaded to take over the leadership again to assist the club in a period of crisis. In 1949, Holmes gave way to M.R.Barton, an Oxford blue of the 1930s and a man of immense charm. Barton, like Holmes, did much to repair a great club that had had its problems. He led them to the shared title, and he suggested to the committee that he should be succeeded in 1952 by an enthusiastic cricketer named Stuart Surridge.

Surrey could have gone outside the county for a captain to succeed Barton, as Leicestershire had done with C.H.Palmer and Northamptonshire had done in enlisting the aid of F.R.Brown. Alternatively, they could have appointed one of the senior professionals like Laurie Fishlock or Jack Parker, although both of these were at the veteran stage and nearing retirement. Warwickshire had just won the Championship in fine style with an all-professional side under the inspiring leadership of Tom Dollery, but the amateur/professional demarcation was still much in evidence, and it was unlikely that such a bastion as The Oval would help to hasten its end.

Ironically, Surridge, like Sellers, whom he admired deeply and resembled in many ways, was what one might call a 'professional amateur'. He was not of the old school. He was in business and not a graduate of Oxford or Cambridge. He had grown up and played with several of the cricketers he was to lead. He had learned his trade in bat-making the hard way, for although his grandfather had founded the business in the nineteenth century and it had been passed from father to son, Stuart was expected to start at the bottom and to learn every aspect of the firm's work. Before one can give orders, one must learn how to take them.

There were misgivings about Surridge when he was appointed captain of Surrey. There were those who doubted if he were a good enough player, but then Sellers had been doubted in the same way, and there were those who considered that he had had too little experience. He had played for the Young Surrey team before the war and had made his first-team debut in 1947. He played in five Championship games in that season and appeared more frequently season by season until he became a regular by 1950.

His exceptional qualities of leadership have tended to overshadow the fact that Stuart Surridge was a very good cricketer. He was a tall, fast-medium pace bowler who used his height to good advantage. In 1952, he took 78 wickets, and in the years that followed, he would have taken many more had he not been so unselfish. He believed that the professionals needed encouragement because they were trying to earn a living, and when there was a chance of cheap wickets it was the professionals who were offered them. Surridge never claimed anything cheap for himself; on the contrary, he would bowl when the wicket was placid and offer full tosses or long hops in an attempt to buy a wicket. His career figures, 506 wickets at 28.89 runs each, do him scant justice and reveal nothing of the man's attacking qualities.

His batting was exuberant. His highest score was 87 and he was essentially a quick-fifty man, but he could terrify fielders and destroy bowlers with the violence of his hitting.

Here, then, was a capable all-rounder, but there was a quality in his game which surpassed all others — his fielding. Surridge admired Sellers because he was tough, stood no nonsense and led by example. 'He wouldn't ask anybody to field closer to the bat than he was prepared to field himself.' That is Surridge talking of Sellers; it could have been anyone who saw or knew him talking of Surridge himself.

Fielding was not a strong point in English cricket in the years immediately after World War Two, but by the early 1950s the Surrey fielding was generally accepted as efficient or satisfactory. In Surridge's opinion it was awful and he set about rectifying it immediately. He insisted on practice and on developing this aspect of the game. His own fielding was supercharged and infectious. The Surrey out-cricket achieved a standard that has become legendary. So aggressive was the Surrey fielding that many of their opponents succumbed to the pressure that was put upon them and became frightened to put bat to ball. *Wisden* was quick to recognise the dynamic effect that Surridge had had on the Surrey fielding and commented after his first season in charge.

'His ability in this direction resulting in the acceptance of some catches which might be regarded by many cricketers as bordering upon the impossible, at times exerted an unnerving effect upon opposing batsmen and paved the way to more than one of the 20 victories.'

Indeed, the Surrey fielding as a whole became the talk of the cricket world with Surridge and Tony Lock, incomparable at short-leg, the two most singled out for special praise.

Certainly Surrey had the strongest and best balanced attack in the club's history. It was an attack that has had no superior and very few equals in the history of the game, and it was supported by brilliant close fielding and catching. The batting was equal to the demands made upon it, and was, according to Peter West, 'virile'. West also recognised 'there was an intangible factor' in the

For five years Stuart Surridge led Surrey, and in each of those years they won the Championship.

team's success, 'a true team spirit, which sprang from the inspiration and boisterous precept of Surridge in his first year of command'.

One cannot overpraise Surridge. He was in complete command of all situations. He captained Surrey for five seasons, and they won the Championship in each one of those seasons. It is a record which has stood unchallenged now for nearly 40 years, and one cannot see it being equalled for many years to come, if ever.

During Surridge's reign the system of deciding the Championship was that each county played 28 games and received 12 points for a win and four points for a first-innings lead in a match drawn or lost. The attitude of Surridge and his Surrey side was that each match was vital and that victory must be sought from the very first ball. They engaged in constant fielding practice before each game, and they maintained a consistently dynamic approach. There was obvious joy and pride in all that they did. It is reflected in the record:

Year	P	W	L	D	N/R	Pts	Margin of Winning Title
1952	28	20	3	5		256	32 points
1953	28	13	4	10	1	184	16 points
1954	28	15	3	8	2	208	22 points
1955	28	23	5	-		284	16 points
1956	28	15	5	6	2	200	20 points
1957	28	21	3	3	1	312	94 points
1958	28	14	5	8	1	212	26 points

The last two titles were won under the captaincy of Peter May.

We have drawn attention to the strength of the Surrey attack at this period, and again the figures are testimony to the quality and the achievement. In his five years as captain of the Championship-winning side, Surridge's figures were 187 wickets at 28.11 runs each. He bowled 2,018.5 overs, of which 413 were maidens. The figures of the other leading bowlers over the seven-year record period in the Championship are as follows:

	Overs	Maidens	Runs	Wickets	Average
G.A.R.Lock	5238.1	2009	10405	817	12.73
J.C.Laker	4836	1678	9830	628	15.65
P.J.Loader	3484.5	837	8030	492	16.32
A.V.Bedser	4932.3	1391	10184	624	16.32
E.A.Bedser	2852.3	943	5759	292	19.72

Tony Lock, whose aggressive slow left-arm bowling and dynamic fielding was a key factor in Surrey's success.

These are astounding figures, and when one considers that the six men were playing together in the same team at the same time they are phenomenal.

Peter Loader had appeared for Surrey once as an amateur in 1951, was offered a professional contract and began to win a place in the side as Alec Bedser's deputy in 1952. He was, in fact, faster than Alec Bedser, was to win 13 Test caps and become one of the few bowlers to perform the hat-trick in Test cricket.

Alec Bedser is one of the legends of English cricket. He was a giant among bowlers and for a period in the late 1940s he *was* the England attack. Bedser was a no frills cricketer, transparently honest in all that he did. Loyal, traditional, conservative, with an immense capacity and appetite for work, he was a big man who hustled to the wicket smoothly off a run that was never exaggerated and with a style that was always economic. For such a big man, he was remarkably quick and agile and an excellent fielder. He was the master of the art of medium-pace bowling in the Barnes-Tate tradition, and he was ever subtle and inventive. He adapted to all surfaces, and there was no batsman in the world, from Bradman to Hutton and Compton, who was not troubled by him.

His twin brother, Eric, has tended to have been overshadowed, but he was an excellent all-rounder, a batsman capable of opening the innings and an off-break bowler who would command a regular place in an England side of today.

The leading exponent of off-spin at the time that the Bedsers were playing was, of course, Jim Laker, and it is doubtful if the game has seen his equal.

He is the only man to have taken 19 wickets in a Test match, and it should be remembered that earlier in the 1956 season when he took his 9 for 37 and 10 for 53 in the Old Trafford Test match against Australia, he had 10 for 88 as Surrey beat the Australians by ten wickets at The Oval. Laker spun the ball with his fingers which often became raw and sore because of the amount of spin he imparted. He was able to turn the ball on any wicket, and the close to the wicket fielders could hear the ball zipping through the air.

His comrade-in-arms was the left-arm spinner Tony Lock. He bowled the ball quicker than most spinners of his type, but perhaps that was characteristic of a man whose energy and enthusiasm bubbled permanently and who attacked from start to finish. He

Lion-hearted Alec Bedser ranks along with Maurice Tate and S.F.Barnes as the greatest of England's medium-pace bowlers. He led Surrey most capably on many occasions.

was not only a great bowler, but a man of such dynamism that he influenced all who came into contact with him, both in England and, later, in Western Australia. To escape the wiles of Laker at one end, only to be confronted by the relentless aggression of Lock at the other, was a daunting prospect for Surrey's opponents in the 1950s.

None has dared to question the quality and balance of the Surrey attack in this golden period, but there are those who have suggested that the batting was far from strong and, indeed, even fallible. Surridge would refute such an argument. He is adamant that his side was always capable of getting just the amount of runs that they needed — one run more than the other side — and a glance at the batting line-up would support his view. Clark, Constable, a brilliant fielder, Whittaker, Parker and Fishlock were fine county batsmen and, as the last three retired, they were replaced by Peter May, Ken Barrington, Mickey Stewart — another brilliant fielder, and, briefly, by Raman Subba Row. This hardly suggests a weakening, as the last four all played for England at a time when there was an abundance of good batsmen.

This great Surrey side was a blend of honest, dedicated hard-working cricketers and genius. They were disparate characters who were fused into a unity by Surridge's flair, personality and instinct for the game. One sensational victory seemed to tumble over another and rarely did the captain not do something that would delight, amuse, astound and bring the victory itself. The most famous instance was at The Oval in August 1954.

Surrey had been in devastating form and when Worcestershire arrived at The Oval on 25 August, victory for the home side meant the retention of the Championship. Rain had affected the wicket and no play was possible before 2pm. Surridge won the toss and asked Worcestershire to bat first. They were all out in 100 minutes for 25. Lock took 5 for 2 in 33 balls as the last eight wickets fell for five runs.

Surrey lost two wickets for 31 runs, but Worcestershire were short of the quality spin attack that was needed in the circumstances, and May and Constable added 46. Barrington then joined May and with wicketkeeper McIntyre, who was an excellent batsman as well as an outstanding keeper, still to come, it looked as if Surrey would build a substantial lead. The pitch was getting considerably easier, but to the astonishment of May and Barrington and the Surrey members and supporters, the captain declared with

Off-spinner supreme — Jim Laker.

the score at 92 for three and the time not yet 5.30pm on the first day. There were suggestions of madness, and the only defence that Surridge offered for his action was that it was going to rain, a reason which hardly placated the Surrey players or supporters. The capture of two wickets before the close still failed to convince them, even though one of them was the wicket of Peter Richardson, the England opener, who, in offering no stroke at a ball from Laker, lifted the bat high above his shoulders, only to see the ball turn and rise so sharply that it took the edge of the bat for him to be caught behind.

The game was all over within an hour on the second morning as Worcestershire were bowled out for 40. The match had lasted little more than five hours in all. Surrey had scored only 92 runs and yet had won by an innings and 27 runs. Perhaps there was a touch of madness in the captaincy of Stuart Surridge. There is a touch of madness in all visionaries.

When he had taken on the job of leading Surrey, Stuart Surridge had told the committee that his side would win the Championship five years in succession and he had kept his word. He stood down because he felt that Peter May, as captain of England, must be allowed to captain his county. He felt, too, that the players of promise in the 2nd XI were growing older without being allowed sufficient opportunity to display their talents. He was confident that he was handing on to May a side that was capable of winning the title for the next three years. As it proved, he was over-optimistic by one year.

Peter May had no easy task. The side that he inherited was essentially Surridge's side, and May himself was more a disciple of Hutton than of Surridge. Having taken over a team that had won the Championship five years in succession, May realised that anything short of winning the title would be seen as failure. There was tremendous pressure on him, but he was a gentle man with a hard streak, and he was uncompromising in his demands and his desire to win. He was to be ably served by his vice-captain, Alec Bedser, and by a mature side who respected him as an intelligent leader and as the greatest batsman of his generation.

Under May, the fielding was as dynamic as it had been under Surridge, and in 1957, Mickey Stewart held 77 catches, mostly at short-leg, while Barrington, at slip, held 64 catches and Lock, in the leg trap, the same number. These are exceptional figures and put the three fielders in the first dozen in the history of the game.

Peter May, the outstanding batsman of his generation.

At Northampton, in what was a vital match, Stewart held a world-record seven catches, and so aggressive was the Surrey fielding in these vintage years that batsmen were in a state of constant uncertainty.

If one has emphasised the quality of Surrey's fielding in this period, it is because it was revolutionary. It had been customary to place the elder statesmen of a side close to the wicket so that they would not have too much running to do. Surridge, and later May, put the youngest players in the positions nearest the wicket and relied upon their quick reflexes, safe hands and courage to hold catches that others would not have dreamed possible. In the 1930s, Yorkshire had set the pattern that fielding was a principle ingredient in a title-winning side, and in the 1950s, Surrey refined that principle to a level which had never before been attained.

May's first season as captain of Surrey was an emphatic success. His side lost one more game than Northamptonshire, but they won six more than their closest rivals and finished an astonishing 94 points ahead of Northamptonshire in the table. In some ways it was the pinnacle of their achievement, yet the seeds of decline were already beginning to take root.

Alec Bedser's great Test career ended in 1955 and, although he performed splendidly in 1957, he was perhaps not quite as fit as he had been before the bout of shingles which had hastened the end of his Test career. Tony Lock was having trouble with an injured knee, and Arthur McIntyre, an outstanding wicketkeeper still, was nearing the end of his career.

McIntyre was to lead the side on several occasions in 1958, his last season, for Alec Bedser, who had captained so shrewdly and encouragingly in May's absence on international duty, went down with pneumonia on the eve of the season and could not play until July. That Surrey were still able to win the Championship by a margin of 26 points was remarkable and of great credit to Peter May who, in a wet summer, towered above all other batsmen in the country.

In the winter of 1958-59, May took the England side to Australia and had with him four other Surrey players, Laker, Lock, Loader and Swetman, the young wicketkeeper. May was unable to play until the end of May, 1959, because of his marriage, and in July, he had to undergo an operation which brought his season to an end. His batting was sorely missed, and none of the bowlers was quite as successful as they had been in previous seasons. Lock's action had come under close scrutiny, particularly the way in which he delivered his quicker ball, and he was in the process of remodelling his style. Laker was growing disenchanted and was to retire at the end of the season. The greatest and most successful cricket team of modern times was in the process of breaking up.

They were still the most feared side in the country and they needed only to win their last two matches in 1959 to take the title for the eighth time in succession. But they won neither and their reign was at an end. At Hove, Yorkshire were left 105 minutes in which to score 215 runs and win the Championship. They took 15 from the first over, and 100 came up in 43 minutes. Stott hit 96 in 86 minutes and he and Padgett put on 141 in an hour. Victory came with seven minutes and five wickets to spare. The Surrey supremacy was broken at last.

The Yorkshire success took everyone by surprise, not least Yorkshire themselves, who had expected a period of rebuilding. There had been rumbles of discontent within the club which had led to the resignation of captain Billy Sutcliffe and the loss of leading batsman Willie Watson. That Yorkshire were neither happy nor united was obvious even to a casual observer. To help re-establish the side, the Yorkshire committee had taken the surprising step of appointing the 40-year old J.R.Burnet to lead the county in 1958. He had never before appeared in first-class cricket.

His first season as captain saw the abrupt dismissal of Johnny Wardle, a slow left-arm bowler of international class and worthy of the great Yorkshire tradition of left-arm spinners. Wardle was a witty and popular cricketer to the public, but in the dressing-room he was a canker, and Yorkshire announced that they would not be retaining him after the 1958 season. Wardle replied in the pages of the *Daily Mail* that he had been sacked because he 'refused to accept the authority of the quite hopeless old man appointed captain'. The newspaper article ended his first-class cricket career, and the 'hopeless old man', fully supported by his men, led Yorkshire to the Championship in 1959. Having had two seasons in first-class cricket and done the job that he had been appointed to do, Burnet retired.

Although Len Hutton had been one of England's most successful captains, he had never been elected captain of Yorkshire, whose great mentor, Lord Hawke, is best remembered by many for saying that he prayed to God that a professional would never captain England. That statement had been made in 1925. Thirty-five years later, in a country still scarred by a second world war, attitudes had changed and were changing still. When Burnet stood down, Yorkshire appointed the senior professional, Vic Wilson, to succeed him as captain.

Wilson led Yorkshire for two seasons. They won the title in 1960 and finished second in 1961, after which Wilson retired and was succeeded by Brian Close. The winners of the Championship in 1961 were Hampshire, and they were captained by Colin Ingleby-Mackenzie.

Changing Times

The End of the Amateur, The Arrival of the One-Day Game

I T WOULD be difficult to justify a place for Ingleby-Mackenzie's Hampshire side of 1961 among the great county sides in cricket history, yet they merit our attention for theirs was a popular win and, in many ways, it represented the end of something. Hampshire had never won the title before, and that a county should at last break the monopoly that had long been held by Surrey and Yorkshire was appealing. Also, they were an entertaining side, an important factor at a time when cricket was becoming dull and its following was dwindling.

The 1961 Hampshire team was mostly a side of seasoned professionals. In Derek Shackleton they had one of the great medium-pace bowlers, and he formed a formidable opening attack with 'Butch' White. Peter Sainsbury was a useful left-arm spinner and a most capable batsman in a line-up that was solid and dependable. Horton, Gray and Livingstone were consistent batsmen, while Ingleby-Mackenzie was capable of quick runs and exciting innings; and there was Roy Marshall.

Marshall was a West Indian who had toured England in 1950 and had scored over 1,000 runs, but he had been unable to win a Test place in a side which boasted Worrell, Weekes, Walcott, Stollmeyer and Rae. He later won four Test caps, but he decided to qualify for Hampshire by residence and became the most exciting opening batsman in the country. He hit the ball with tremendous power, had a wide range of strokes and was a most vibrant cricketer who had a popular following.

Colin Ingleby-Mackenzie was a survivor from a lost age. An Old

Etonian, he was a cavalier. He led with dash and daring and hit the ball hard. He had the reputation of being something of a gambler and of enjoying life to the full. He won public affection when, asked about discipline, he was quoted as saying, 'I always insist that my team be in bed before breakfast.' He was a personality who aroused in people a vision of what they believed to be the Golden Age of the Edwardians. He was the last of the amateurs. He was certainly the last amateur to lead a county side to a trophy victory.

In 1962, the distinction between amateur and professional was abolished. It was the first of several radical changes that were introduced in order to boost a game that was flagging in its appeal to the public and was facing a financial crisis. In 1963 came the knock-out competition sponsored by Gillette, and six years later came the John Player Sunday League. A third one-day competition, the Benson and Hedges Cup, began in 1972. Before this, in 1968, counties were allowed to recruit one overseas player on immediate registration.

These immense changes in the game were brought about by the administrators being forced into an awareness of the need to present cricket as an entertainment which needed sponsorship, television coverage and more effective public relations. Within a few short years the whole concept of the game was changed. Where once there had been just a single honour for which the 17 counties had vied, many without ever nourishing any real hope of success, there were now four trophies for which sides could compete. There were, too, now great financial incentives to win a major competition.

Some of the greatest cricketers the game has known — Wally Hammond, C.B.Fry, Maurice Tate, Les Ames, Bob Wyatt, 'Tich' Freeman, Godfrey Evans and Trevor Bailey among them — had enjoyed careers which lasted for over 20 years, but they had never been a member of a title-winning side during all of that time. Most were reconciled to this state of affairs as were those who watched them.

People went to see a county side out of affection and loyalty and because they loved the game. They went to watch the skills of great players like Compton, Hutton and Hammond and, although it was glory if one of the lesser counties gained a surprise victory over one of the 'big six', winning was not considered all that important by the followers of the game. It was recognised

Sparkle and fun and one golden year for Hampshire under Colin Ingleby-Mackenzie.

that cricket had an intrinsic value in itself and that the winning of the County Championship was effectively the monopoly of a mighty few.

From the mid-1960s and the advent of the one-day game, attitudes began to change. Where once supporters had been content to follow a county through years of drought, the majority of them now demanded success. If that success was not forthcoming, support dwindled. Allegiance to a county side became more partisan, more demanding — and louder. Those counties who were slow to realise this change in emphasis suffered accordingly.

The revolution was not immediate. Vic Wilson led Yorkshire to the Championship in 1962, his last season. He handed over the captaincy to Brian Close, under whose leadership Yorkshire took the title four times in seven years. They were the last county to dominate the Championship in such a manner.

Remarkably, the side changed little between 1963 and 1968. Geoff Boycott, the outstanding batsman of his generation, was just coming to the fore at the beginning of the period and was England's established opener and leading batsman by the end of it. His name was not yet linked with controversy. Ken Taylor, Doug Padgett, Jackie Hampshire and Phil Sharpe, all Test cricketers, gave substance to the rest of the batting, and there were two all-rounders of top quality in Ray Illingworth and Brian Close. Don Wilson, if not a Rhodes, Verity or Wardle, was a slow left-arm bowler good enough to play six times for England. Behind the stumps was Jimmy Binks, another Test cricketer, who, in the opinion of many judges, had no superior in the country and was who desperately unlucky not to gain more than the two Test caps he won against India in 1964. He is one of only seven wicketkeepers to have claimed 100 victims or more in a season.

Many of his catches were taken off the bowling of Freddie Trueman, one of the truly great fast bowlers in the history of the game. Trueman was not only fast and accurate with the ability to move the ball, he was an unquenchable enthusiast. His ardour for the game and for Yorkshire cricket lost none of its fervour over the years. He was a fierce, friendly and fair adversary.

His new-ball partner was Tony Nicholson, the only member of the side not to win a Test cap. Nicholson was a brisk medium-pace, naggingly accurate, just short of a length and constantly hostile.

The fielding was in the Yorkshire tradition with Sharpe, Close

Highly capable and competitive, ever controversial — Brian Close.

and Trueman outstanding in the close-to-the-wicket positions. Like Sellers and Surridge, Close led by example and his fearless fielding became legendary. He also shared with Sellers and Surridge a hatred for defeat or finishing second. His zealousness on behalf of Yorkshire was to cost him dearly.

In 1967, Yorkshire began badly in defence of their title, but they emerged among the leaders in mid-season. They were third at the beginning of August and went to the top of the table on 15 August. The following day they went to Edgbaston to play Warwickshire. Yorkshire were bowled out for 238, and Warwickshire took a first-innings lead of four runs. When Yorkshire batted for a second time they slumped against Tom Cartwright and David Cook, a left-arm medium-pace bowler who played only nine games for Warwickshire in a period of six years. Yorkshire were all out for 145, and Warwickshire had 102 minutes in which to score 142 to win the match.

Under the scheme in operation at the time, a win gave a side eight points and there were four points for a first-innings lead whatever the final outcome of the match. A drawn match gave each side two points. As Yorkshire had lost first-innings points, they could only hope to gain points by winning or drawing with Warwickshire. There seemed no likelihood of them winning, so that the best that they could hope for was two points for a draw, welcome in a Championship race which was very close indeed.

Thanks to Amiss and Jameson, Warwickshire scored at the required rate, but in 102 minutes Yorkshire bowled only 24 overs. At one time they left the field during a shower of rain, although umpires Elliott and Gray remained in the middle with the two batsmen, and one of the two overs bowled in that last 15 minutes was bowled by Trueman who conceded two no-balls, so lengthening the over, and sent down three bouncers. Warwickshire failed by nine runs to reach their target, and the game ended in acrimony.

The Cricketer described the events at Edgbaston and the turmoil which followed as 'one of the unhappiest ten days in the game's history'. An executive committee of former county captains, Sellers among them, investigated the umpires' report on the match and announced unanimously that: 'Yorkshire had used delaying tactics during the second Warwickshire innings and that these tactics constituted unfair play and were against the best interests of the game.'

Close was held entirely responsible for the tactics and was severely censured. Moreover, he was deprived of the England captaincy. He had held the position for a year and had become something of a national hero. He had been named as captain of the side to tour West Indies in the winter 1967-68, but, following the Edgbaston incident and the subsequent censure, the invitation to him was withdrawn and Colin Cowdrey took the side to the Caribbean.

It is somewhat amusing to reflect now that Close and Yorkshire were condemned because they had bowled at an over-rate of 15 overs an hour, a rate which would often be welcome today. It was accepted in 1967 that the optimum over-rate was 20 overs an hour and Close's tactics brought about this being written into the laws for the last hour of a game.

Yorkshire took the title by a margin of ten points in 1967, but they could not be sure of the Championship until they had claimed first-innings points in the final match against Gloucestershire.

Their margin of victory the following season, with a more elaborate point-scoring system in operation, was by 14 points, and once again much depended on the final fixture. This was against Surrey at Hull and, although Yorkshire were never in danger of defeat, they had to fight to gain victory by 60 runs with five minutes of extra-time remaining. Three wickets in two overs at the close gave them the win and helped them to retain the Championship. They had been held up by Younis Ahmed and Arnold Long, who batted for 105 minutes while 61 runs were scored for the eighth wicket. This stubborn partnership was eventually broken when Younis pulled Wilson hard, but the ball hit Brian Close on the arm and rebounded into the hands of Binks behind the wicket for a simple catch. It was a fittingly symbolic piece of Close fielding with which to mark the twilight of Yorkshire's success. In the 22 years since 1968, they have not added to their 29 official titles and in recent years, often divided by controversy and public pain, they have frequently struggled in the lower half of the table.

Few would put the Yorkshire side of the 1960s on a par with the great sides of the past. Boycott apart, the batting could not compare in quality with the likes of Hutton, Sutcliffe and Leyland while the attack rested heavily on Trueman, Illingworth and Wilson, of whom only Trueman was in the very top flight.

Yorkshire had supported the new legislation regarding the immediate registration of overseas players in principle, although they affirmed their policy of playing only those born within the county would continue. Through the tribulations of recent years they have maintained that policy while others have imported success.

Yorkshire's Championship triumphs of the 1960s were punctuated by Worcestershire who took the title in 1964 and 1965. For much of the 1930s, the Midland county had been vying for the wooden spoon in the Championship, and their elevation to the position of leading county was as welcome as it was well prepared. Much of the preparation was done by Don Kenyon, a seasoned professional, an inspiring captain, intelligent and tactically shrewd, and, in the opinion of the majority of Worcestershire's older supporters, the finest batsman ever to play for the county, a county which can boast Cyril Walters, Tom Graveney and Graeme Hick.

Kenyon believed in a strong squad of players and, like all the successful captains since Sellers, he placed a keen emphasis on fielding and on the value of the 'bits and pieces, bread and butter' cricketer. He saw Jim Standen, a goalkeeper with Arsenal and West Ham United, as the type of player essential to a successful side. Standen was a medium-pace bowler of above average ability, a capable lower-order batsman who was able to vary his game according to the needs of the side, and a fielder supreme with an athleticism which turned any ball not played into the ground a potential catch.

Worcestershire were also served by two front-line pace bowlers, Flavell and Coldwell, both of whom played for England and represented the most potent new-ball attack in the country. They were ably supported by Brian Brain, a medium-pacer, and by Norman Gifford, a left-arm spinner of international standing. Martin Horton, who opened the innings with Kenyon, was a fine off-break bowler, and there was quality batting in the form of West Indian Ron Headley, son of the great George, Tom Graveney, a master stylist and experienced Test player who joined Worcestershire after a rift with his native Gloucestershire, Dick Richardson and Alan Ormrod. Roy Booth was an excellent wicketkeeper and capable batsman, and the whole side had balance and that delicate blend of youth and experience which is a necessary quality in a good side.

At 3.12pm on Tuesday, 25 August 1964, Roy Booth stumped Ken Graveney off the bowling of Norman Gifford and Worcestershire had beaten Gloucestershire at New Road by an

Don Kenyon (right) who led Worcestershire to their first title in 1964, here opening the innings with Eddie Cooper.

innings and two runs. Few people left the ground, for they huddled in front of the pavilion awaiting news of the match at Southampton where Warwickshire, who had been fighting Worcestershire tenaciously for the title all season, were playing Hampshire. Warwickshire had been set to score 314 at 90 runs an hour, a most difficult task but one which they came close to accomplishing. They lost by 17 runs, and Worcestershire were Champions for the first time in their history.

They retained their title the following season in spectacular and dramatic fashion, winning ten of their last 11 matches and overtaking Northamptonshire at the death. Worcestershire gained a sensational victory over Hampshire at Bournemouth in the penultimate game of the season. A blank second day due to rain led Kenyon to declare after one ball of his side's second innings and leave Hampshire with the seemingly simple task of scoring 147 in 160 minutes. But suddenly the sun came out to dry the damp pitch. The wicket became a minefield for batsmen. Flavell and Coldwell, backed by some dynamic close-catching, were unplayable. Flavell took 5 for 9 and Coldwell 5 for 22, and Hampshire were bowled out for 31 in an hour and five minutes.

Northamptonshire, who had completed their programme, still led the table, and Worcestershire needed to win their last match, against Sussex at Hove, to rob Northamptonshire of the title. They began well at Hove and bowled out Sussex before lunch on the first day, but Worcestershire found the going hard when it was their turn to bat. It was only some disciplined batting by the middle order which gave them a first-innings lead of 94. The feature of the Sussex second innings was a splendid innings of 60 by their captain, the Nawab of Pataudi, and the home side reached 225 before they were bowled out. This meant that Worcestershire needed 132 in 260 minutes to take the match and the Championship. They began disastrously as Kenyon, Ormrod, Headley and Graveney were out with 36 scored, and D'Oliveira went at 70.

Basil D'Oliveira had qualified to play for Worcestershire by residence and 1965 was his first season. His all-round ability gave the side a greater dimension than it had had in the previous year. His dismissal meant that Worcestershire were still 62 short of their target with Dick Richardson the only front-line batsman left. To support him, he had Roy Booth, Doug Slade, the left-arm spinner who often played alongside Gifford to give two bowlers of the same type in the side, Gifford himself, Coldwell and Flavell. Neither

Richardson nor Booth had enjoyed a good season with the bat, but they batted with great resilience in difficult circumstances to take their side to within 11 runs of victory before Booth fell to Snow, the bowler who had caused the earlier damage. Slade joined Dick Richardson and the winning hit was made with only seven minutes of the season remaining.

The following year, Worcestershire found themselves in a reversal of roles, deprived of the Championship by Yorkshire on the last afternoon of the season.

It would be wrong to claim for Kenyon's side a place among the giants of the game, but in many respects they were the first outstanding team of the modern era, the first to comprehend and embrace the demands of the limited-over game as well as of the first-class game. They were runners-up in the first Gillette Cup in 1963 and runners-up again in 1966, while, in 1971, with Norman Gifford now leading the side, they won the John Player League. No other side of the period was so consistently competitive and successful in all three competitions.

Kenyon, a professional, had been captain of Worcestershire before the distinction between amateur and professional was eradicated, and certainly cricket after 1962 became more professional in both substance and attitude. Some would say that this has been to the detriment of the game. As we have already indicated, the abolition of the distinction between amateurs and professionals was only one of a variety of reforms that were brought about as a result of investigations into the state of cricket and its finances. An MCC committee under H.S.Altham also recommended that a new national knock-out tournament should be introduced, and that it should be a one-day limited-over competition.

This was a radical step, for although the idea of a cricket equivalent to soccer's FA Cup had long been mooted, it had always been envisaged within the frame-work of the three-day first-class game. The idea of a limitation on the length of an innings and of the number of overs a bowler could bowl was seen by many followers of the game as a betrayal of cricket's basic principles but the financial state of cricket and its ever declining appeal called for drastic measures, and the first knock-out competition came into existence in 1963. Significantly for the future of English cricket, it was sponsored by the Gillette company.

The initial competition was restricted to the 17 first-class counties and consisted of a 65-over match with no bowler allowed to bowl more than 15 overs. By the second season the number of overs was reduced to 60 and the bowler's quota to 13. In 1966, the bowler's maximum was reduced to 12, the format unchanged since then.

The first Gillette Cup had its teething troubles, but by the time Worcestershire and Sussex reached the Final at Lord's at the beginning of September, the public's imagination had been captured. When Sussex played Yorkshire in the second round at Hove in June there were 15,000 people present, a crowd the like of which had not been seen at a county game for several years, and they sat until 7.45pm to witness an exciting finish.

The attendance at Hove had equalled the ground record, and there was a capacity crowd of 25,000 for the Final at Lord's. The weather was cold and cloudy with periods of drizzle, but no-one left before the end which came in the 64th over of the Worcestershire innings when Carter was run out to leave Sussex winners by 14 runs. There were scenes of great jubilation, and Ted Dexter, the Sussex captain, held the Gillette Cup aloft in the manner of the winning captain at a Wembley Final. Dexter's tactics had had much to do with Sussex's victory, for in the closing stages of the match he had posted all his fielders round the boundary in an attempt to prevent Worcestershire from scoring at a brisk rate. The individual award went to Norman Gifford of Worcestershire, who took 4 for 33 with his left-arm spin, and it is interesting that whereas many counties had dispensed with their spinners and played an all-seam attack, Worcestershire fielded both Gifford and Slade, who bowled most economically, and used Martin Horton's off-breaks as support for the pace attack of Flavell and Carter.

A new form of cricket had been born that was to prove increasingly popular and that was to help revitalise the game. More importantly, two sides who had never won the County Championship were the finalists in the first Gillette Cup. When Dexter held the trophy aloft he was celebrating a triumph for the south coast county which the likes of Ranjitsinhji, Duleepsinhji, Tate, J.H.Parks, Bowley and the Cornfords had never tasted. Sussex retained the Gillette Cup in 1964, and they have won it twice since then as well as the John Player League in 1982. They have still to win the County Championship, but since 1963 we have needed to assess a side on qualities other than those required solely to succeed in the three-day game. Cricket has taken on a new dimension and no side has been able to dominate the game so totally as Surrey and Yorkshire did in the past.

Ted Dexter who, with Sussex, was one of the first to evolve tactics for the one-day game.

The First Kings of
One-Day Cricket

The Lancashire of Bond and Rhoades

YORKSHIRE added to their lustre of the late 1960s by winning the Gillette Cup in 1965 and 1969. Their dominance in the first Final was total. They hit 317 for four and bowled out Surrey for 142. Geoff Boycott played one of the finest innings in a Lord's Final that one can remember. Noted as a batsman of ruthless resolve and concentration, he batted with a gaiety of character and a wealth of shots, hitting three sixes and 15 fours, and this was in a season when, remarkably, he had failed to score a first-class century. He was to miss the 1969 Final with a fractured left hand, but Close's tactical awareness brought victory over Derbyshire. This marked the end of Yorkshire's position of power in English cricket, and it is no coincidence that their reign ended the year after legislation had come into force allowing counties to recruit one overseas player on immediate registration. It was legislation to which Yorkshire gave their support but of which they have refused to take advantage.

It is surprising that several counties failed to realise fully the opportunity that the new legislation gave them to build a side capable of winning one of the major competitions. Even Tony Lewis, captain of Glamorgan when they took the Championship in 1969, commented that although they were both delighted and lucky in the contribution that Majid Khan made to their success, there had been no particular planning when Glamorgan decided to sign him on immediate registration. Others were more thoughtful in their acquistions.

Warwickshire were unambiguous in their desires. Motivated by the personal ambition of a wealthy man, Derrick Robins, a man who has given much to the game and not received the recognition he deserves, and sparked by the energy of chairman Cyril Goodway, Warwickshire sought success. Robins passionately wanted the county to win the Championship and he used every opportunity he could to build a side capable of fulfilling this ambition. Lance Gibbs, the great West Indian off-spinner, had begun a residential qualification in 1967 and was available to play in 1968 when he was joined by the exciting West Indian batsman Rohan Kanhai, who came on immediate registration. By 1970, Kanhai had been living in England for five years and Warwickshire brought this fact to the attention of the TCCB, who agreed that this now made it possible for the county to register another overseas player on immediate registration. Alvin Kallicharran became the third West Indian to join the Warwickshire staff. A fourth came in 1972, Deryck Murray, the wicketkeeper who had been at the universities of Cambridge and Nottingham and had played for Nottinghamshire. He was allowed immediate registration to play for Warwickshire.

As well as these four West Indian Test players, Warwickshire had the Pakistani Test batsman, Billy Ibadulla, in their side, and although they were narrowly beaten for the Championship in 1971, they won it the following season. Success had been bought and an ambition realised, yet not even this acquired strength was able to dominate the County Championship in the manner of the masters of the past, and Warwickshire were one of eight counties who took the title in the eight years following Yorkshire's last Championship in 1968. To seek the dominant side of the late 1960s and early 1970s we must turn to the one-day game.

Warwickshire had been one of the counties quick to assess the demands of limited-over cricket. They won the Gillette Cup in 1966 and 1968 and were runners-up to Sussex in 1964, the second year of the competition. Their semi-final victory over Lancashire at Old Trafford in that season aroused much ill-feeling and had considerable repercussions. Bob Barber, the left-handed England opener and a former Lancashire player, hit 76 and helped to take Warwickshire to a formidable 294 for seven. Lancashire began well enough in reply, as Green and Worsley scored 67 in the first 12 overs. Worsley was out at 67, and from that point Lancashire fell apart. Mike Smith, the Warwickshire captain, took two good leg-side catches to account for Entwistle and Grieves, and he then set fielders all round the boundary as his bowlers maintained an accurate length. Frustrated and angered by these defensive tactics, the Lancashire batsmen demonstrated their displeasure by making little or no attempt to score. Marner and Clayton, in particular, exaggeratedly blocked the ball, and the game ended with Lancashire on 209 for seven and a large crowd angrily barracking both sides.

This was not the end of the affair. The Lancashire committee asked team manager Cyril Washbrook for a report which was to make special reference to the behaviour of several players following complaints by opponents and following the way in which the side had batted in the Gillette Cup semi-final. The outcome of the report was that Lancashire dispensed with the services of skipper Ken Grieves and dismissed Marner and Clayton, both of whom were to find other counties. These were not the first players to leave a club where much was wrong behind the scenes.

A fierce critic of the administration was Cedric Rhoades. He won a place on the committee and quickly rose to become first vice-chairman and then chairman. His passion in life was the well-being of Lancashire cricket and it was he who helped to save the club financially. He was now determined that Lancashire should become a major cricketing force in the land. He drew up terms of contract for players which gave both incentive to success and pride in playing for Lancashire, and he was quick to comprehend the impact that the immediate registration of an overseas player could have.

Thwarted in his attempt to sign Gary Sobers, who was to prove to be less of a county cricketer than he was a Test player, Rhoades acquired Farokh Engineer, the Indian wicketkeeper-batsman, and signed Clive Lloyd to qualify by residence in time for the 1969 season. Both were surprise signings; both transpired to be inspirational acquisitions.

The importation of Engineer was particularly surprising in that he was a wicketkeeper, and most counties had little difficulty in finding a wicketkeeper adequate to their requirements without having to import a Test player. But as well as being a very fine wicketkeeper, Engineer was an unorthodox, aggressive batsman capable of lifting the spirits of a side by the way in which he tore an attack apart at the start of an innings. By the time he arrived at Lancashire, Engineer had been a Test player for seven years. He had disappointed with his batting on India's tour of England in 1967, but he was not to disappoint Lancashire and the eight years that he spent with the county were indeed a golden age in Lancashire cricket.

*The Indian Test wicketkeeper/batsman Farokh Engineer was an inspired importation
by Lancashire in the 1960s.*

Clive Lloyd was already known to the Lancastrians when he began to play for them in 1969, for he had been the only batsman in the Lancashire League to hit a 1,000 runs in 1968, the year of his residential qualification when he played for Haslingden. He had made his Test debut in 1966, but when Lancashire had invited him to qualify for them he was still very much an unknown quantity. Like Engineer, he was signed by Lancashire because he was seen as being an integral part of a conceived pattern which would bring glory and honour to the county.

Following the dismissal of Grieves in 1964, Lancashire had turned to Brian Statham, one of the great England fast bowlers, to lead them. He was not an ideal captain in his tactical sense and in his personality, which leaned towards the self-effacing, but he was liked and respected by the players and he did an excellent job in encouraging young men so that the nucleus of a new team began to emerge. He stepped down after the 1967 season and was succeeded by Jack Bond. If the signing of Engineer and Clive Lloyd had caused a surprise, the appointment of Bond as captain was sensational.

Bond was born at Kearsley, near Bolton, in 1932, and he first played for Lancashire in 1955, making 1 and 0 on his debut. He did not win a regular place in the side until 1961, and for two seasons he performed well as a batsman. In 1963, he had his wrist broken by a ball from the West Indian fast bowler, Wes Hall, and for the next four years he was never sure of a place in the side, nor even of being retained on the staff. Frequently he captained the 2nd XI and he did so most impressively. He proved to be a man capable of getting the best out of others, and such men are not often found. Rhoades and his fellows on the Lancashire committee saw in Bond qualities which others had failed to perceive. They had brought about the revolution in the committee room; Bond was to bring about the revolution on the field. If Rhoades was an inspirational father-figure behind the scenes, Bond was the man of sense and judgement on the field. In every respect, what Bond and Lancashire achieved on the cricket field in those years between 1969 and 1975 was revolutionary. Bond himself was the first cricketer to win fame and fortune on the strength of his performances in and attitude to limited-over cricket.

There had been very little original thinking or perception of the different demands that the one-day game made as opposed to the three-day variety. As we have noted, few concessions had been

Clive Lloyd. Lancashire thrilled to the West Indian's batting and fielding.

made to the limited-over game except, unwisely, to omit slow bowlers from a side and to set fielders deep to guard the boundaries. It was Lancashire, and Bond, who pioneered changed. He selected sides for a situation and manipulated batting orders to suit an occasion. He had no obsession for pace. If a bowler was accurate enough, he was good enough.

Of the side that Bond inherited in 1968, only Pullar, Higgs and Statham were capped players of long-standing, and all three were to leave the county within 18 months. The faithful Statham was to retire, and Pullar and Higgs were to find pastures new. David Lloyd, Barry Wood, Farokh Engineer and Ken Shuttleworth were capped in 1968, and Clive Lloyd and John Sullivan the following year when Jack Simmons began to earn a regular place in the side.

Bond adopted a realistic approach to his team and to the game. He admitted the weaknesses of his side and forced individuals to face their limitations. He demanded a fresh approach and fresh attitudes in order to remedy shortcomings. One of the outstanding fielders in the history of the game, he realised the vital importance of fielding in one-day cricket. He made it quite clear to all concerned that he was not prepared to consider anyone for a place in the side who was not totally committed to raising the standard of fielding to a level not previously attained. He insisted on physical fitness and set the example himself.

It was this emphasis on fielding which made Farokh Engineer such an important acquisition. He was an exotic extrovert of a wicketkeeper, and energetic pivot around whom the field revolved. There was an exuberance in his keeping which was an inspiration to the fielders and a threat to the batsman. The same could be said of Clive Lloyd, the cat in the covers, prowling menacingly and ready to swoop and kill at the instant.

These two, Engineer and Clive Lloyd, were perfectly suited to Bond's second demand, that the approach to batting should be zestful so that a brisk scoring rate would be maintained.

The joyous batting was complemented by accurate bowling and intelligent field-placing. The sloth which had devoured Lanchashire cricket was at an end, and crowds flocked to Old Trafford in numbers which had not been seen since the years immediately following World War Two.

Bond and Lancashire gained instant reward for their planning and for their approach to the one-day game. They won the John

Jack Bond revived Lancashire cricket and brought a passion, commitment and tactical awareness to the one-day game which set a model for all.

Player League in its inaugural year, 1969, and retained the title in 1970. They were third the following year. The Gillette Cup became their own special preserve. They won it three years in succession, 1970 to 1972, were runners-up in 1974 and 1976 and won it again in 1975. These were the most glorious years in Lancashire's cricket history since McDonald and the 1920s.

They finished third in the County Championship in 1970 and 1971, but their strengths were best suited to the one-day game. Bond revelled in limited-over cricket, and it was said that he hated the placidity of Monday after the excitement and huge crowds of Sunday. Despite the presence of Engineer and Clive Lloyd, who had brought a necessary spark and personality to the side which had previously been lacking, Lancashire had no stars. Their triumphs were team triumphs. Both Engineer and Lloyd were quickly absorbed by the county and its supporters, and it is no accident that when their playing days were finished, both men settled in the county which had embraced them.

There was the tang of Lancashire in the team's play and in its character. Barry Wood was a Yorkshireman, and he was later to play for Derbyshire, but he, like Engineer and Clive Lloyd, became as Lancastrian as those around him. From Rhoades, through Bond and his players, to those who paid to come through the turnstile there was a common cause, the honour of the Red Rose and the success of Lancashire cricket.

The first John Player League in 1969 was won by a margin of one point, but this is a deceptively narrow margin, for Lancashire became Champions when they beat Warwickshire at Nuneaton on 24 August with three Sundays of the programme still remaining. They retained the title the following year by a margin of five points and again they were Champions with matches remaining.

The deciding match in this 1970 season was against Yorkshire at Old Trafford on 30 August, and if one needed evidence as to how great a hold Lancashire and the limited-over game now had on the public, one needed only to refer to this match. Before the game started the gates had to be closed with 33,000 people locked inside. This was the first time that the gates had had to be closed at Old Trafford since Washbrook's benefit game against the Australians 22 years earlier.

Yorkshire reached 111 before they lost their third wicket, with Boycott making 81, but as they attempted to force the pace wickets tumbled, and they were bowled out in 37.5 overs for 165. Peter

Barry Wood — true grit and determination in all he did.

Lever and Ken Shuttleworth, the opening bowlers, conceded 46 runs in 14 overs, but it was nagging off-breaks of Jack Simmons and the left-arm spin of David Hughes which really nullified the Yorkshire attempt to score quick runs. There was, too, of course, the exciting Lancashire fielding which was always worth 20-30 runs. The emphasis was not on brilliant close catching as it had been with Sellers' Yorkshire and Surridge's Surrey, although the catching was consistent and thrilling, it was more on dynamic ground fielding and accurate throwing that made taking a run against Lancashire a hazardous business.

Farokh Engineer was out for six. It was said of him by writer John Kay that it was his inconsistent streak which made him such an entertaining player. Snellgrove went at 65, and Clive Lloyd at 94, but there was little doubt that Lancashire would win, and Pilling and Sullivan hit 50s and victory came with seven wickets standing and 4.1 overs remaining.

During the course of his 55 not out, Harry Pilling became the first batsman to reach a 1,000 runs in the Sunday League, and he was given a cheque for £100 in recognition of the achievement. He was the leading run-scorer in the League in 1970, hitting 625 runs, average 52.08. In 13 years in the competition, he was to hit 2,270 runs, but he never made a century.

Harry Pilling was one of the delights of the Lancashire crowd and of crowds everywhere. He was the smallest man in cricket, standing 5ft 2in. It was his diminutive stature, allied to his sheer application and personality, which won the hearts of the cricket public. He had strong arms, a keen eye and a big heart. He was a fighter with a great sense of fun and an awareness that he was part of the entertainment industry. Six days after he had reached 1,000 runs in the John Player League and Lancashire had taken the trophy for the second time, he was named Man-of-the-Match in the Gillette Cup Final as Lancashire won the trophy for the first time.

The crowds that engulfed Old Trafford after the game against Yorkshire and had stood cheering for nearly an hour, as Bond held the trophy, now engulfed Lord's to celebrate in similar manner. Sussex, winners of the Gillette Cup in its first two years, were well beaten. They lost Geoffrey Greenidge and Richard Langridge for 34, but by lunch, with Jim Parks and Tony Greig looking well set, they had recovered. By the 37th over, they had reached 113 for three, but now came the need to accelerate, and that was

A Lancashire hero — 'Flat Jack' Simmons.

the most difficult task that any side found when batting against Lancashire. In quick succession David Hughes bowled Parks, Greig and Graves with his slow left-arm teasing deliveries. Suttle, Griffith and Snow were run out, the victims of Lancashire's electric fielding, and Sussex had to settle for 184 for 9 from their 60 overs.

Barry Wood and David Lloyd started cautiously when Lancashire began their reply, and even though Clive Lloyd hit Spencer over mid-wicket for six and drove him straight for four, Lancashire were 113 for four in 40 overs. Sussex had been 115 for five at the same stage. Harry Pilling and Farokh Engineer, batting at number six, now seized the initiative. In the next 15.1 overs, they hit the 72 runs needed for victory, and the Gillette Cup was Lancashire's with 4.5 overs to spare. Engineer batted with his customary panache, and Pilling was as determined as ever for his 70 not out, but the real difference between the two sides was in the quality of the out-cricket. It was also worth noting that while Sussex relied on a mainly seam attack of medium pace, Lancashire had an off-spinner and a left-arm spinner at the heart of their attack.

They came close to repeating the one-day double in 1971, but eventually finished third in the John Player League. All the excitement of the season was concentrated into the Gillette Cup and the matches involving Lancashire. They survived a Roy Virgin century and several crises in a first-round match at Taunton which was spread over two days to beat Somerset by six wickets. They won by the same margin in the second round at Worcester, where Glenn Turner hit a century and Clive Lloyd hit a match-winning 83 not out. The West Indian left-hander was also to be at the centre of events in the quarter-final match against Essex at Chelmsford.

Eight thousand people packed into Chelmsford to see the match, a crowd the like of which had never been seen on the ground before. They were entertained by some pulsating and controversial cricket. It was an occasion charged with high drama.

Batting first, Lancashire were soon in trouble. Keith Boyce, a gloriously lithe and enthusiastic all-rounder of high quality, bowled Wood for one and had Pilling caught behind for nought. David Lloyd and Clive Lloyd took the score to 16 when the West Indian went for an impossible run. In the excitement which followed the Essex players were convinced that they had run out Clive Lloyd, but it was David Lloyd who set off for the pavilion. Umpires Jakeman and Constant rejected the Essex appeals that it was Clive Lloyd who should be out, and he remained to hit 109.

The controversial run out apart, it was a magnificent innings. Sullivan went for ten, Engineer for nought and Bond for three, so that Lancashire were 59 for six, and it was not until Jack Simmons came in that Lloyd received adequate support. Simmons, ever a fighter, helped in a stand of 91, and Hughes shared a partnership of 23 which was ended when Lloyd was caught and bowled by Stuart Turner. Lancashire ended with 203 for nine from their 60 overs, by no means a formidable score.

At the time, Essex were a side inexperienced in winning, and they fretted too soon for quick runs. The result was that they lost Ward, Bruce Francis, the Australian, skipper Brian Taylor and Keith Fletcher with only 34 scored. The durable Graham Saville and Keith Boyce, who batted like a spring uncoiling, added 51 to raise Essex spirits. Six wickets were down for 112 when Robin Hobbs joined Stuart Turner in a stand which nearly turned the course of the match. In 13 overs, they added 74. It was a stand fraught with excitement and tempers ran high. The home crowd bayed in disapproval as Barry Wood, bowling 12 overs of medium pace, appeared to take every opportunity of impeding Hobbs as the batsmen ran between the wickets. In the end, Essex ran out of quality batting. When Ray East was caught off David Hughes on the second ball of the last over Essex were still 13 runs short of their target.

When the passions quietened and the game was analysed with cold and sensible logic it was apparent that once more Lancashire had snatched victory because of the standard of their out-cricket and the control which Bond exerted over it. In an age obsessed with seam, he had saved the young left-arm spinner David Hughes to bowl the closing overs of the innings, and Hughes had responded with admirable control. A month later, in the semi-final, Hughes was to make a different kind of response, this time as a batsman.

The Gillette Cup semi-final between Lancashire and Gloucestershire at Old Trafford on 28 July 1971, has passed into cricket legend. Twenty years on, the game is remembered as vividly as it was on the day. The gates were again closed before the start. The attendance was officially given as 23,520, although one would believe this was a conservative estimate. The receipts were £9,728, a huge amount 20 years ago. Rain was to cause an hour's delay at lunch time, and the game was to last from 11.00am to 8.59pm, an unheard of hour for the end of a cricket match, and television programmes were to be delayed or cancelled so that the closing stages of the match could be shown.

Tony Brown won the toss and decided to bat first. The Gloucestershire opening pair were Green, the former Lancashire player, and Nicholls. They successfully countered the opening thrust of Peter Lever and Ken Shuttleworth. These two were both England bowlers by this time.

Lever was a whole-hearted bowler who maintained a good length and could be very quick. He was a prolific wicket-taker in the one-day game, and his partnership with Shuttleworth was a formidable one. Shuttleworth looked to be another Fred Trueman in fire and aggression, and he could be both fast and hostile, but although he was an integral part of the Lancashire success, he never established himself as the bowling force in English cricket that had been predicted.

For a pair of opening batsman to survive the attack of Lever and Shuttleworth was a necessity if a side was to have any hope of success. Green and Nicholls survived admirably and put on 57 for the first wicket. It seemed they would extend their partnership further, but they were not the first to become victims of the quality of the unexpected in the Lancashire fielding. Green pushed Simmons to mid-on and called for a run. Clive Lloyd glided in from mid-wicket and pounced on the ball before it could reach Sullivan at mid-on. In one movement he threw down the stumps at the bowler's end to run out David Green.

Nicholls played well until he was bowled by Simmons for 53, and his dismissal brought in Mike Procter, the great South African all-rounder, a ferocious fast bowler and a magnificent hitter. Procter paced and dominated the rest of the Gloucestershire innings. He was particularly severe on David Hughes, and his innings of 65 included a six and nine fours. His dismissal was again testimony to the quality of the Lancashire fielding. He got an edge to a ball from Peter Lever and was astonishingly caught by Farokh Engineer diving to his left.

Gloucestershire finished with 229 for six from their 60 overs. Jack Simmons took the honours for Lancashire with the wickets of Nicholls and David Shepherd at a cost of 25 runs in his 12 overs, three of which were maidens.

Procter was a most difficult bowler from whom to score runs in any circumstances, and he was well supported by Davey. It took David Lloyd and Barry Wood 17 overs in which to score 50, but they kept their wickets intact. Lancashire realised from the start of the one-day competitions that it is always possible to chase a target and increase the tempo at the end of an innings, so long as you have sufficient wickets in hand.

Wood was a tigerish, tenacious competitor, admirably suited to limited-over cricket. He bowled gentle medium pace, always keeping a nagging length and able to wobble the ball a little, and as a batsman he had a defiant gruffness which was frequently translated into crashing shots. David Lloyd was a more amiable character, and it reflected in his batting. As a left-hander, he was the perfect foil for Wood. He had a wider range of shots than the Yorkshireman and a greater fluency.

They were separated at 61 when David Lloyd was leg-before to Tony Brown, but Wood and Pilling began to lift the tempo and took the score to 105 before Pilling became Brown's second victim. Clive Lloyd looked as if he meant to settle the match on his own, attacking the bowling from the start. He took 16 runs off five balls from the mighty Procter, but on the last ball of the same over, Barry Wood was run out as the batsmen attempted a quick bye.

Gloucestershire were now brought back into the game by off-spinner John Mortimore. He beat Clive Lloyd in the flight and bowled him for 34. He deceived Engineer and prompted him to hit his wicket as he dithered for a shot. Sullivan was bowled by Davey, and Lancashire were 163 for six in the 46th over with the time 7.30pm and the light worsening minute by minute.

Umpires Bird and Jepson asked Bond if he would like to go off and finish the game the following morning. He declined. He reasoned that the Gloucestershire bowlers would be refreshed by the morrow, and his own batsmen unlikely to get the required runs. It was a calculated risk, but he and Simmons gave it some validity by adding 40 runs from seven overs. Simmons clouted lustily, but when he was bowled by Mortimore 27 runs were still needed from just over five overs. The next man in was David Hughes.

David Hughes was primarily a slow left-arm bowler. He was 24 years old, and his bowling thrived under Bond's captaincy. He drank from Bond's fountain, and the Bond-Lancashire philosophy became part of his blood. Nearly 20 years after this day he was to fill the role that Bond filled in the early 1970s and, like Bond, lead Lancashire out of the wilderness. In 1971, however, he was a young first-class cricketer with a batting average of just over 13, and a highest score in limited-over cricket of 38.

In an attempt to acclimatise himself to the light, Hughes had sat in a gloomy corner of the dressing-room before he went out to bat. Legend has it that when he reached the middle, Bond said to him, 'Don't go daft. Take things as they come.' To which he replied, 'If I can see them skipper, I think I can hit them.' He could see them and he proceeded to play one of the most remarkable overs in the history of the game.

John Mortimore began the 56th over of the Lancashire innings with figures of 3 for 57 from ten overs. Unwisely, perhaps, he continued to toss the ball up invitingly, but it was the tactic which had brought him the wickets of Clive Lloyd, Farokh Engineer and the redoubtable Jack Simmons. Quick on his feet, Hughes moved down the wicket and hit the first ball beyond extra cover for four. The next ball went high over long-on for six. With the lights in the pavilion and from the neighbouring railway station twinkling through the darkness, Hughes slashed the third ball into the off-side for two, and the fourth was hit wide of mid-on for another two. This was excitement of the highest order, and the Lancashire crowd erupted when Hughes drove the fifth ball of the over to the cover boundary in classical manner. The last ball of the over was pulled high over mid-on for six, and the scores were level. Hughes had taken 24 runs from the over.

There was no need for further drama, and Bond played the first four deliveries of Procter's next over with calm before nudging the next ball past gully for the winning run on the fifth ball.

The Final contained excitement and drama of a different nature with the result in doubt until close to the very end. Lancashire's opponents were Kent, the county destined to succeed them as the outstanding side in the country.

Bond won the toss and decided to bat first, but Lancashire began disastrously with Barry Wood falling leg-before to Dye's second ball of the match. David Lloyd stood firm, and Harry Pilling attempted to play some shots in a second-wicket stand of 45, but the going was grim as Asif Iqbal began with five maiden overs.

Clive Lloyd attempted to wrest the initiative and opened his account by hooking Asif for six, but John Shepherd and Derek Underwood were relentlessly accurate and economic and in spite of Clive Lloyd's 66, Kent still had a grip on the match. The accuracy of the Kent bowling can be gleaned from the fact that the usually

David Hughes tasted success under Bond and 20 years on was to revive former glories.

aggressive Engineer was restricted to eight runs in 50 minutes during the course of his innings of 24. He was finally bowled by Woolmer, who proved to be the soft belly of the Kent bowling, and Lancashire were 179 for seven in the 54th over.

Jack Simmons was now joined by David Hughes and together they plundered 45 runs, 39 of them coming from the last four overs. It proved to be a priceless contribution.

The careers of Simmons and Hughes ran almost parallel, and both played until the veteran stage. They complemented each other in bowling — off-spinner and left-arm leg-spinner — and they were like comrades-in-arms as batsmen. Jack Simmons was 28 before he first played for Lancashire, although the county had first wanted to sign him when he was 18. He had cricket and Lancashire in his blood and, like his father and his grandfather, he played for Enfield in the Lancashire League. He was a thick-set, honest cricketer, the stuff of which county success is made. He had a reputation for big eating, for flat off-spin of unerring accuracy and for the ability to clout the ball hard and uncompromisingly. He won and saved many a match for Lancashire.

Simmons and Hughes had raised the Lancashire score to 224, and the Kent innings began as badly as the Lancashire innings had done, Luckhurst falling in the first over, caught behind off Peter Lever. Nicholls fell at 19, and the first four Kent batsmen were out for 68.

Lancashire appeared to have taken control of the game, but Asif Iqbal, who was to take the individual award, played a glorious innings. In company with Alan Knott, he added 37, and they looked likely to put Kent in a commanding position until Knott foolishly ran himself out, venturing a run which Asif had never anticipated and falling well short of the crease when he was sent back.

As long as Asif remained, however, Kent had high hopes of victory, and he gave a masterly display of cutting, hooking, pulling and driving. He had hit 89 and taken Kent to a point where they needed only 28 to win from the last six overs of the innings with four wickets standing when he drove powerfully at Jack Simmons.

Simmons was bowling to a strong leg-side field, his attack being aimed at the leg stump. Asif gave himself room to hit to the sparsely populated off side and hit the ball cleanly and with considerable force. Jack Bond was fielding at extra cover, virtually patrolling the off side on his own. The ball seemed well wide of Bond, but he leapt to his right and plucked it out of the air. He was knocked back by the strength of the drive and rolled over as he hit the ground, but he had achieved one of the most famous catches to be seen in the long history of Lord's.

The three remaining Kent wickets fell for three runs in the space of 14 balls, and Lancashire retained the Gillette Cup with victory by 24 runs. Eight days later they had only to beat Glamorgan at Old Trafford to complete the one-day double for the second year in succession. Once more a crowd of 30,000 packed into the Manchester ground. Initially, all went well for Lancashire as they bowled out Glamorgan for a meagre 143. Engineer was out quickly, but Snellgrove and David Lloyd appeared to be well settled. Then came an inexplicable collapse, and Lancashire were beaten by 34 runs to leave Worcestershire as John Player League Champions.

If one has dwelt long and in detail on this Lancashire Gillette Cup campaign of 1971, it is becausee it encapsulates the virtues of all great sides. There was inspiration and motivation from above which manifested itself in a corporate pride of the county and its cricket. There was outstanding leadership on the field which created both confidence in self and in each other and which led to a meaningful discipline. Like the Yorkshire side of the 1930s and the Surrey side of the 1950s, there was a standard of fielding that no other side could match. The team itself had balance, and there was that substance of honest professionalism in the cricket of men like Hughes and Simmons, the bread and butter players, that is the essence of any successful side. There was, too, in Bond a tactical awareness which had a particular relevance to the new form of cricket which first began to capture the imagination of the public in the late 1960s and early 1970s.

Lancashire created a record the following season, 1972, when they took the Gillette Cup for the third year in succession. They had no easy path to the Final, and their way was strewn with narrow victories. Somerset were beaten by nine runs in a high-scoring game at Old Trafford, and Hampshire were beaten by four wickets with nine balls to spare. The semi-final was spread over two days because of rain, and the adjudication for Man-of-the-Match was made by umpires Pope and Bird. George Pope, the former Derbyshire all-rounder, said before he made the award that he would like to pay tribute to Denness and Cowdrey of Kent who, when asked if they would like to go off in very bad light on the Thursday evening, replied, 'There are 20,000 people on this ground and we will stay on.' Lancashire won by seven runs, and one of their heroes was Peter Lee, who took 2 for 16 in his 12 overs and broke the Cowdrey-Denness stand.

Lee was a medium-pace bowler who had been signed from Northamptonshire as a back-up for Lever and Shuttleworth, but with Shuttleworth in decline, Lee established himself as the number-one strike bowler. He was unerringly accurate and a prolific wicket-taker. He was also in the Lancashire mould, the dedicated professional.

In the Final, Lancashire faced Warwickshire, the County Champions. Warwickshire hit 234 for nine in their 60 overs, so that Lancashire faced a target which had never before been attained by victors batting second in a Gillette Cup match. The target may well have been greater, had not Bond manipulated his bowlers so intelligently, once more demonstrating the value of a varied attack which included two spinners.

Lancashire lost David Lloyd and Barry Wood for 26 in ten overs, and Clive Lloyd made a quiet start scoring only six runs in the next eight overs. Then he drove David Brown with tremendous power to the boundary and hooked the next ball for six. This seemed to ignite him, and first with Pilling and then with Frank Hayes, a fair-haired, handsome stroke player who had established himself in the side, he shared partnerships of 97 and 86. He had begun the match with 12 economic overs, and now he gave an enchanting display of batting, a fusion of power and feline grace. In two and a half hours, 42 overs, he hit 126, an innings which included three sixes and 14 fours.

When Clive Lloyd was finally leg-before to Bob Willis, Lancashire needed only 16 from eight overs. Farokh Engineer was out straight away, but victory came by four wickets with 22 balls to spare.

This was the end for Bond, who announced his retirement. He had shaped Lancashire into the most exciting and successful side in the country. He had grasped at what was offered by the one-day game and had brought about a renaissance in Lancashire cricket. He and his side thrilled to play in front of large crowds, and the crowds thrilled to them.

By the time he became captain of Lancashire, Bond's best days as a cricketer were over. Invariably he batted low down. He did not bowl, and his highest score in limited-over cricket was 43, and that was made against Derbyshire in the first year of the John Player League, 1969. To look at his figures would suggest that he was not worth a place in the side, which would be the gravest of mistakes.

He was the first man to realise the extra dimensions provided by the one-day game, and he saw that positivity and intelligence were needed to take advantage of them. Where once there had been just the County Championship, there were now, by 1972, four competitions, and in the minds of many they were of equal worth. Indeed, the grounds were fuller on Sundays and for the Gillette Cup matches than they were for the Championship honours. In the years ahead, players would begin to speak of their greatest ambition as being able to play in a Final at Lord's.

Bond grasped the full implications of the one-day game. He maintained an attack that was balanced and varied, a fact that many of his successors in other counties failed to grasp, and his players moved to their positions in the field without any apparent direction. Those positions had been determined by clinical analysis and meticulous pre-planning. Runs were saved and batsmen frustrated to destruction by Bond's carefully set fields.

David Lloyd succeeded Bond as captain of Lancashire, and for the first time in five years the county was not to win a trophy. There were extenuating circumstances in that Clive Lloyd was with the West Indian side for the second half of the season, Lever was often out of the side through injury, Hayes was on Test duty and Shuttleworth's form and fitness deserted him completely. Nevertheless, Lancashire were semi-finalists in the Benson and Hedges Cup, losing by one wicket to Worcestershire at Old Trafford, and they were quarter-finalists in the Gillette Cup. They lost to Middlesex at Lord's, their first defeat in the competition for four years, and were handicapped when David Lloyd was forced to retire hurt with only three runs scored. The following season they were back at Lord's for the Gillette Cup Final.

In 1974, they were certainly not the power that they had been, but many counties would have envied their record. They were semi-finalists in the Benson and Hedges Cup and they were the only unbeaten side in the County Championship, although their five wins in 20 matches could take them no higher than eighth. Their fourth appearance in the Gillette Cup in the space of five years turned out to be a bitter disappointment. Rain caused the match to be held over until the Monday, and Lancashire were bowled out for 118, the lowest score made by a side in the Final. Kent won by four wickets with more than 13 overs to spare.

With senior players finding more consistency in 1975, Lancashire came close to winning the County Championship. They finished fourth, but this was again a disappointment, for, until August, they had looked certain to take the title. They were compensated for this loss in the Gillette Cup Final, where they totally dominated Middlesex to win by seven wickets. Clive Lloyd hit 73 not out and took the individual award, and Barry Wood hit 51. The Lancashire side remained much as it had done throughout the golden period, with Kennedy and Ratcliffe the only newcomers.

Clive Lloyd was unavailable for the 1976 season because he was leading the West Indian side on the tour of England, and this was the year that finally marked the end of the great Lancashire side. They played badly in the Championship and finished second-to-bottom, and in the John Player League they were down to eighth. They were quarter-finalists in the Benson and Hedges Cup, and, for the sixth time in seven years, a record that had never been approached, they were Finalists at Lord's in the 60-over competition.

The opponents in 1976 were Northamponshire, who had never won a trophy in senior cricket. There was a strong Indian sub-continent flavour in the Northamptonshire side with Pakistani Test cricketers Mushtaq Mohammad, the captain, and Sarfraz Nawaz, and the great Indian left-arm spinner, Bishen Bedi. The early successes were all in favour of Northamptonshire. Dye bowled Engineer for nought, and Pilling fell to Sarfraz for three. The worst disaster for Lancashire, however, was when Barry Wood was forced to retire from the match with a broken finger. Not only did this disrupt the Lancashire batting, it also deprived them of a bowler, for Wood's medium pace had been an integral part of the attack in the earlier rounds.

The last over of the Lancashire innings arrived with the score on 169 for seven. Mushtaq gave the last over to Bedi, who had taken 3 for 26 in ten overs although he could have turned to the left-arm seam bowler John Dye, whose movement had caused problems early in the day and had allowed him to rest after conceding only nine runs in seven overs and accounting for Engineer. Hughes faced Bedi's last over and evoked memories of the famous innings against Gloucestershire in 1971. He hit Bedi for 4, 6, 2, 2, 6, 6 and with these 26 runs lifted Lancashire to a defensible 195, but this time Hughes' magnificent effort proved to be the last glow of twilight in Lancashire's reign of supremacy, not the match-winning knock it had been five years earlier.

Willey and Virgin began Northamptonshire's innings with a partnership of 103. There was a minor collapse in mid-innings, but Sharp and Sarfraz took them to victory with four wickets and 11 balls to spare.

Lancashire's dominance of one-day cricket which had lasted for nearly eight years was at an end.

Kent's Vintage Years

The Team of the Seventies

NORTHAMPTONSHIRE'S victory in the Gillette Cup Final of 1976 was significant in that it showed how much more open cricket had become, how much difficult it now was for one county to dominate all others in the way that Yorkshire and Surrey had done in the past. Northamptonshire had been runners-up in the County Championship in 1912 and were runners-up again in 1957, 1965 and 1976, but for most of their history they had languished among the Cinderellas of the game. As we have recorded, between May 1935 and May 1939, they went without a victory in the County Championship. In the 1930s, they were bottom of the table seven times, second to bottom twice and reached the elevated position of 13th in 1933. Their post-war record was only slightly better until the mid-1950s.

The one-day game, however, changed cricket totally and for a side to achieve success in the four competitions, versatility, adaptability and application were needed as they had never been needed before.

Brian Close had left Yorkshire in 1970 because, reputedly, he was neither willing nor able to adapt his captaincy to the needs of limited-over cricket. In the next seven years, however, he captained Somerset, whose one-day record improved considerably under his leadership.

Another to leave Yorkshire for fresh fields was Ray Illingworth. At the end of the 1968 season he had differences with the Yorkshire committee which led him to depart his native county and accept the position as captain of Leicestershire, a post he had been denied at Yorkshire when Geoff Boycott was appointed to succeed Brian Close.

Like Northamptonshire, Leicestershire had been among the Cinderellas of cricket for most of their existence. There had been signs of revival before Illingworth's arrival, but the club had never won a senior trophy. In 1972, they became the first winners of the Benson and Hedges Cup. The county had been in existence since 1895, but they had never enjoyed a season such as they enjoyed 1972.

They were knocked out of the Gillette Cup by Warwickshire, the margin being three runs, and this was the same margin by which they lost to Yorkshire in their last John Player League match. Had they won that game, they would have taken the Sunday League, for they had headed the table since 18 June. At one time, they had also led the County Championship, and they suffered only two defeats, but in the end they slipped to sixth place. In the Benson and Hedges Cup, it was glory all the way.

They headed the Midland group with crashing victories over all their opponents, Northamptonshire, Warwickshire, Worcestershire and Cambridge University. In the quarter-final, before a huge crowd at Grace Road, they comfortably beat the mighty Lancashire. Warwickshire were the visitors in the semi-final, and a capacity crowd of 10,000 saw Leicestershire sweep to the easiest of victories. Warwickshire were bowled out for 96 on a drying wicket, and Leicestershire won by seven wickets in late afternoon. Yorkshire were swept aside in the Final, on a rather damp day at Lord's, and Leicestershire had claimed their first trophy. It was not to be their last.

They took the Sunday League in 1974 and 1977, and in 1975 won the Championship for the first and only time in their history and completed a double by winning the Benson and Hedges Cup for the second time.

There were certain mainstays in the Leicestershire side throughout most of this period. Ray Illingworth was the backbone. His experience and tactical expertise lifted those around him, and it was not a side short of experience. So successful was Illingworth as a skipper that within months of taking over at Leicester, he was captain of England. A naggingly accurate off-break bowler and a highly capable batsman, he will best be remembered for his qualities of leadership. He was totally professional in his approach to the game and to those in his charge. He prepared and schemed meticulously, and he was a stubborn and relentless adversary.

He had two other dependable Yorkshiremen in the side with him, Chris Balderstone and Jack Birkenshaw. Balderstone was a right-handed opening batsman and useful slow left-arm bowler who joined Leicestershire in 1971. He was brave, sound and adaptable. A soccer player, he was superbly fit, and his one mischance was that when he was picked to play for England in 1976, it was against a West Indian side at their strongest and all about him were failing.

Birkenshaw was an excellent off-spinner who twice topped 100 wickets in a season and a very good left-handed middle-order batsman. John Steele complemented both Illingworth and Birkenshaw with his slow left-arm bowling and right-handed batting.

Brian Davidson, Barry Dudleston and Roger Tolchard were all batsmen sound in technique and capable of scoring quick runs. Tolchard was also the wicketkeeper, adequate although not in the top flight, and the fielding was sound without ever reaching the heights of Lancashire or Surrey of earlier days.

From 1969 to 1975, Leicestershire had the services of Graham McKenzie, the Australian Test bowler of pace and beauty. 'Garth' McKenzie purred to the wicket and his delivery was classical and economic, his pace deceptively fast and his late movement unnerving. He was a gentle giant among men and a team man of the first order.

His new-ball partner was most often Ken Higgs, who had tasted success with Lancashire. His burly frame and big bottom marked him as a fastish bowler, and his short approach to the wicket disguised deliveries which came sharply off the pitch. He was relentlessly accurate, and he made history in the 1974 Benson and Hedges Cup when he finished the Surrey innings by dismissing Butcher, Pocock and Long to complete the hat-trick. This was the second of Leicestershire's three appearances in the Benson and Hedges Cup Final within the space of four years, and their one defeat. Facing a target of 171, they were bowled out for 143.

Leicestershire's success at this period was remarkable. This was a seasoned side and, under Illingworth, Leicestershire enjoyed the most prosperous playing time in their history, yet it would be unjust to name them as the outstanding side of the 1970s. That accolade must go to Kent, for whom the period from 1970 to 1978 was indeed a golden age.

When Kent won the Gillette Cup in 1967, it was their first honour since 1913. In the nine seasons beginning with 1970, their record was as follows:

1970   won County Championship
1971   runners-up in the Gillette Cup
1972   won the John Player League; runners-up in the County Championship
1973   won both the John Player League and the Benson and Hedges Cup
1974   won the Gillette Cup
1975   third in the John Player League
1976   won both the John Player League and the Benson and Hedges Cup
1977   joint County Champions with Middlesex and runners-up in the Benson and Hedges Cup
1978   won County Championship and the Benson and Hedges Cup

This is a total of ten trophies in nine years for a county who could claim only five trophies in the previous 100 years. Strangely, Kent were led by four different captains during their years of success.

Colin Cowdrey stepped down after the 1971 season, and Mike Denness was skipper from 1972 to 1976. Asif Iqbal was captain in 1977, and Alan Ealham took over in 1978.

Cowdrey's side achieved one of the most spectacular County Championship successes in the history of the competition. On 1 July 1970, Kent were bottom of the table and, with Test calls now about to fall heavily upon them, there seemed little chance that they would be able to celebrate their centenary year in an appropriate manner. Colin Cowdrey had believed from the outset that, to stand any chance of winning the Championship, Kent had to make a good start to the season before the international series began to take its toll.

The 'Test' matches were, in fact, unofficial. Political pressures had forced the cancellation of the proposed series against South Africa, and matches against the Rest of the World side, which included five South Africans, were arranged to take its place. Cowdrey, Luckhurst, Knott, Underwood and, for the first match in June, Denness were all called upon by the England selectors, thereby weakening Kent severely after the beginning of July, by which time, as we have said, they were already bottom of the County Championship.

With four players on duty for England, Mike Denness led Kent against Essex at Harlow in the match which began on 1 July. He hit 167, Ealham made 88, and Kent won by an innings, but this was followed by defeat at the hands of Middlesex at Lord's and a humiliating reverse by Sussex in the Gillette Cup match at Canterbury.

During the next match, against Derbyshire at Maidstone, team manager Les Ames called a meeting in order to discuss the side's shortcomings. The principal criticism was the lack of positivity in the batting. There was a desperate need to score runs more quickly in order to gain more batting points than the paltry 13 that they gained from the seven matches.

The meeting had the desired effect. Kent had been beaten five times in their first 11 games. They were not to be beaten in the Championship again for the remainder of the season. Their form in the John Player League ran almost parallel to this as they won six matches in a row before losing their final fixture.

In August, the winning of the Championship still seemed little more than a very remote possibility, but then came a wonderful victory at Cheltenham. Kent were without Cowdrey, Luckhurst, Knott and Shepherd, and, despite Derek Underwood's 6 for 68, Gloucestershire made 289. Kent's ninth wicket fell at 130, and it was Underwood, aided by Dye, who did not score, who managed to make the ten runs needed to avoid the follow-on.

Underwood was still the Kent hero as Gloucestershire were bowled out for 190 in the second innings, but a target of 340 on a wicket that was crumbling looked far beyond Kent's capabilities. That victory became possible was due to Mike Denness and Asif Iqbal. Three wickets had fallen for 116 when they came together, and in 95 minutes they added 105.

Asif attacked the bowling zealously, and his 109 included a six and 13 fours. Denness, too, played splendidly for his 97, and at tea, Kent were 329 for 6 with victory within their grasp. Gloucestershire fought back to take three wickets for nine runs, but the last pair, Leary and Dye, proved obdurate and scored the six runs needed to win the match.

Such victories are of immense value to a side in the confidence that they bring. Suddenly, all seemed possible. There was a draw at Northampton, but this was followed by three scintillating home victories and a draw in the rain-affected match at The Oval which clinched the title.

Mike Denness, an intelligent, decisive captain of Kent in the county's most successful period.

Under Cowdrey, and at full strength for these last four games, Kent played exhilarating cricket and looked a fine side and worthy Champions. At Blackheath, against Surrey, Denness set the tempo on a rain-interrupted first day, and Cowdrey and Asif maintained it with a stand of 104 in 22 overs. Asif was again in sparkling form and hit 106 not out in two hours. Johnson was the main destroyer as Surrey were bowled out for 211 to give Kent a first-innings lead of 114. Cowdrey's declaration eventually left Surrey with the task of scoring 263 in three and a half hours. He bowled his spinners virtually throughout the innings, and Surrey batted to win to the very end. They were within 13 runs of victory with the last pair together and seven balls remaining when Pat Pocock was brilliantly caught on the long-off boundary by Asif Iqbal, off the bowling of Johnson, who finished with match figures of 12 for 151.

There was equal excitement in the first match of Folkestone week. Nottinghamshire were the visitors and Gary Sobers hammered a glorious century on the opening day. Kent looked doomed when they lost their first five wickets for 27 runs, three of the wickets falling to the former Kent medium-pace bowler David Halfyard. Brian Luckhurst stood firm and batted for five and a quarter hours for his 156 not out, sharing century partnerships with Ealham and Shepherd. Cowdrey declared 76 in arrears after his side had claimed a fifth batting point. Sobers was again in belligerent mood and after scoring freely he asked Kent to make 282 to win in three hours. Denness and Luckhurst gave them a fine start with a partnership of 103, and Asif Iqbal hit 56 out of 94 in 50 minutes. With 20 overs remaining, Kent needed 112 to win. Wickets fell in the race for runs, but three boundaries from Alan Knott clinched the issue with eight balls left.

The last home match of the season confirmed Kent's status. Leicestershire were bowled out for 152 and 229, and Kent made 421 for 7 off 105 overs, claiming eight batting bonus points on the way.

An examination of Kent's full strength side in those last four matches reveals what an astonishingly powerful combination it was: Denness, Luckhurst, Johnson, Cowdrey, Asif Iqbal, Ealham, Shepherd, Knott, Woolmer, Underwood and Dye. Both Denness and Luckhurst were England openers, while Woolmer, number-nine in this side, was to be an England middle-order batsman within five years and an England opener within six. He was a most accurate

Asif Iqbal, an inspiration for the Kent side of the 1970s in every department of the game.

medium-pace bowler, who had prodigious success in one-day cricket. Like Johnson, an off-break bowler and highly competent 1,000-runs-a-year batsman, and Ealham, a batsman and fielder in the Jackie Bond class, Woolmer had forced his way to a regular place in the side in 1970 and had been awarded his county cap.

Colin Cowdrey had already played more than 100 Test matches and was one of the greatest batsmen of his generation, while Asif Iqbal and John Shepherd were all-rounders of international class. Asif, a captain of Pakistan, was a thrilling batsman, a dynamic fielder and a medium-pace bowler who could swing the ball venomously. Shepherd, too, was a medium-pace bowler and hard-hitting batsman, a most accomplished bits and pieces player.

In the opinion of many, Alan Knott was the finest wicketkeeper to have appeared in cricket since the end of World War Two. He was also a most adaptable batsman who rarely failed to make a significant contribution in any form of cricket. His partnership with 'Deadly' Derek Underwood, a left-arm spinner who bowled more quickly than most of his type and who was in the very highest class, became legendary throughout the cricket world.

John Dye was a left-arm seam bowler, and a very good one, who was much troubled by injury and who later went to Northamptonshire. He would share the new ball with Shepherd and sometimes with Asif.

What is most significant about the side for those last four matches of the 1970 season, however, is the players who were not included in this strongest eleven but who appeared frequently in the Championship year — Leary, Nicholls, Brown, Graham and the veteran Dixon. If it is argued that the side was not strong in pace bowling, it undeniably had one of the most vital qualities of a successful side — strength in depth. No county side had attained anything approaching greatness without this quality.

When Mike Denness took over the Kent side from Colin Cowdrey in 1972, he assessed the strengths and weaknesses of the playing staff and believed that the county were better equipped to succeed in limited-over cricket than they were in the three-day game. His assessment proved to be correct and, although his team were no stragglers in the Championship, in five years under Denness, Kent took six one-day titles.

The reasons for Denness deciding to emphasize his side's challenge in the limited-over competitions are apparent. John Dye had departed, so leaving the new-ball department thinner than

'Deadly' Derek Underwood, a man for all seasons and all forms of cricket.

ever, and Colin Cowdrey, the most experienced and technically accomplished batsman in the side, was nearing the end of his career. The bowling was immensely strong in medium pace. Bernard Julien had joined fellow West Indian, John Shepherd, in the side. Julien was a fast-medium pace left-arm bowler and a right-handed batsman whose explosions could win any match. Bob Woolmer, Norman Graham, the incomparable Derek Underwood and Asif Iqbal completed a sextet of medium pace bowlers of unerring accuracy.

Woolmer first won his place in the limited-over side because of his medium-pace bowling. He bowled just short of a length, moved the ball a little and was a very difficult proposition when a batsman was trying to force quick runs. He bowled for Kent in first-class cricket and took 334 wickets for them in his career which lasted until 1984. In the same period, in the John Player League alone, he took 220 wickets. When one considers that a bowler was never allowed to bowl more than eight overs in a match, this is a phenomenal figure, one and a half wickets per game for a man who was not a main strike bowler.

The strength of the batting was in its ability to score at a very quick rate. Asif Iqbal, Bernard Julien, John Shepherd, Graham Johnson and Denness himself were all capable of tearing an attack apart, and Alan Knott, who could and did bat anywhere in the order, fashioned quick runs in a style that was all his own. His running between the wickets was like an inspirational dynamo to his side. Behind the stumps he was an inspiration to any side and a mighty asset to any bowler.

We have already mentioned that Alan Ealham was in the Jack Bond class as a fielder, and none realised better than Denness that Lancashire had set a standard in fielding which had to be emulated if a county was to prosper in one-day cricket. Ealham was magnificent, both as a catcher and a ground fielder, and he thrilled crowds at Canterbury with his stops and sensational catches in the outfield. He was closely rivalled by Asif Iqbal, and one of the characteristics of this Kent side was how hard they worked at their fielding. Johnson turned himself into a fine fielder and Woolmer persevered to bring himself up to the level of the rest of the side.

With the success in the one-day game came fanatical support and long before the start of a day's play, Canterbury was packed with excited Kent followers. They could not have wished for a more thrilling finish to the season than was given them in Denness' first year as skipper, 1972.

Worth his place in any side on the strength of his fielding alone — Kent's Alan Ealham.

Before the second week in July, Kent suffered four defeats and a no-result in the John Player League and were seemingly out of the contest. Then they won five matches in succession, including victory over Leicestershire, the current leaders, so that when Worcestershire, the reigning Sunday Champions, arrived at Canterbury on the last Sunday of the season, Kent knew that victory would give them the title by a margin of one point over Leicestershire. A crowd of some 12,000 people swarmed into the St Lawrence ground to see the match.

Worcestershire hit 190 for five in their 40 overs, which was the highest score that had been made in a Sunday League game in Kent that season. The visitors were particularly severe on Underwood.

Needing to score at 4.75 runs an over, Kent were given a splendid start by Luckhurst and Johnson, who hit 43 in eight overs. Then Luckhurst and Nicholls added 108 in 22 overs. Both were out in the 30th over, and Julien and Denness did not last long, but Asif Iqbal took Kent to victory and the title with two overs to spare.

The winning of the John Player League in 1972 was only a sample of success, for the following season, even though Julien had to spend most of his time with the West Indian tourists, Kent took two of the four major trophies and there were times when the newspapers were talking in terms of a 'grand slam'. Only two defeats were suffered in the John Player League and the title was won by 12 August, the earliest the League has been claimed.

Although he was unavailable for the Benson and Hedges Cup competition after the quarter-final stage, because of his commitment to the West Indies, Bernard Julien did much to help Kent to reach the later stages of the tournament. A devastating spell of new-ball bowling at The Oval reduced Surrey to 15 for five, and Julien finished with figures of 5 for 21 from his 11 overs. He also played a significant part in the quarter-final victory over Hampshire at Southampton. This was a thrilling match in which Kent gained a narrow victory by 11 runs. Julien and Asif provided the backbone of the Kent innings with a brisk fourth-wicket partnership of 82, and Julien later broke the Hampshire opening stand when he had Gordon Greenidge caught.

More than anything it was Kent's magnificent fielding and their unquenchable team spirit which took them into the Final with victory over Essex at Canterbury. Kent made only 169 in their 55 overs, but Ealham took a spectacular running, diving catch to dismiss Edmeades, and Cooke and Pont were run out. The Essex nerve cracked against such dynamic fielding, and they were all out for 123 in 44 overs.

In the Lord's Final against Worcestershire on 21 July, Kent began very slowly and after 20 overs the score was a meagre 34 for two. It was over an hour before Luckhurst hit the first boundary of the innings, a six into the Tavern area, and this heralded a pulsating partnership of 166 in 29 overs between Luckhurst and Asif Iqbal. The running between the wickets was masterly, although the stand was broken when a tiring Luckhurst was beaten by D'Oliveira's long throw to the wicketkeeper. Asif was yorked for 59 shortly afterwards, but the tempo was maintained. From the last eight overs, 53 runs were scored. Colin Cowdrey, not a cricketer that one associates with the one-day game and batting as low as number seven, made 29 of them with some delicate placing.

Facing a score of 225, Worcestershire were never really in the hunt. Asif Iqbal followed his belligerent innings with four wickets for 43 runs, and Kent won by 39 runs.

Asif Iqbal was an 'electric' cricketer. He exuded energy and sparks flew when he was batting, bowling or fielding. His appearances for Kent were limited in 1974, as he was a member of the Pakistan touring side, but the county were at Lord's again, and this time took the Gillette Cup with victory over Lancashire in a game we have already mentioned.

The following season was the one barren season for Kent during Denness' period of captaincy, but in 1979 they were back to their winning ways, even though they were hard hit by Test calls and injuries.

In the Sunday League they lost five of their first nine games, but only one thereafter. They finished with 40 points, as did four other sides. They had the same number of away wins as Essex, but their run rate was 0.427 better than their closest rivals. Somerset would have won the League on the last day of the season had they beaten or tied with Glamorgan. As it was, Dredge was run out on the last ball of the match and Somerset lost by one run to give Kent their third, and last, John Player Championship.

Kent began their campaign in the Benson and Hedges Cup rather uncertainly, too. They were overwhelmed by Yorkshire in their opening match, but victories over Surrey, Oxford and Cambridge, and Sussex took them to the head of their group, helped by the fact that the combined Oxford and Cambridge side beat Yorkshire at Barnsley. Nottinghamshire were comfortably beaten in the quarter-final with Kevin Jarvis, just establishing himself as a regular fast medium bowler in the side, taking four wickets and the Gold Award.

The semi-final at The Oval was a splendid match and notable for an outstanding innings by Mike Denness, who hit 104 out of 173 in two hours. There was some steady play by Johnson, and Asif and Ealham thrashed 83 runs at the close of the innings. Surrey were faced by a target of 281, a task that had never been accomplished in the short history of the tournament. They came very close to it. Kent won by 16 runs, and the game finished at 7.15pm. There was a crowd of 14,000 at The Oval to see the game, for Kent now attracted a large following wherever they went.

Worcestershire were again Kent's opponents in the Final, and when he won the toss, Gifford asked Kent to bat first. Woolmer had by now moved up from number nine to open the innings. His partner was Johnson, and they created a record by becoming the first opening pair to share a three-figure stand in a Lord's Final. In 30 overs they scored 110 before Woolmer was caught at deep mid-on for 61. He had hit D'Oliveira for 15 in one over, but shortly after this D'Oliveira had had to leave the field with a damaged hamstring which he suffered when chasing an overthrow to the boundary.

This was a severe handicap to Worcestershire, who now flung their field far and wide to prevent boundaries. The circle rule was still some years away. Between the 36th and the 52nd over, Kent did not score a boundary, but swift running between the wickets kept the score moving.

Johnson was bowled in the 44th over for 78, but Asif contributed his customary late plunder, and Kent reached 236 for five in their 55 overs.

Worcestershire started strongly, but Shepherd and Woolmer joined the attack and the run rate slowed.

Shepherd had Glenn Turner caught low down by Knott in the 13th over, and Neale, frustrated, was caught at cover by Johnson when he swatted at the same bowler. This began a remarkable sequence as Underwood kept the batsmen in a vice-like grip and Ormrod, Imran and Hemsley were all caught as they attempted to pull him. The catcher in each case was Graham Johnson, who judged all three catches beautifully on the boundary's edge. His fielding allied to his batting was to earn him the Gold Award.

Tenacious as a batsman; accurate as a bowler — Bob Woolmer.

There followed one of the bravest innings seen at Lord's as D'Oliveira, his leg strapped and batting with Glenn Turner as runner, hit 50 out of 75 in 14 overs before he was bowled by Jarvis. Kent went on to win by 43 runs.

Mike Denness' reign coincided with a glorious period in Kent history, yet it ended in doubt and mystery. It was rumoured that there were those who were not satisfied with six trophies in five years because the County Championship pennant was not among them, and they remained in that past age when that was all that mattered. Denness had recognised the county's strengths and weaknesses. He saw the ability to score runs quickly, to field to the highest level and to bowl for containment or wickets as the situation demanded were the qualities best suited to limited-over cricket and that his side had those qualities. His record proved he was correct in his aims and judgements, but at the end of the 1976 season he resigned as captain. Nor was it certain that he would make himself available for the following season.

In the event, Denness left Kent and joined Essex, while Asif Iqbal succeeded him as captain with Graham Johnson as his vice-captain, the first time such an appointment had been made by the county.

Asif took his side to a Lord's Final at the first attempt, but they were no match for Gloucestershire who, inspired by Mike Procter and Andy Stovold, won the Benson and Hedges Cup by 64 runs with 45 balls of Kent's innings left unused.

There was ample compensation, however, for by beating Warwickshire at Edgbaston in the last match of the season, Kent were able to share the County Championship with Middlesex. It was a fine achievement, for, as well as the departure of Denness, Kent had lost Colin Cowdrey and Brian Luckhurst through retirement. Yet there was an unease. The success had been brought about mainly by the form of the senior players, Ealham, Asif and Shepherd in particular, and there were problems on the horizon.

Asif Iqbal, Derek Underwood, Alan Knott, Bob Woolmer and Bernard Julien all signed to play for the Packer organization in World Series Cricket and their futures with Kent were initially in doubt. Asif was deprived of the captaincy and Alan Ealham appointed in his place for the 1978 season. The fears over the impact of Packer cricket soon diminished when it was realised that, with Kent having renewed the players' contracts, they would be available for the entire season as they would not be selected for Test matches.

Wicketkeeper supreme — Alan Knott.

Only Alan Knott did not return, although he was to do so later, and he had a highly competent deputy in Paul Downton.

There was a further bonus for Kent in the rapid progress of batsman Chris Tavare, in his first full season down from Oxford. The result of all this was that the county used only 15 players in the Championship matches in the whole of the season, and of these, Clinton, Dilley and Kemp appeared in only eight matches between them. Invariably, the side that took the field was Woolmer, Rowe, Tavare, Asif Iqbal, Johnson, Ealham, Shepherd, Downton, Underwood and Jarvis, with the last place between Chris Cowdrey and Hills.

Tavare and Woolmer scored more than a 1,000 runs in Championship matches and Underwood took 110 wickets. The title was won by a margin of 19 points from Essex, nor did success end there.

They won their group in the Benson and Hedges Cup and gained revenge for the one defeat that they had suffered when they overwhelmed Nottinghamshire in the quarter-final. Somerset were also well beaten in a semi-final that was badly mauled by the weather. The Final was the most one-sided seen at Lord's and Derbyshire, enjoying something of a revival under Eddie Barlow's leadership, were beaten by six wickets with 13.2 overs to spare. This was the third time in six years that Kent had taken the Cup. They had dominated the early years of the Benson and Hedges competition much in the way that Lancashire had dominated the early years of the Gillette Cup.

There was talk of discord in the boardroom, but the team spirit seemed as good as ever, and years of success appeared to loom ahead. It was not to be. Kent have won nothing since 1978, and no county in modern times, save Glamorgan, have gone longer without winning a trophy.

The 1979 season seemed merely a temporary aberration and had they beaten Middlesex on the last day of the season, Kent would have won the John Player League again.

Thereafter there were suggestions of a lack of unity as older players began to lose form and younger ones did not fulfil their promise. Ealham's place in the side became uncertain and he was sacked as captain, with Asif reinstated. This proved to be only a temporary measure and indecision and uncertainly prevailed. The great days of Kent cricket were over.

The Kent team of the 1970s were never a balanced side in the sense that outstanding sides of the past like Surrey and Yorkshire had been, or even the fine Lancashire one-day side had been. Kent's virtues were different. They had an all-round ability which allowed the team to move as a unit so that if one department failed, another was always ready to fill the breach. Batting order was flexible; bowlers there were in abundance.

It was under Mike Denness that they revealed their virtues to the full and played over and above the potential of their individual worth. For much of the 1970s they were supreme among English counties.

Middlesex

The Age of Brearley and the Discipleship of Gatting

IN 1971, while Lancashire were at their peak and Kent just beginning their period of ascendancy, Middlesex appointed Mike Brearley as captain. The county had been in the doldrums for some time. They could field a side which included five Test cricketers — Titmus, Parfitt, Murray, Russell and Price — but they had won nothing nor looked like winning anything. They lacked a strike bowler, and they lacked leadership. Senior members of the Middlesex committee were acutely aware of the problems that the club faced and of the need to reorganise in order to bring the side closer to the demands of the game as it was now being played. To turn to Brearley was part of a calculated policy that was to help move the county into the most consistently successful period in its history.

Brearley was an academic who had shown tremendous form as a batsman in his years at Cambridge, hitting centuries in the Varsity matches of 1962 and 1964. He was seen as a future England Test player, but he had left the game temporarily to continue his studies and then taken up an appointment teaching philosophy in Newcastle, appearing for Middlesex in the summer holidays. It was the offer of the captaincy which lured him back to cricket full time.

He was fascinated by the tactics of the game and by his desire to get the best out of other people. His was an enquiring, alert mind and was excited by the manipulation of men and the cut and thrust of battle. He was not the seasoned 'professional' in the sense that Sellers and Surridge had been or that Bond was. To Brearley, cricket was an art, a game of chess or the composition of a piece of music, but he was no romantic in a world of his own distant from the realities and the needs of the moment.

He acknowledged immediately that the side he inherited was not strong enough in bowling, that there were divisions with the playing staff that could not be tolerated, that the committee structure was unwieldly and that the side was playing unattractive cricket. It was this last factor that was the first to be changed. Brearley insisted upon robust and adventurous cricket. The side responded and players and opponents began to enjoy the game more. It also meant that Middlesex could attract new players more easily.

There was a buoyancy that initially took the side to the top of the table only for them to fade. The pattern was repeated in 1972, but these were formative years. Parfitt and Russell retired and Price played less and less, and such men are not easily replaced, but new faces began to appear. Phil Edmonds, a slow left-arm bowler and highly capable batsman, came down from Cambridge. He was a tempestuous spirit, but an invaluable addition the side, and his partnership with off-spinner John Emburey, destined to succeed Titmus, became one of the most potent in the game.

Barlow, Butcher, Gatting and Gould were others who began to appear, and there was the incomparable Clive Radley, a batsman who dictated the length at which the bowler should bowl, who was a model of consistency and who has had no superior in his commitment to the county game. Moreover, Radley was able to adapt himself to the needs of the game be it 40 overs or three days.

By 1975, Middlesex were good enough to reach the Finals of both the Benson and Hedges Cup and the Gillette Cup, but they were well beaten by Leicestershire in the first and Lancashire in the second. John Murray, one of the greatest and most graceful of wicketkeepers, retired, and still the side was being reshaped. Selvey and Brearley became England cricketers; the talents of Gatting and Gould began to shine. Wayne Daniel, the West Indian pace bowler, was registered to qualify for the 1977 season, and A.A. Jones was signed from Somerset.

The acquisition of Jones was one of Brearley's most astute moves. A pace bowler, Jones had the reputation of being temperamental and lazy in the field. He had been sacked by two counties. Brearley convinced Middlesex that they had need of Jones, and they backed him. It proved a most successful move. Jones was leading wicket-taker with 69 wickets, and Middlesex won the Championship. Brearley prophesied that the county would remain at the top for the next five years. He was too conservative in his estimate.

Mike Smith, Brearley, Barlow, Featherstone and Radley had provided admirable batting strength, and Roland Butcher and Mike Gatting had shown the quality of the reserve strengh. Jones and Selvey were a fine and penetrative opening attack, with Tim Lamb a good support on occasions. Titmus, in his last season, Edmonds and Featherstone supplied a complementary spin attack, and Emburey, who played in four matches, hovered in the wings.

The price of success is that a side loses some of its better players to Test calls. In 1977, for example, Brearley could play in only 11 Championship matches because he was involved in all five Tests against Australia, and Barlow played in one Test and in all three one-day internationals. Over the next few years, the demands on the club were to become even greater.

In the absence of Brearley, Smith led the side well, but six of the nine Championship wins were to be gained when Brearley was captain of the eleven. He was a master at judging a player, his strengths and weaknesses, at reading a wicket and at divining how a game could be won.

The most astonishing example of Brearley's enterprise in winning a match came in the game against Surrey at Lord's at the beginning of August. No play was possible on the first day and only five overs were bowled on the second, during which time Surrey lost Alan Butcher. On the last morning the Surrey batsmen displayed neither the tenacity nor the technique to cope with the Middlesex seam attack of Daniel, Selvey and Gatting on a damp wicket. By 12.15pm, Surrey were all out for 49.

Emburey and Gould opened the Middlesex innings, and after Emburey had faced one ball Brearley declared. Batting again, with the pitch still damp, Surrey wilted for a second time against an attack that was as inspired as it was determined. Monte Lynch suffered the misfortune of recording a 'pair' before lunch, and Surrey showed no signs of resistance until Arnold joined Richards in a ninth wicket stand of 24. By tea they were all out for 89. Incredibly, Middlesex had reached the final interval on the last day without having scored a run but having taken 20 wickets. They had 88 minutes in which to score 139 to win the match. Brearley and Smith took 47 runs from the first seven overs, and the opening partnership realised 101 before Smith was stumped.

The grey eminence of English cricket — Mike Brearley.

Radley and Brearley moved to a comfortable victory with 11 balls to spare.

This was an outstanding and amazing win, and one which played a significant part in Middlesex sharing the County Championship with Kent.

If this was an example of Brearley's capacity to win a game against heavy odds, then his trust in Gatting and Emburey was testimony to his ability to judge a player. Brearley had supreme confidence in Gatting, a confidence which was not shared by others, and Gatting responded with a 1,000 runs in 1977 although he did not hit a century. At Brearley's insistence, Gatting was chosen for the England tour of Pakistan and he was later to establish himself as one of his country's leading batsmen.

Few people on the county circuit had a high opinion of John Emburey when he played a few matches before 1977, but Brearley always insisted that he was an off-spinner of international class. He was not in the Middlesex side at the beginning of the 1977 season, but Jones sustained a back injury and Emburey was drafted into the side. Jones, Daniel and Selvey had formed a most hostile pace attack in the early part of the season, but the alliance between Edmonds and Emburey gave the side a balance which was the envy of all. In Championship matches alone, Edmonds took 72 wickets and Emburey 68, while Selvey had 72 and Daniel 71.

Wayne Daniel was among the fastest bowlers in the world at this time. He was Middlesex's first astute overseas signing. He was able to make the ball rear uncomfortably from a length and maintained consistent hostility.

Gatting and Featherstone were able to supply support to the main line bowlers in seam and spin, and the strength of this Middlesex side was that it was a side for all seasons. It was as successful in the one-day knock-out competitions as it was in the Championship, and, in 1977, Middlesex claimed the Gillette Cup as well as their share in the Championship.

They had a narrow win over Kent in the first round, although Jones took three wickets in five balls to reduce Kent to 47 for five at the start of the match. Warwickshire and Hampshire were the next victims, but the semi-final against Gloucestershire was postponed for six days and was finally decided by a 15-over thrash on the morning of Friday, 26 August. Middlesex beat Somerset by six wickets with more than three overs to spare.

Brearley created history in the Final when he became the first

The young John Emburey in whom Middlesex and Brearley showed great faith. They were well rewarded.

captain to win the toss and ask the opposition to bat. It seemed that he might have erred, for the softness of the pitch nullified Daniel's efforts, but Selvey bowled admirably. Edmonds and Emburey exerted immaculate control even though Emburey was hit for one massive six into the pavilion by Llewellyn. Featherstone picked up three wickets as Glamorgan's innings fretted to a close, and Middlesex faced a score of 177 for nine.

Brearley was caught behind off the first ball of the innings, and Radley was dropped at slip by Collis King, but there were few real alarms for Middlesex. Radley pushed, nudged, dabbed and drove his way to 85 not out and the Man-of-the-Match award, and Middlesex won by five wickets with 4.2 overs to spare. Gatting took the fielding prize, but this was an area in which the whole side excelled. There was a joy in their cricket.

They had now won three prizes in two years and were looked upon as the leading county along with Kent. The calls on players became heavier as, in 1978, Middlesex lost Brearley, Edmonds and Radley for six Tests, that is 12 of the 21 Championship games, and Emburey also played for England against New Zealand at The Oval.

Middlesex dropped to third in the Championship which was won by a Kent side untroubled by Test calls.

In 1979, perplexed by bad weather and the demands of a Test series and of the World Cup, Middlesex had their poorest season since Brearley had taken over, but the following season they were back at the top with another County Championship/Gillette Cup double. As they also finished third in the John Player League and were semi-finalists in the Benson and Hedges Cup, it could be said that they enjoyed the most successful year by any county in the nine seasons that four trophies had been offered for competition.

The county enjoyed a tremendous bonus in 1980 which had a considerable influence on their success. Believing that Wayne Daniel would be a member of the West Indian side to tour England, Middlesex recruited the South African pace bowler Vincent van der Bijl. Daniel was a surprise omission from the West Indian party, Croft and Marshall being preferred, and Middlesex were able to play both Daniel and van der Bijl in 1980, so giving them one of the most potent attacks in their history.

Vincent van der Bijl was a gentle giant of a man. He ambled in off a long run, clutching the ball as if he were unwilling to

Clive Radley, the heart and sinew of the Middlesex batting in the county's finest years.

let it go. He brought the ball down from a full height, which meant about nine feet, was far quicker than the batsman could have anticipated from his leisurely approach to the wicket, was unerringly straight and made the ball both move and lift disconcertingly. His 85 County Championship wickets at 14.72 runs each are evidence of his quality, and he was, too, a wonderfully encouraging team man. There was something courteous about van der Bijl in all that he did.

Another newcomer to the side was Paul Downton, who had been signed from Kent on the recommendation of John Murray who rated him very highly. He was not given an automatic place behind the stumps, but he took over from Gould in mid-season and proved himself to be an excellent opening batsman as well as a wicketkeeper of Test class.

Although Edmonds missed much of the season because of a knee operation, the Middlesex attack was the most formidable in the country. Daniel, van der Bijl and Emburey were to the fore, but Selvey, Maru, Hughes, Merry and Titmus, who had returned from his sojourn as coach at The Oval to assist when required, provided the strongest possible reserve strength.

Gatting was often on Test call, but Brearley, Radley and Barlow gave substance to the batting with Roland Butcher adding lustre on occasions. Butcher was never a consistent batsman, but he would play three or four innings a year which would win a match and clinch the Championship. In July 1980, he played two such innings within a week which were to be decisive in the ultimate outcome of the title.

At Lord's, Hampshire set Middlesex the formidable task of scoring 296 in 220 minutes to win the match. They were looking lost at 54 for three when Butcher came to the wicket. In 144 minutes, he hit 153 not out, an innings which included nine sixes and eight fours, and Middlesex won with eight overs to spare. This was followed by an innings of 179 in under three hours at Scarborough, where Middlesex won by eight wickets. This time Butcher hit eight sixes and 21 fours.

A brilliant innings victory over Essex at Lord's at the beginning of August seemed to have clinched the title for Middlesex, but defeats at the hands of Leicestershire and Gloucestershire threw the Championship race open again as Surrey moved into their best form.

On 30 August, Middlesex began their match against Glamorgan

at Cardiff knowing that victory would bring them the Championship and that failure to win might well mean that Surrey would take the title. Middlesex were handicapped by the absence of Gatting and Emburey, who were playing in the Centenary Test against Australia, and from the start things did not go well. No play was possible until 5.15pm on the Saturday. Middlesex lost the toss, were put in to bat and closed at a miserable 41 for three. Vincent van der Bijl hit a robust 40 on the Monday and they reached 163.

Glamorgan then fell to the Middlesex pace attack. Simon Hughes, fresh from Durham University and looking at this time as if he would become a genuine pace bowler, took four wickets, as did van der Bijl, and Glamorgan were bowled out for 140. Middlesex were five points away from the title, but only six and a half hours of the match remained.

Brearley led by example, hitting 124 not out when Middlesex batted for a second time, 113 of them before lunch on the last morning at which point he declared. Glamorgan had four hours in which to score 235. More important, Middlesex had four hours in which to bowl Glamorgan out and win the title. Hughes made an early breakthrough when he bowled Alan Lewis Jones, and the home side was reduced to 84 for five. Holmes battled bravely and he and Moseley put on 52, but van der Bijl broke the stand, and when Edmonds found the edge of Perry's bat Downton took the catch and Middlesex had won the Championship.

They drew their final match, against Kent at Canterbury, and returned to Lord's for the Gillette Cup Final. This was the last year in with the 60-over competition was sponsored by Gillette, National Westminster Bank succeeding them for 1981.

Surrey, who had chased Middlesex so hard in the Championship, were the other Finalists, and they batted first. Tight bowling and astute captaincy restricted them to 201 in their 60 overs. Brearley's worth was never more apparent than in the way in which he handled and encouraged the 20-year-old Simon Hughes as he came in for some punishment in the closing overs.

Brearley went on to score 96 not out and take the individual award as Middlesex won by seven wickets and with considerable ease.

There was an inevitable anti-climax in 1981, a year of some controversy for the county. The controversy arose because Middlesex signed Jeff Thomson, the Australian pace bowler, on a one-year contract as replacement for van der Bijl, who had said from the start that he would play only one season of county cricket. This was interpreted by many as a cynical gesture more associated with soccer than with cricket, an attempt to buy success at any price and a hinderance to the development of young English cricketers. But it was symptomatic of the times and for the now insatiable appetite for success which was at the very heart of the game and pervaded all its gestures and all its acts.

The argument over Thomson became irrelevant as he was injured and played in only six Championship matches, yet when he took the field with the Middlesex side for the opening match against Essex at Lord's it revealed the enormous strength of the Middlesex side. The team was: Brearley, Downton, Radley, Gatting, Butcher, Barlow, Emburey, Edmonds, Selvey, Thomson and Daniel. Each one was a Test cricketer, and the first eight in the order were to score more than one first-class century in their careers. Later in the season, following Thomson's breakdown, more opportunity was given to fast bowler Norman Cowans who was to find a place in the England team very quickly.

Another bonus from the disappointments of the 1981 season was to be the emergence of Barlow and Slack as an opening pair of distinction. Unfortunately, the partnership did not survive into the 1982 season when Barlow, troubled by injury and loss of form, played in only four matches.

This was Mike Brearley's last season and Middlesex did not suffer defeat in any competition until the middle of June, so that there were dreams of the 'grand slam'. Those dreams were shattered when Lancashire won the Benson and Hedges Cup quarter-final match, and there were three defeats in the John Player League at the end of July and the beginning of August, which meant that Sussex and not Middlesex took the Sunday title. Nevertheless, in finishing second, Middlesex attained the highest position that they have ever reached in the 40-over League.

Two very close victories took Middlesex to the semi-final of the Natwest Bank Trophy, but Surrey were emphatic winners by 125 runs, so that Middlesex were left with only the County Championship.

Good early season form was followed by a slight lapse, but Middlesex began August at the top of the Championship table with Surrey in second place. By the end of the month, the Middlesex lead had been increased to 31 points and Leicestershire were in

Wayne Daniel, the arch-destroyer.

second place, although when Surrey arrived at Lord's their challenge was still very much alive.

This was to be Brearley's last match at Lord's and when he inspected the wicket, he was certain that it was so worn that it would take spin on the last day. Fred Titmus, three months short of his 50th birthday, had called in at the Middlesex dressing-room for a cup of coffee. On seeing him, Brearley asked him to play, so sure was he that the wicket would be of benefit to the veteran off-spinner. Titmus had not appeared in a first-class match since 1980 but he accepted Brearley's assessment, borrowed kit from his former colleagues and played.

Middlesex batted laboriously on the opening day and rain interfered with the second. Eventually, Brearley declared on the last afternoon and asked Surrey to score 161 in 135 minutes. Like Surridge, he had a nose for victory.

Surrey were in trouble from the start. They were 49 for five before Sylvester Clarke was promoted to try to hit some quick runs. He did, scoring all 35 that were made while he was at the wicket and hitting three sixes and a four. It was to no avail. Titmus had him caught at long-on and soon added the wickets of Thomas and Monkhouse. Emburey had Needham caught in the outfield, and Middlesex had won a sensational victory by 58 runs. Titmus finished with 3 for 43 in the second innings. Brearley's judgement of a pitch and of a game was second to nobody.

Hampshire were beaten at Uxbridge, and only four points were needed from the final game at Worcester to confirm the Championship belonged to Middlesex. They were not long in coming and so Mike Brearley's career ended as most of it had been, in glory. In 12 seasons of captaincy he had rebuilt the Middlesex club to make it the best county side of a generation. The successes were packed into the last eight years of his leadership — four County Championships (one of them shared) and two Gillette Cups. The county had never enjoyed a period remotely comparable, yet in many ways the trophies that he brought to Middlesex were the least of Brearley's achievements. He had infected the club with the ambition which was his own great driving force, the ambition to do nothing unless he did it well. When he retired he left no vacuum behind but a thriving county in which success could, and would, continue.

With the backing of a number of young and intelligent committee men, Brearley had helped to create an infrastructure at Middlesex so essential if a county club is to thrive in the commercial world of cricket in the 1980s and 1990s. He had insisted on a realistic and fair pay structure and on the players' voices being heard at committee level. In effect, he had helped to bring about an effective and friendly management system within the club, a well-oiled machine which would ensure that success should be continuous. A system which Liverpool had displayed so magnificently in the world of soccer.

It was this system which allowed Mike Gatting to succeed Brearley at a time when rifts and dissension could have caused havoc in another club. Phil Edmonds had been vice-captain to Brearley for a time, but his tempestuous character and brand of eccentricity were not qualities best suited to leadership, and Emburey looked destined to be captain of Middlesex after Brearley.

Emburey was a tough, intelligent cricketer who, while following Brearley and respecting him, had ideas of his own. His decision to participate in the tour of South Africa sponsored by South African Breweries cost him dearly, however. He was banned from Test cricket for three years and was deprived of the vice-captaincy of his county at a time when he was close to succeeding Brearley. Gatting took over from Emburey and was promoted to take on the mantle of leadership after Brearley, who had long been one of his most ardent champions.

The transition was smooth. Gatting was a very different captain from Brearley. He has been dubbed more of an NCO than one of the officers' mess, whereas Brearley was something of a patrician, despite himself. Gatting had not Brearley's astute awareness of the game, few have had that, but he was tough, uncompromising and with nothing to distract from the one thing he had always wanted to do, play cricket.

Gatting had advantages and disadvantages in succeeding Brearley. The obvious disadvantage was Brearley was a popular leader who had enjoyed years of success and any who followed him would be measured by his standards. The advantages were that Gatting inherited a good side who were used to winning and were eager to continue to win in an age where rewards were high and that he was also backed by an excellent organisation. He was a straightforward, no-nonsense captain, and his first edict was that the side would be picked on merit. Middlesex were as powerful and determined under Gatting as they had been under Brearley, and the success continued.

The first season of his leadership, 1983, saw Middlesex move to the top of the County Championship in June with six victories in succession, but then there was a decline of which Essex took full advantage. They took over the lead in late August when Gatting's inexperience led to surprising caution, and they maintained that lead until the end of the season when the last day of Middlesex's game at Trent Bridge was abandoned through rain to leave Essex as undisputed Champions.

Unquestionably, Middlesex and Essex were the best two sides in the country, and when they met in the Benson and Hedges Cup Final at Lord's in July it was probably the first occasion when two such sides of outstanding ability have met in a Lord's Final. Middlesex's path to the Final had been bizarre. They had completed only one of their zonal matches, beating Kent at Canterbury, won the quarter-final at Bristol on the toss of a coin and beaten Lancashire in the semi-final on a gloomy day before a sparse crowd, the match finishing in near darkness at 7.50pm. The Final, though, was to prove to be a classic.

Middlesex were without Roland Butcher, who had been hit in the face by a ball from Ferris of Leicestershire and was unable to play for the remainder of the season. An exciting batsman and a brilliant fielder, he was greatly missed.

Early-morning drizzle caused the start of the match to be delayed for 50 minutes, and when Fletcher, the Essex captain, won the toss he asked Middlesex to bat first in steamy conditions. John Lever, the Essex and England left-arm pace bowler, had been in doubt until the morning of the match, for he had undergone an operation only a week before the match. Barlow suggested that there were doubts as to his fitness when he hit him for three boundaries through the off-side field in his first three overs. It was Foster who was to dismiss Barlow, knocking back his middle stump, having earlier had Slack brilliantly taken at slip by Gooch.

Radley was an unobtrusive as ever, but he began to move consistently on to the front foot, nudging and deflecting, always dictating his own length and edging the score along. Gatting began to fret as Turner and Gooch embarked on accurate and economic spells. The run-rate sagged, and with the score on 74 in the 29th over, Radley turned Gooch to the Mound Stand boundary, Gatting went for an improbable third run and was beaten by Foster's chase and throw to the wicketkeeper. Keith Tomlins was leg-before first ball, and Essex had seized the initiative.

Emburey willed himself into being a batsman. He defied limitations in technique and created shots of his own. His powers of concentration were enormous and his desire to succeed unquenchable. He provided the ideal foil for Radley, who crouched lower and lower with determination and began to score more rapidly. Radley and Emburey added 49 in 15 overs before Emburey was caught behind off Lever, and Radley, who finished on 89 not out, cajoled Downton, Edmonds, Williams and Daniel into helping him to add 73 in the last 11 overs. They were aided by some dropped catches, and the final score of 196 for eight was not large, but it was far better than had looked possible at one time.

When the Essex innings began the Middlesex score soon appeared to be diminutive. Hardie crashed Daniel for four in the first over of the innings, and the second saw Gooch bludgeon Cowans to the mid-wicket boundary three times and take 16 off the over. Gatting had set an attacking off-side field, but Cowans bowled short, and Gooch murdered the bowling. After ten overs Essex were 71 for nought and an early end apparently in sight.

Neil Williams had replaced Cowans at the Nursery end, but Gooch drove him straight for four. He aimed to repeat the shot, but he edged low to Downton, who took a fine catch. Essex were 79 for 1 in the 12th over, the massacre temporarily halted.

It was Edmonds who had applied the brakes with some accurate spin bowling, but at tea the score was 113 for one from 25 overs. Edmonds took two wickets immediately after tea, having McEwan taken at mid-on and Fletcher at silly mid-off as he pushed forward, but with 23 overs remaining, Essex needed only 61 to win and had seven wickets in hand.

Pont was dropped, but then he lost a bouncer from Williams, was hit on the side of the helmet and dropped his bat on his wicket. Hardie had lost his timing and was out in the 41st over for 49, and Middlesex now moved on to the attack. Gatting jettisoned the idea of containing one-day field-placing and positioned his men as if it were a three-day Championship match. Emburey induced strokelessness, and Turner and Pringle were very much on the defensive. Nevertheless, when Daniel had Pringle leg before on the first ball of the 52nd over an Essex victory still looked assured as they needed but 12 runs from 23 balls and had four wickets remaining.

Stuart Turner had batted with uncustomary restraint, and when he finally threw bat at the ball he was well caught on the run by substitute John Carr at mid-on. David East touched a ball to the fine-leg boundary, and Essex needed only six for victory with three wickets in hand and more than two overs left. Having hit the leg-side boundary, David East attempted to hit Cowans's next ball over mid-wicket for four. Cowans was now operating from the Pavilion end, and Gatting was fielding half-way back to the boundary. He got a hand to East's shot and, spinning around, brought off a remarkable catch as the ball was dropping behind him.

Daniel began the penultimate over with a wide, but thereafter, in the gloom, his pace was too much for Ray East. The fifth ball hit the batsman on the pad. East charged down the wicket and was run out by Radley's throw from square on the off-side. Lever played out the last ball, so leaving five runs to be scored from the final over with Foster on strike. One ball was sufficient for Middlesex as a Cowans' yorker splattered Foster's stumps to give Middlesex a dramatic victory. It was 8.50pm, and the night was already asserting itself.

Middlesex were to feel the pain that Essex must have felt that day at Lord's when, a few weeks later, they lost their NatWest Trophy semi-final match to Somerset by dint of having lost more wickets in a game where the scores finished level, but they could well feel pleased with their first season under Gatting's leadership.

So satiated had Middlesex become with success that finishing third in the Championship in 1984 without ever really being in a position to challenge was seen as comparative failure, but form was found at an appropriate time and on 1 September, Middlesex found themselves in the NatWest Bank Trophy Final. It was their sixth Lord's final in nine years.

The opponents were Kent, led by Chris Tavare, and fighting hard to regain former glory. Kent won the toss and batted first. Benson and Taylor began confidently and 50 was on the board in 17 overs. This climbed to 96 in 30 overs, but then Benson was splendidly stumped by Downton off Emburey, and Slack, who had replaced an Edmonds unable to find a length, bowled Taylor. One of the great qualities of the Middlesex side was its adaptability. Wilf Slack bowled his full quota, 12 overs of gentle medium pace and conceded only 33 runs while dismissing an opening batsman who had scored 49. Neither Gatting nor Butcher bowled, although both were capable of doing so, and this gave Gatting the option

Purpose, panache and determination — Mike Gatting.

of nine bowlers in his side in a one-day game. Many sides struggled to find a fifth.

Kent ended with 232 for six from their 60 overs, less than might have been expected at one time, but still a useful score.

Underwood bowled a typically frustrating spell, and when Gatting was fourth out at 124, Middlesex appeared to have lost their way. Inevitably, it was Radley who came to the rescue, hurrying and scurrying and finding the gaps in the field. He was most ably supported by Downton as 87 runs were scored in 15 overs. They were out in successive overs, and Emburey and Edmonds came together with 16 needed off 23 balls.

They ran briskly and intelligently and pushed and dabbed to perfection, but an excellent penultimate over by Jarvis meant that seven were needed off the last over, which was bowled by Richard Ellison.

The first ball produced a leg-bye, and Edmonds pushed the ball square on the off side for a single off the second. Emburey straight drove for two and pushed a single to cover. Edmonds levelled the scores when he guided the fifth ball to third man. Rightly, Ellison pitched the last ball well up, but it was not as full a length as he would have wished, and Emburey turned it to the square-leg boundary, where it was engulfed by the crowds swarming on to the pitch. In his second year as captain, Gatting again held a trophy aloft; and Clive Radley took the individual award for the third time in the six Lord's Finals in which he had appeared.

The demands on a side increase in proportion to the success it achieves. Supporters want to win everything, all the time, and make their criticisms apparent if this is not achieved. Opponents are less generous than they might once have been and are eager to beat a side who has monopolised winning. The players themselves are in danger of becoming jaded. They have had a surfeit of delights and, in theory, it becomes harder to motivate them. But if one may turn again to the soccer analogy, Liverpool have never found problems in motivating their players after years of unending glory. A first-team squad of excellence means that each player has to keep on top of form and fitness if he is to hold his place. No one is sacrosanct. The Middlesex system was very similar.

By the beginning of the 1985 season they had won eight trophies in nine years. During the season, five Middlesex players — Gatting, Cowans, Downton, Edmonds and Emburey — appeared in the

Test series against Australia. Three of them played in six Tests, Edmonds in five. Despite this, Middlesex were able to call upon 13 capped players, all of whom had helped to win the Championship in 1982. This nucleus was supplemented by some exciting young talent in Carr, Rose, Miller, Metson and Brown. So abundant was the talent at Lord's that Maru had moved to Hampshire as had Kevan James, and Metson and Rose were both to go elsewhere in their desire for a regular first-team place.

The side reached the semi-final of the Benson and Hedges Cup where they were beaten by Essex, who also knocked them out of the NatWest Bank Trophy, but there was still the Championship. Hampshire and Gloucestershire had been early pacemakers but Middlesex climbed above them both and began their last game one point ahead of Hampshire.

The Middlesex recipe for success was simple but effective. They scored runs quickly, so that their bowlers would have as much time as possible in which to bowl out the opposition. This was the policy that was adopted in the last match of the season, at Edgbaston.

Warwickshire batted first and began soundly, but Neil Williams accounted for both openers and Emburey destroyed the middle order so that they were all out for 187. Middlesex were batting by late afternoon on the first day, and Slack and Brown gave them a good start. This was followed by Gatting's assault on the bowling and some violent hitting from Emburey, a batsman who drives bowlers to despair with his unorthodoxy. Middlesex led by 258 runs with a day remaining.

Robin Dyer and Andy Lloyd again began confidently for Warwickshire, but Phil Edmonds started to extract turn and bowled Dyer. John Emburey joined him in the attack and Warwickshire were hurried to defeat. Middlesex were Champions for the fifth time in ten years.

In 1986, Gatting became captain of England and this factor, and others like Test calls and injuries, began to take its toll. The most serious of the injuries forced Barlow, a wonderful club man, to retire, and Neil Williams was severely handicapped and played little cricket. There were compensations, like the appearance of Angus Fraser, a most promising fast bowler, but Middlesex were never in the Championship race. Despite that, for the fifth year in succession, they lifted a trophy.

In the Benson and Hedges Cup, they swept through their zonal matches with a 100-per-cent record, brushed aside Sussex and Nottinghamshire with ease and faced Kent in a Lord's Final for the second time in three years.

The Final was played for the most part in subdued light and ended in rain. Put in to bat in overcast conditions, Middlesex batted with uncharacteristic hesitancy. They were encouraged by Kent's generosity in bowling a plethora of wides and no-balls. In all, Kent conceded the equivalent of two and a half extra overs, unforgivable in limited-over cricket and total suicide in the context of this match.

It was Clive Radley who resurrected the Middlesex innings when it threatened to flounder. As ever, he dictated the length at which he would play the ball, constantly moving down the wicket. When he was brilliantly run out for 54, he had taken Middlesex towards their final score of 199 for 7.

Middlesex bowled straighter and tighter than Kent had done, and the batsmen struggled painfully until Graham Cowdrey and Richard Ellison added 69 in 12 overs for the sixth wicket. With rain falling heavily, Kent arrived at the last two overs of their innings requiring 19 to win. This was reduced to 14 runs from the last over.

Simon Hughes was the bowler and Steve Marsh the batsman. Marsh missed the first ball, took two off the second and pulled the third high into the Grandstand for six. Hughes almost yorked Marsh with his fourth ball, and the batsmen could only scramble a single from the fifth. Needing to hit the last ball for six, Dilley clouted to square-leg, but the shot earned him only two and Middlesex had won their tenth trophy in 11 seasons.

It seemed that there the relentless pursuit of trophies which had begun under Mike Brearley's leadership must cease. Middlesex won nothing and never looked like winning anything in 1987. Williams was slow to regain fitness, and Cowans was recovering from an operation. Radley decided he would retire at the end of the year, and Wayne Daniel's bowling was waning in pace and penetration. At the end of the 1987 season, Phil Edmonds could not come to agreement over a new contract with the county and retired from first-class cricket.

There were encouraging signs in the advancement of Angus Fraser, despite injury, and in the advent of Phil Tufnell, a slow left-arm bowler who promised to be an adequate replacement for Edmonds, but there was a sense that the great era in Middlesex

Phil Edmonds. He and Emburey formed the most lethal spin combination in England in the late 1970s and early 1980s.

cricket was at a close and that patience would be needed over a period of rebuilding.

To the astonishment of all, including themselves, the period of patience was not needed. In 1988, Middlesex were back in the winner's enclosure. They improved their position in the County Championship, were quarter-finalists in the Benson and Hedges Cup, led the Sunday League for much of the season before finishing fourth to qualify for the new Refuge Assurance Cup and won the NatWest Bank Trophy by comfortably beating Worcestershire towards the end of the season.

Fraser confirmed all that had been hoped for him and was on the verge of the England side. There was a revival for Cowans, and Ramprakash, in particular, and Roseberry suggested that a new generation of exciting batsmen had arrived. Indeed, Mark Ramprakash took the individual award in the NatWest Bank Trophy Final.

Fraser and Hughes had bowled splendidly to restrict Worcestershire to 161 for nine in their 60 overs, but Middlesex lost Carr, Needham, Gatting and Slack for 25, and Butcher ran himself out at 64. Ramprakash then played a most stylish and mature innings of 56, which made victory a formality. He was only two days away from his 19th birthday.

The appetite for success was as keen as ever and when Middlesex failed to take a trophy in 1989, there was acute disappointment. Few other counties would have been disappointed with a season which saw the side finish third in the County Championship, contest the Refuge Assurance Sunday League until the end of the season and fail to hold on to the NatWest Bank Trophy only because they were beaten by Warwickshire in the last over.

These achievements were all the more remarkable in that the county had suffered several traumas, not the least of which was the tragic death of batsman Wilf Slack during the close season.

Desmond Haynes had replaced Wayne Daniel as the overseas player and immediately proved himself to be a great team man and an asset to the club on and off the field. Ramprakash, Roseberry and Tufnell continued to develop. Fraser was quickly establishing his place as England's leading strike bowler and there was some excellent pace bowling by Ricardo Ellcock, who had been acquired from Worcestershire.

It had not been a Middlesex policy to join the 'transfer' market which now takes at the end of every cricket season, but Ellcock, although prone to injury, proved a good acquisition. He was selected for the England party to tour West Indies, but he broke down on arrival in the Caribbean and took no part in the tour, nor in the England season of 1990.

This did not stop Middlesex from reasserting themselves as the leading county in England. They won the County Championship and the Refuge Assurance Cup, having led the Sunday League for much of the season, and they were semi-finalists in the NatWest Bank Trophy. Gatting and Emburey were regularly available as they had debarred themselves from Test cricket by going to South Africa, and the side had strength in depth, balance and a happy blend of youth and experience.

Roseberry was promoted to open the innings with Haynes and this proved to be a most fruitful partnership. Gatting, who has never quite captured the public imagination in the same way that Gower and Gooch have done, continued to bludgeon, carve and destroy attacks at number three and remained one of the most prolific scorers in the history of county cricket. Ramprakash continued to excite with the exquisiteness of his stroke play at number four, and at number five Keith Brown had taken on the mantle of Clive Radley, a batsman to whom one looked in any crisis. Downton and Emburey still defied and broke bowlers' hearts. Fraser and Williams both played for England and with Cowans, Emburey and Tufnell constituted the best balanced and most penetrative attack in the country. They were magnificently supported in the field, with Brown and Roseberry exciting close catchers. In Gatting's words, success was all based on team work.

There appears to be no logical reason why the Middlesex era of success should cease. They captured 13 trophies in the period between 1976 and 1990. It is a formidable record and one which gives them the right to assert that they have been the outstanding side of modern times. There are those who would challenge this assertion, and that challenge would come most vehemently from Middlesex's near-neighbours and rivals — Essex.

Vintage Essex

Cinderella Arrives At The Ball

ON 17 September,1989, Essex beat Nottinghamshire by five runs in the Final of the Refuge Assurance Cup at Edgbaston. This was the second year of the competition, a knock-out tournament between the top four teams in the Refuge Assurance League. In the inaugural year, the Cup had been won by Lancashire who, thereby, became the first county to win all five competitions. Essex equalled that feat in 1989, but, astonishingly, they had won all five trophies within the space of ten years. and during that period they had won more matches in all competitions than any other county. It was triumph tinged with romance and achieved after years of considerable agony and disappointment.

Formed in 1876, Essex County Cricket Club could boast some great players in the course of their first century, men like J.W.H.T.Douglas, Percy Perrin, Morris Nichols, Ken Farnes, Tom Pearce, Trevor Bailey, Jack O'Connor and Doug Insole, but they had won nothing. For 80 years they had to be content with third place in 1898 as their best performance in the County Championship.

The club had had its traumas and, for financial reasons, had come close to extinction on several occasions. The most disturbing crisis in recent times came in 1966, when Trevor Bailey retired. Brian Taylor was named as his successor, which caused the England all-rounder, Barry Knight, to move to Leicestershire. Other retirements followed and an examination of the club's financial state revealed a need for ruthless economies. Second XI cricket was virtually abandoned and Brian Taylor was asked to operate with a playing staff of 13, which included the captain himself.

Brian Taylor was neither a great cricketer nor a great tactician, but he was very much what Essex needed to lead them in this difficult period. He was a strong diciplinarian, a fitness fanatic and he had an awareness of what his side was capable of doing. As Mike Denness had realised at Kent, the one-day competitions offered teams another dimension and demanded particular skills, skills which Taylor believed were possessed by Essex.

The small playing staff had its benefits as well as its disadvantages. First, as John Lever was to point out, he and others had an intense period of training in first-class cricket itself. He bowled day in and day out and had to learn how to bowl because there was nobody to replace him. Second, the small staff engendered a feeling of togetherness, a passionate team spirit between young men who virtually grew up together. This spirit was to play a significant part in the golden age that was to come. Essex's appetite for victory was to be sharper than most.

The first year of the John Player League, 1969, saw them finish third, and in the second year they were fourth. In 1971, they were cruelly beaten into second place. They finished their programme on 29 August and were four points ahead of their nearest rivals. The following Sunday, Worcestershire beat Warwickshire inside 18 overs at Dudley, finished level on points with Essex and took the title with a run-rate that was 0.003 faster than that of Essex.

There were similar narrow and emotional failures in the 60-over competition and in the Benson and Hedges Cup, and when Brian Taylor stood down in 1974, Essex were still without a trophy. There had been some astute team-building, however, and if Essex had been forced to economise, they had husbanded their limited wealth with wisdom. They signed three players, Hardie from Scotland, Smith, a wicketkeeper from Yorkshire, and Cooke from Cheshire, who was the only one of the three not to establish himself permanently in the side. They were forced, too, to sign a replacement for Keith Boyce, a magnificent West Indian all-rounder who had been forced to end his career through injury. And to take the place of Australian opening batsman Bruce Francis, they acquired the services of a South African batsman Ken McEwan, of whom little was known. In 1977, Mike Denness, the former Kent and England captain, arrived on a three-year contract and a jigsaw puzzle was complete. Yet still the trophies did not come.

In 1977, Essex went to Scarborough to meet Yorkshire in the penultimate match in the John Player Sunday League. They lost in the last over after they had looked to be certain winners for most of the match. The following week they beat Worcestershire at Chelmsford, but Leicestershire also won. Both counties had finished on 52 points, but Leicestershire took the title with more victories. This was the second year in succession that Essex had been runners-up in the League. They surrendered the title to Kent in 1976 with a run-rate that was 0.427 below the winners in a year when five counties finished level on points.

The season of 1978 was more successful and more frustrating than ever before. Essex suffered only one defeat in the County Championship, by Surrey at The Oval, and they chased Kent to the end of the season, but they finished nine points behind in the second place. This was the highest that they had achieved in their history, but it still left them without a trophy.

The agony of the Gillette Cup was even greater. Essex reached the semi-final of the 60-over competition for the first time in their history and were drawn against Somerset at Taunton. Somerset made 287, with Viv Richards hitting 116. In reply, Gooch, who batted 30 overs for 61, McEwan and, in particular, Fletcher, gave Essex a sound platform for a challenge. Fletcher and Pont added 80 in 12 overs and Essex needed 42 from five overs.

Ian Botham ran out Pont and caught and bowled Fletcher in successive overs, and the last over arrived with 12 needed and two wickets standing. Neil Smith hit a single, Ray East edged a boundary and was then bowled by Colin Dredge. Dredge conceded a no-ball which, in the stage of high excitement which now existed, brought an overthrow and a total of three. Lever faced the last ball with three needed for an Essex victory. He turned the ball to the leg-side boundary, where Rose failed to gather cleanly, but he recovered and his throw just beat Neil Smith's dive so that Essex were all out for 287 and had lost the match by virtue of having lost more wickets than Somerset.

The chairman's reports in the *Essex Yearbook* had become more plaintive each year. 'Enterprising cricket, unstinting effort, superb fielding, outstanding individual performances, promising young players — nothing to show for it all. Nothing, that is, if the winning of a competition — any competition — is the overriding consideration in the support of a side which, year in year out, provides entertainment unsurpassed by any other county.'

The point was, of course, that, by 1979, winning a competition had become the overriding consideration in supporting a side for all but the faithful core of members. For Essex, and for Somerset, the drought was to be over in 1979. If we first consider the attitude of Somerset, we will see how important winning had now become.

Somerset had never finished higher than third in the County Championship, and, having beaten Essex in that momentous semi-final of the Gillette Cup in 1978, they lost the Final to Sussex. By the start of the 1979 season, Essex and Somerset were the only two first-class counties not to have won any of the four competitions. Somerset possessed an exciting side, and the powerful hitting of Richards and Botham, in particular, drew large crowds in expectation.

On 24 May 1979, Somerset went to Worcester for their final zonal match in the Benson and Hedges Cup. In Somerset's group were Gloucestershire, who had finished their programme and were out of the reckoning, Glamorgan, Worcestershire and Minor Counties (South). Somerset had won their first three matches, and Worcestershire and Glamorgan had won two each. Glamorgan's last fixture was against Minor Counties (South) and they were expected to win with ease. This meant that if Worcestershire beat Somerset, three counties would finish level with nine points each, and the two places for the quarter-finals would be decided on bowlers' striking rate. In this area, Somerset were ahead of their rivals.

Batting first against Worcestershire, Somerset opened with skipper Brian Rose and Peter Denning. The first over was bowled by the West Indian paceman, Vanburn Holder, and it produced one run, a no-ball. At the end of the over Rose declared. There was the customary ten-minute interval, after which Worcestershire began their innings. It lasted for ten balls, and Glenn Turner scored the two runs needed for victory. The whole match had lasted for under 20 minutes. Rose had deliberately forfeited the game, but, in doing so, he had preserved his side's superior strike rate in bowling and assured them of a place in the quarter-finals. As it transpired, Somerset were disqualifed from the competition for having violated the spirit, although not the rules, of the game.

In answer to the angry outcry that greeted his action at Worcester, Rose stated that his sole concern was that Somerset should win a trophy and that he had intended to take every means within the laws of the game to bring that about. One cannot think that Rose took his action without first consulting committee members and other officers of the club. Winning had become that important.

Ironically, Somerset broke their duck in 1979 by winning the

Gillette Cup and, the following day, the John Player League, a competition in which they, like Essex, had had their share of agonies and twice been denied although they had the same number of points as the winners. In 1981 and 1982, they won the Benson and Hedges Cup, and they took the Gillette Cup in 1983, but after that things began to fall apart.

They were never a great side, but for a few years they were a vastly entertaining one. They lacked balance and variety in attack and, in spite of the presence of the admirable Denning and Rose, they were too temperamentally reliant on the explosions of Viv Richards and Ian Botham. Joel Garner was a potent striking force, and the genial Vic Marks was an excellent off-break bowler, particularly effective in the one-day game, but there was an undercurrent of instability in the side. Perhaps that was one of the factors that made them exciting and entertaining to watch. The years of glory were short, for Essex, on the other hand, the period of success has lasted considerably longer.

One of the principle qualities of the 1979 Essex side was its hunger. Fletcher, Ray East, Lever, Acfield and Turner had all been with the side in those lean years of the late 1960s. Gooch, McEwan, Hardie, Pont and Smith had been trained under Taylor and had shared the years of frustration with the older players. Denness and Phillip were the comparative newcomers, but each brought a component that Essex cricket had lacked.

Norbert Phillip never quite excited the imagination as Keith Boyce had done, but, for four or five years, he provided the pace that the Essex attack had lacked, was to be the ideal new-ball partner for John Lever and played some invaluably ferocious innings. Mike Denness brought a less tangible quality. He had been a member of a highly successful team. He was used to winning, and he brought an experience of winning to a side whose greatest enemy was a lack of self-belief and self-confidence.

At the beginning of the 1979 season, Fletcher had decided that Alan Lilley would open with Gooch in the one-day matches and Mike Denness would play in the Championship games, but Lilley, a promising youngster, had shown a vulnerability outside the off stump which knowing bowlers had been quick to exploit, and Denness took over for the Benson and Hedges Cup Final.

By the time that they reached the Benson and Hedges Final, Essex were already well ahead in the County Championship. Rain had interfered with the early matches of the season, but there had

Keith Fletcher, astute captain and master tactician.

been some significant achievements. In the opening county game, Stuart Turner had hit a whirlwind century and Essex had taken six points to Kent's five. This may appear a trivial matter, but Kent had so long been the Essex bogey side that to finish a point ahead of them and lead them on the first innings was a considerable boost to morale.

There was a draw at Lord's, a crushing win at Chesterfield and then a devastating performance in a match at Ilford which was reduced to one day by rain. Glamorgan made 184 for seven declared in 74 overs, and Essex hit off the runs in under 28 overs. Gooch (93) and McEwan (67) shared an unbroken second-wicket stand of 141. In the second match of Ilford week, Lancashire were beaten by an innings in two days. McEwan hit 88 and Brian Hardie scored an unbeaten century.

How invaluable Brian Hardie was to Essex at this time, and over the next ten years, cannot be over-estimated. He had come down from Scotland in 1973 and on the strength of one innings had gained an unjustified reputation of being a slow scorer, a dour batsman. He was initially, and latterly, used as an opener, but he provided the solidity and the adaptability that Essex had desperately needed at number five, the concrete in the middle. Mike Brearley had said at Westcliff in the early 1970s that if Essex could find more substance at number five, they would be a fine side. Hardie provided that substance. He was a somewhat unorthodox player, resolutely determined to push forward, head held high, and mingled some glorious cover drives with some slices to third man that all seemed an integral part of his game. He was, above all, a most joyful cricketer and the best short-leg of his generation.

The victory over Lancashire came at the beginning of June. It was a match in which John Lever took nine wickets, and he followed this with 13 against Leicestershire and 13 against Warwickshire. He was to take 53 wickets in the month at the end of which Essex led the County Championship by the huge margin of 67 points.

Lever's contribution to Essex cricket was immense. A fast-medium pace left-arm bowler with the most economic and smoothest of actions, Lever could, and often would, bowl all day. His appetite for the game and for work was insatiable. He played in 21 Test matches, far fewer than he should have done, and took 73 wickets at a cost far cheaper than more vaunted contemporaries.

The rock on which the Essex attack was founded — John Lever.

More important, whereas people like Willis and Snow had found it hard to motivate themselves at county level and had been essentially big-occasion men, Lever was unstinting in effort and achievement day after day on the county circuit. It was no surprise that he was, in the eyes of his fellow professionals, the model professional.

Lever did not need incentives, but he was stung into even greater action in 1979 by the England selectors' incomprehensible decision to omit him from the World Cup squad, a decision which they were to regret most bitterly when it came to the Final and Willis' non-availability. The competition occupied most of June, so that when he might have been taking wickets for England Lever was bowling Essex to an unassailable lead in the Championship.

What was equally important for Essex was that the side was well balanced. Ray East, the team's court jester, was an excellent slow left-arm bowler with a lovely looping flight and with the character to enliven any cricket match. David Acfield was a fine off-spinner who, like East, came very close to international honours. Acfield had a dry wit and was a great contributor to a side whose cricket was essentially fun.

In the all-rounder category, as well as Norbert Phillip, there was Keith Pont, a hard-hitting batsman and useful medium-pace bowler, and Stuart Turner. Pont took the individual award when Essex beat Yorkshire in the semi-final of the Benson and Hedges Cup and played some fine aggressive innings over the years without ever quite fulfilling the promise that had been expected. Turner produced more than could have been expected.

He bowled medium-fast, hit hard and fielded anywhere. He scored quick runs, bowled accurately and with hostility and could produce some inspiring moments. He played the game to a standard above his innate ability, and he stood for all that is good in county cricket. In the one-day game he was to become a giant. In the John Player League alone, he scored over 3,000 runs and took more than 300 wickets, the only cricketer to accomplish this feat in the League. He held 82 catches and batted in every position from one to ten. Les Hatton, author of the history of the John Player League, named him as the outstanding cricketer of the competition. Stuart Turner was the essential bread and butter player on whom county success is so indisputably founded.

When Essex arrived at Lord's for the Benson and Hedges Cup Final, the County Championship was virtually won already

An all-rounder who bristled with endeavour and was the embodiment of the Essex spirit — Stuart Turner.

although they did not know that at the time. Essex's opponents at Lord's were Surrey, rich in tradition and in past success. Roger Knight won the toss, asked Essex to bat first, and Gooch and Denness were greeted with a roar of welcome the like of which had never been heard at Lord's before. Cinderella had at last arrived at the ball.

Denness and Gooch put on 48 stylish runs for the first wicket, and Gooch and McEwan then shared a stand of 124. In the beauty and the power of its execution it was batting to stir the heart. Fletcher hit a stunning 34 off 30 balls, a glorious miniature, and Gooch was finally out for 120 in the 53rd over. He had hit three sixes and 11 fours in a mighty innings. Essex made 296 for six in their 55 overs, a record for a Benson and Hedges Final. Howarth and Knight batted bravely in reply, but Surrey were all out for 255. Essex had won the first trophy in their history.

The second, the County Championship, was achieved a few weeks later, and they had, in fact, accumulated enough points to take the Championship before the end of July.

Their team contained two batsmen of world class, a luxury in any county side, Graham Gooch and Ken McEwan. McEwan, the South African was a gentle, self-effacing man whose modesty never allowed him to realise quite how great a batsman he was. He batted like the ancients, upright, classical, majestic in movement. There was no lovelier sight in cricket in the 1980s than Ken McEwan at the crease.

By 1979, Graham Gooch, just rehabilitated in the England side, was quickly becoming an international batsman of stature. A batsman of immense power, he seemed capable of destroying any attack with a lazy disdain. Within two years he was to become the most exciting batsman in English cricket and he was to remain at the top for the rest of the decade, although his batting was to change in character. Like Lever, Gooch's special strength was his willingness and ability to give as much at county level as he gave at international level, even when he had become a regular member of the England side. It has not been the same with all of his contemporaries.

However prolific his scoring at county level, Gooch's appearances for Essex were limited by the calls of the national selectors, and when the title was won in 1979 he was able to play in only ten of the 21 Championship matches. This underlines the debt that was owed to the bread and butter men and the less acclaimed batsmen like Brian Hardie who hit 1,111 runs, average 42.73, and topped the Championship averages.

Keith Fletcher, too, his Test career behind him, or so it was thought at the time, scored consistently and always hit runs when needed. If he was no longer the great batsman he had been, he was still a most capable one and his captaincy earned the highest praise and, eventually, briefly, the leadership of England. He knew the county circuit intimately and had grown up with Essex and most of the players whom he now led. He was a shrewd tactician, firm, although not as strong a disciplinarian as Taylor had been, and his knowledge and leadership were deeply respected by his men. He was not a Surridge, Sellers or Brearley, men whom one feels could have led any side, but essentially a county captain of the highest order, whose particular moment was to lead Essex in the 1980s.

The importance of Essex's twin triumphs in 1979 was that a sound barrier had been broken, a four-minute mile had been run. What has been done once can be done again.

In 1980, Essex were narrowly beaten in the Benson and Hedges Cup Final and even more narrowly beaten in the quarter-final of the Gillette Cup, a season that would have been greeted with joy ten years earlier, but was now an anti-climax.

The next year they were back on the trophy trail. There was an early exit from the Benson and Hedges Cup, but Essex challenged strongly in the other three competitions. Their challenge for the County Championship faded in August, but they won a fine victory over Sussex in the quarter-final of the NatWest Bank Trophy at Hove and went to the top of the John Player League on 19 July.

The semi-final of the NatWest Bank Trophy at Derby spread into a second day, due to bad light, and the game was decided on the final ball when Derbyshire needed one run to win. Newman was only able to push forward at Norbert Phillip's good length delivery, and the bowler gathered the ball on his follow-through. A gentle lob to Hardie, who had taken up position by the bowler's wicket, would have won the game, but Phillip threw wildly and Derbyshire won the match.

Villain at Derby, Phillip was the hero a few weeks later at The Oval. He hit five sixes and eight fours in an innings of 80 not out, 34 of his runs coming out of the 37 scored in the last two overs. The innings put the game out of Surrey's reach and Essex were the winners of the John Player League. For a team that had been runners-up on three occasions in the 1970s, it was a particularly gratifying win.

The side had begun to show some gradual changes. Neil Smith, who had been one of the best wicketkeepers in the country for two seasons, maintaining form day in and day out, now lost form and was replaced by the ebullient David East. Derek Pringle, Cambridge University and England, an all-rounder of immense potential, was now a regular in the side, and pace bowler Neil Foster had overcome several setbacks to take over from Norbert Phillip as the joint spearhead of the Essex attack.

In 1983, Essex were Benson and Hedges Cup Finalists for the third time in five years. They lost an extraordinary and thrilling Final to Middlesex in circumstances which we have already described. This defeat ended an unhappy week for them when their temperament was called into question, for not only had they snatched defeat from the jaws of victory against Middlesex, they had also done the same thing against Kent in the second round of the NatWest Bank Trophy three days earlier. They were also trailing in the Championship race, but some positive cricket allowed them to overtake Middlesex and win the title by a margin of 16 points.

They were fortunate in that Gooch and Lever were available for the whole of the season, having been banned from Test cricket following their sojourn in South Africa, and Neil Foster was the only Essex player upon whom the selectors called. When one considers that by 1981 the demands of international cricket had become so great that Gooch was able to play in only nine of his county's Championship matches, the domestic advantages of having a player banned from Test cricket are apparent.

Gooch did not reach his best form until late in the 1983 season, but this was at the very time when Esex made their strongest challenge. McEwan was in magnificent form and became the first Essex batsman for 28 years to score 2,000 runs in the Championship. Fletcher, too, batted well while Lever (98 wickets) and Phillips (68) continued as the spearheads of the attack.

There was a sense of solidity about the Essex side, a happy blend of youth and experience which was well led. There was, too, good provision for the future and a continuance of success with replacements for older players being intelligently blooded. By 1984, two young batsmen, Prichard and Gladwin, had established themselves in the side. Introducing young men into a winning side is far easier than bringing them into losing one, and both batsmen were encouraged and able to play their shots from the beginning of their careers. Gladwin's span of success, sadly, was to last for a comparatively short period, but there was a time in the mid-1980s when he was close to being an England opener.

In 1984, Essex won the John Player League for the second time. They were assured of the title with two weeks of the season still remaining, and they finished eight points ahead of Nottinghamshire and Sussex. On 11 September, they became the first county to win both the Championship and the Sunday League in the same season.

The season reached a most exciting climax. At Old Trafford, Essex beat Lancashire inside two days. Paul Prichard, the only uncapped player in the side, hit a century as did Ken McEwan, whose 100 was within two minutes of being the fastest of the season. In the closing stages of their innings, Essex scored at eight runs an over. Essex's win meant that they were now four points ahead of Nottinghamshire, who were still engaged in a struggle with Somerset at Taunton. If Nottinghamshire won this match, they would take the title. Botham set the visitors a target of 297 in what transpired to be 60 overs. Clive Rice played a magnificent innings of 98, and Hadlee and French maintained the momentum, but 36 were needed from the last three overs. Bore hit mightily and 14 were needed from the last over. He hit 4, 4, 2 before being caught on the straight boundary by substitute Richard Ollis. Somerset had won by three runs, and Essex had held on to their title, the first county to do this outright for 16 years.

Gooch scored more runs in the season than any Essex player had done before, and Lever took 106 Championship wickets alone. Ray East had retired, and Essex's one concern regarding future success appeared to be in the spin bowling department.

To fill the gap left by East's departure, Essex signed the slow left-arm bowler, John Childs, who had not been retained by Gloucestershire, for whom he had played for nine years. Childs was far from being an immediate success, taking only three Championship wickets for 377 runs in 1985, but his time was to come.

In a wet summer, with Gooch and Foster missing half the Championship matches because of Test calls, Essex still powered their way to unprecedented success in 1985. In mid-July, with only one win to their credit, they were bottom of the Championship, but they fought their way back with customary tenacity to finish fourth. They reached the Final of the Benson and Hedges Cup, but, without the injured Fletcher, they lost to Leicestershire with a rather lack-lustre performance. They had, however, reached the NatWest Bank Trophy Final for the first time, and on the last Sunday of the season they retained their John Player League title with an exciting win over Yorkshire.

Nottinghamshire were Essex's opponents in the NatWest Final. It was a marvellous match which began with Gooch and Hardie establishing a record for a Lord's Final with a partnership of 202. Hardie hit 110 off 149 balls and played what was probably the best innings of his career. When Nottinghamshire threatened to restrict Essex, McEwan, in his last season in county cricket, and Pringle added 56 from the last four overs. Broad and Robinson gave Nottinghamshire a good start, but there seemed little hope of them reaching the target of 281.

The last over arrived with Derek Randall facing Derek Pringle and 18 needed for victory. Randall took 16 off the first five deliveries, but he was caught at mid-wicket off the last and Essex had won by one run. In seven years, they had captured eight titles, and Keith Fletcher had led them to success in all four competitions, an unique and remarkable record among county captains.

Fletcher decided to hand over the captaincy to Graham Gooch at the end of the 1985 season when it was also announced that Allan Border would be the overseas player to replace Ken McEwan. What was more significant was that Essex now had such strength in depth that they were able to overcome difficulties that would have left other counties struggling. In 1986, the England selectors often deprived them of two or three players, and both Hardie and Fletcher suffered injuries, but Essex finished second in the John Player League and won the County Championship for the third time in four years. John Stephenson and Don Topley were younger players to make their mark, but it was Foster, who took 100 Championship wickets, Border, who did not play in the last month of the season, and Childs, who really took the honours. The Championship was won in an astonishing manner in late August with improbable victories over Somerset at Taunton and Kent at Folkestone. Essex trailed by 71 runs on the first innings at Taunton, but Gooch was eventually able to set Somerset a target of 273

One of the most glorious sights in cricket in the late 1970s and early 1980s, the South African batsman Ken McEwan, an integral part of the Essex success.

in 68 overs. With 18 overs remaining, the home side needed only 20 runs to win and had five wickets standing, but those five wickets fell to Childs and Pringle in just over nine overs for ten runs, and Essex won by nine runs.

At Folkestone, Kent were asked to make 184 in 47 overs and reached tea with 47 without loss. In the final session of the match, they lost all ten wickets, seven of them to Childs, for 113 runs, and Essex had again won an improbable victory by 23 runs.

They needed only four points now to make certain of the Championship, and these were claimed in Nottinghamshire's first innings at Trent Bridge. A string of injuries and Test calls took their toll at Essex in 1987, when they had their worst season of the decade, and it was Nottinghamshire who took both the County Championship and the NatWest Bank Trophy. Nottinghamshire enjoyed one of the best periods in their history in the 1980s, winning the Championship twice, the NatWest Trophy and the Benson and Hedges Cup. They had a consistent and prolific opening pair in Robinson and Broad, arguably the best captain in county cricket in Clive Rice, an all-rounder of world class, and the great Richard Hadlee. With Hadlee in the side in 1981 and 1982, they finished first and fourth; without him in 1983, they were 14th.

Essex scrambled back into contention in 1988. Fletcher had taken over the captaincy again for two seasons, and he led the side to third place in the Championship and the semi-final of the Benson and Hedges Cup in 1988 before passing over to Gooch for a second time, this time for good as he announced his retirement from first-class cricket after leading Essex throughout their greatest days. He richly deserved the accolades that were showered upon him.

With Fletcher's retirement, Essex entered 1989 with only Gooch, Hardie, Lever and Lilley remaining from the vintage side of ten years earlier, yet so gradual had been the changes, so effective and subtle the planning that metamorphosis had been almost imperceptible. They remained the team that others were most eager to beat.

Essex won all four of their zonal matches in the Benson and Hedges Cup by substantial margins, and although the victory over Lancashire in the quarter-final was by three wickets, Essex had actually levelled the scores with only five wickets down. The semi-final at Taunton was a thrilling affair with John Lever bowling

Graham Gooch — power and authority.

Darren Foster with the last ball of the match to give Essex victory by four runs.

The early loss of Hardie in the Final against Nottinghamshire did not stop Essex reaching a creditable 243 for seven in their 55 overs. Alan Lilley made 95 not out, but there was a criticism that he had not succeeded in lifting the tempo over the closing overs as he might have done. Lever quickly dismissed Broad and Pollard, but Robinson and Johnson batted well, and Nottinghamshire always had their target in sight. An accurate last over by John Lever tilted the game in favour of Essex, and Hemmings faced the last ball needing to hit it for four to give his side victory. He did just that, square-driving the ball past Hardie, who scampered after it in vain pursuit. This was Essex's fourth defeat in as many Benson and Hedges finals in the space of ten years.

In the County Championship, Essex surged ahead of the field. They won eight and drew five of their first 13 matches, and when Kent were beaten inside two days in the first match of the Southend Festival, there seemed to be no possibility that they could be caught. Yorkshire were the next victims at Southchurch Park, and they, too, were beaten, but the pitch had been reported to the TCCB as being sub-standard, and Essex were deducted 25 points.

This penalty was received with a mixture of anger and frustration, for, having bowled out Yorkshire for 115 on the opening day, Essex had hit 248, which was two more runs than any side had scored in an innings at New Road, Worcester, so far during the season. Disappointed, they lost one and drew two of their next three games, and they eventually lost the Championship to Worcestershire by a margin of six points although the comparative records of the two counties were: Worcestershire P22, Won 12, Lost 3, Drawn 7; Essex P22, Won 13, Lost 2, Drawn 7.

Worcestershire had 127 bonus points; Essex 130. None close to the game could have been happy with what had happened.

There was to be some consolation. Essex were never far away from the top of the Sunday League, now sponsored by Refuge Assurance, and finished in third place with the same number of points as Worcestershire. This meant that they qualified for the Refuge Assurance Cup, which had been initiated the previous season. There was great satisfaction in overwhelming Worcestershire in the semi-final at New Road, and equal satisfaction in gaining revenge over Nottinghamshire by winning the Final by five runs. Every title that cricket has to offer had been won by Essex within the space of 11 years. They could justifiably claim to be the team of the 1980s and to take their place alongside the outstanding county sides in history.

Had they beaten Kent at Chelmsford in the penultimate match of the 1990 season, they might well have won the Championship for the fifth time, but, in truth, they did not look the side they had once been. Those lean years under Taylor had produced an appetite and a zest in the side of the early 1980s which were hard to reawaken in young men who had known only the fat times. Lever had retired, a good and faithful servant, and Hardie went at the end of 1990, so that only Gooch of the great side that had created cricket history for Essex remained.

There were plenty of talented young men — Hussain, Stephenson, Prichard, Shahid, Ilott — but whether they have the hunger or the discipline remains to be seen. One had the feeling that the curtain has come down on one of the great sides of the modern era.

Conclusion

WHO will rank with these giants of the past in the years to come? Worcestershire may well argue that they have already staked their claim by taking the Sunday League in 1987 and 1988 and the County Championship in 1988 and 1989. They have also been losing Finalists in the three other competitions during that period.

Shrewdly governed, Worcestershire have the strength in depth which Don Kenyon realised was so essential when he led the county to their first successes in the mid-1960s. They have a formidable array of seam bowling, although Radford, Dilley and Botham may well be past their best years, and they have a highly capable left-arm spinner in Illingworth. The batting has been so dominated by Graeme Hick, except on the occasions of the big Finals, that one wonders what will happen if he becomes an England regular as most predict he will. Will a thinness then appear as it surely must in the Essex bowling if Foster's wearing limbs at last give out?

One cannot see any side again having the total dominance that Surrey and Yorkshire had in their great years. The game has changed much. The stakes are high and the competition fiercer. And who was the greatest side among those we have touched upon? One can only conjecture.

Was it Hambledon with their lyrical fervour, and their ability to drink ale at twopence a pint which 'flared like turpentine'? Or was it the grand old Kent XI with Alfred Mynn, the farmer's boy of 20st? Or Shaw's Nottinghamshire? Or Shuter's Surrey?

Many would claim strongly for the Yorkshire of Lord Hawke. Created and nurtured by him, they set new standards of professionalism and attainment. Their descendants of the 1930s are still held in awe by those who saw them, and the record of Sellers' side was mightily impressive.

From across the Pennines there will be advocates for the Lancashire of Green and McDonald, but this was a side, surely, which, dominant though it was, relied heavily on one great fast bowler.

If one were forced to make a selection, to raise one county side above all others in the history of the game, then the final selection must rest between the Yorkshire of Hawke, the Yorkshire of Sellers and the Surrey of Surridge. There is a common denominator in the greatest of sides. They have all been led by men of exceptional qualities in the vision and discipline of captaincy. They have all been fielding sides of a standard that their rivals could not approach. They have all possessed character, both in the sense of richness or quaintness and in the sense of determination and resolve. They have all had an insatiable appetite for success and a common trust in and respect for each other. They have all had strength in depth and have been acutely conscious of the worth of the bread and butter men, the unsung heroes who are the backbone of the county game. They have had batsmen who could consistently score sufficent runs without necessarily aiming for the record books, and, above all, they have possessed attacks which were as sharp and penetrative as they were balanced. Catches may win matches, but bowlers win Championships.

Certainly Sellers' side of the 1930s had the majority of these qualities in abundance. *The Cricketer* described it as 'the strongest, most efficient and the best example of what an XI can be'. Sellers' team inherited the traditions of Yorkshire cricket which had been set down by Lord Hawke, and Hawke insisted on an eleven of good temper and good manners. Sellers' side had these things, and it had a unity of spirit and purpose, yet in the final analysis it is doubtful whether it was as strong as Hawke's great side, and it certainly did not have quite the balance in attack. And Hawke's side did not have the balance enjoyed by Surridge's sides of the 1950s.

It is doubtful if any county side has ever possessed the balance and quality that the Surrey attack of that period possessed. Alec Bedser was the supreme medium-pace bowler in the world. Peter Loader took the new ball for England, and Jim Laker and Tony Lock were the most feared spin pair of the age, one with off-breaks, the other slow left-arm. They were ably supported by Stuart

Surridge himself, and his aggressive medium pace, and the off-breaks of Eric Bedser. A half-century against that attack was a mighty achievement, for a batsman was offered no respite.

This is not to say that Lock was a better bowler than Wilfred Rhodes, nor that Loader was better than George Hirst. Quite obviously that was not the case, but there has never been a better balanced, more varied, more potent attack than the Surrey attack of the 1950s.

Surridge refuted the suggestion that his side's batting was not strong enough. 'We always got enough,' he said. 'Why score 400 when 250 will do?' In any case, a side that could offer good runs as far down as number ten and that possessed Peter May, the greatest batsman of his generation, and later Barrington and Stewart, had batting that was the envy of most. If one had to pick the finest of all county sides, one would go for the Surrey of Stuart Surridge.

There will be protests from the White Rose county, who will point out that not all of Surridge's side were born within the county boundaries. This is true, but they all qualified for Surrey by periods of residence under the existing rules of the day. For Surrey, like Yorkshire, resources came from within. There was no summer transfer market or overseas-player importation to facilitate the rectifying of weaknesses.

The great sides of Surrey and Yorkshire generated their power from within. Take them for all in all, we shall not look upon their like again.

The finest of all county sides? Surrey's 1955 team, in the middle of their remarkable run of Championship successes. Back row (left to right): R.C.E.Pratt, D.F.Cox, P.J.Loader, T.H.Clark, G.A.R.Lock, D.G.W.Fletcher, K.F.Barrington, M.D.Willett, B.Constable. Front row: M.J.Stewart, E.A.Bedser, A.J.McIntyre, P.B.H.May, W.S.Surridge (captain), A.V.Bedser, J.C.Laker, R.Swetman.

Some, though, would argue that Yorkshire's pre-war side was the best county team the game has seen. This line-up won the Championship in 1938, their sixth title triumph of the decade, and they were again victorious the following year. Back row (left to right): A.Hayhurst (masseur), W.Barber, E.P.Robinson, W.E.Bowes, T.F.Smailes, C.Turner, Mr Ringrose (scorer). Front row: A.Mitchell, H.Sutcliffe, A.B.Sellers (captain), M.Leyland, A.Wood. On ground: F.Wilkinson, H.Halliday. Len Hutton and Hedley Verity were on England duty.

Honou

Year	County Championship
1890	Surrey
1891	Surrey
1892	Surrey
1893	Yorkshire
1894	Surrey
1895	Surrey
1896	Yorkshire
1897	Lancashire
1898	Yorkshire
1899	Surrey
1900	Yorkshire
1901	Yorkshire
1902	Yorkshire
1903	Middlesex
1904	Lancashire
1905	Yorkshire
1906	Kent
1907	Nottinghamshire
1908	Yorkshire
1909	Kent
1910	Kent
1911	Warwickshire
1912	Yorkshire
1913	Kent
1914	Surrey
1919	Yorkshire
1920	Middlesex
1921	Middlesex
1922	Yorkshire
1923	Yorkshire
1924	Yorkshire
1925	Yorkshire
1926	Lancashire
1927	Lancashire
1928	Lancashire
1929	Nottinghamshire
1930	Lancashire
1931	Yorkshire
1932	Yorkshire
1933	Yorkshire
1934	Lancashire
1935	Yorkshire
1936	Derbyshire
1937	Yorkshire
1938	Yorkshire
1939	Yorkshire
1946	Yorkshire
1947	Middlesex
1948	Glamorgan
1949	Middlesex and Yorkshire
1950	Lancashire and Surrey
1951	Warwickshire

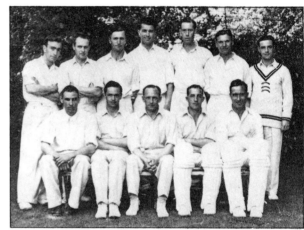

Middlesex, County Champions in 1947.

Sussex retain the Gillette Cup in 1964.

Former Lancashire player Barry Wood holds aloft the first NatWest Bank Trophy, won by Derbyshire in 1981.

Board

Year	County Championship	Gillette Cup/ NatWest Trophy	Sunday League	Benson and Hedges Cup
1952	Surrey			
1953	Surrey			
1954	Surrey			
1955	Surrey			
1956	Surrey			
1957	Surrey			
1958	Surrey			
1959	Yorkshire			
1960	Yorkshire			
1961	Hampshire			
1962	Yorkshire			
1963	Yorkshire	Sussex		
1964	Worcestershire	Sussex		
1965	Worcestershire	Yorkshire		
1966	Yorkshire	Warwickshire		
1967	Yorkshire	Kent		
1968	Yorkshire	Warwickshire		
1969	Glamorgan	Yorkshire	Lancashire	
1970	Kent	Lancashire	Lancashire	
1971	Surrey	Lancashire	Worcestershire	
1972	Warwickshire	Lancashire	Kent	Leicestershire
1973	Hampshire	Gloucestershire	Kent	Kent
1974	Worcestershire	Kent	Leicestershire	Surrey
1975	Leicestershire	Lancashire	Hampshire	Leicestershire
1976	Middlesex	Northamptonshire	Kent	Kent
1977	Middlesex and Kent	Middlesex	Leicestershire	Gloucestershire
1978	Kent	Sussex	Hampshire	Kent
1979	Essex	Somerset	Somerset	Essex
1980	Middlesex	Middlesex	Warwickshire	Northamptonshire
1981	Nottinghamshire	Derbyshire	Essex	Somerset
1982	Middlesex	Surrey	Sussex	Somerset
1983	Essex	Somerset	Yorkshire	Middlesex
1984	Essex	Middlesex	Essex	Lancashire
1985	Middlesex	Essex	Essex	Lancashire
1986	Essex	Sussex	Hampshire	Middlesex
1987	Nottinghamshire	Nottinghamshire	Worcestershire	Yorkshire
1988	Worcestershire	Middlesex	Worcestershire	Hampshire
1989	Worcestershire	Warwickshire	Lancashire	Nottinghamshire
1990	Middlesex	Lancashire	Derbyshire	Lancashire

The County Championship was sponsored by Schweppes from 1977 to 1983 and has been sponsored by Britannic Assurance since 1984.

From 1963 to 1980, the knock-out competition was sponsored by Gillette. Since 1981 it has been sponsored by National Westminster Bank. In 1963, it was a 65-overs competition. Since 1964 it has been 60-overs.

The Sunday League was sponsored by John Player from 1969 to 1986. It has been sponsored by Refuge Assurance since 1987.

The Refuge Assurance Cup was initiated in 1988. The top four sides in the Refuge Assurance Sunday League play in a knock-out competition, first versus fourth, second versus third, with the final at Edgbaston.

Refuge Assurance Cup Winners

1988	Lancashire	(third)
1989	Essex	(third)
1990	Middlesex	(third)

Essex and Lancashire are the only two counties to have won all five competitions. Kent and Yorkshire have won four of the competitions.

Methods By Which The County Championship Has Been Decided

1890 – 1894
Losses were deducted from wins, drawn games were ignored. The county with the highest number of points won the championship.

1895 – 1909
One point was awarded for a win and one point deducted for a loss. Drawn games were ignored. Championship was decided by the greatest proportionate number of points in finished games.

1895	P	W	L	D	Pts	%	
Surrey	26	17	4	5	13	61.90	(13/21)
Lancashire	21	14	4	3	10	55.55	(10/18)

1910
Percentage of wins to matches played.

1911 – 1914
Five points for a win; three points for first innings lead; one point for losing on first innings. Final placing determined by taking percentage of points obtained to number of points possible.

1919
Percentage of wins to matches played

1920 – 1923
Five points for a win; two points for first innings lead in drawn match. Order decided by percentage of points obtained to points possible.

1924 – 1926
Slight amendment in points to system in operation in the previous four seasons. Three points for first innings lead in drawn match; one point if behind on first innings in drawn match.

1927 – 1928
Eight points for a win. Five points to side leading on first innings in a drawn match; three points to side behind on first innings in a drawn match. Four points each for all other games in which

at least six hours play had been possible but no result achieved. Matches in which less than six hours had been played were discounted. Order decided by percentage of points gained to maximum points possible.

1929 – 1930
Each county to play 28 matches and championship decided on points won. Points awarded as for 1927 to 1928, but four points for tie on first innings or in the match or for abandoned games and games in which no first innings result was achieved.

1931 – 1932
Amendment to points system. 15 points for a win; seven and a half points each in a match finishing level. Five points for first innings lead in a drawn match; three points if behind on first innings in drawn match. Four points awarded as in 1929-1930.

1933 – 1937
The same points system was retained with the addition of ten points for the side winning on first innings and three points to their opponents in a match restricted to the third day only. Counties could now play as many matches as they wished, but had to play a minimum of 24. No county was allowed to play another county more than twice in a season. Order decided by percentage of points gained to points possible.

1938 – 1939
No county to play less than 24 matches. Order decided by dividing the number of points gained by the number of matches played. 12 points for a win. Six points to each side if scores ended level. Four points for first innings lead in match drawn or lost. Two points for a tie on first innings in match drawn or lost. Eight points for first innings lead in a match restricted to third day.

1946 – 1948
Each county to play 26 matches with points obtained determining order. 12 points for a win. Four points for first innings lead in match drawn or lost; two points if tie on first innings in game lost or drawn. Eight points for first innings lead in match restricted to third day. Six points for a match in which scores finish level.

1949
System as for 1946-48 except that in a match in which the scores

finished level, eight points were now awarded for the side which led on the first innings and four to the side which trailed on the first innings.

1950 – 1952
Number of matches played by each county increased to 28.

1953 – 1956
Scoring in a match in which the scored finished level reduced to six points each.

1957 – 1959
Bonus point system introduced by which the side that scored at the faster rate in the first innings should gain two points if they led on the first innings. If sides ended the season level on points, order would be decided by most wins and, secondly, number of bonus points.

1960 – 1962
Counties could play as many as 32 matches with final placing decided by average number of points obtained from each match.

1963 – 1966
Each county to play 28 matches with points obtained to determine order. Ten points for a win. Five points for a match in which scores finished level. Two points for first innings lead if match drawn or lost.

1967
Eight points for a win. Four points for a win on first innings (two each if tied). Two points for a draw in which both first innings have been completed. Two points for a side batting second in a drawn match where first innings has been completed.

1968 – 1969
Ten points for a win; five for a match in which scores finished level; five for a draw. In the first innings of the match, the following bonus points were introduced for achievements *within the first 85 overs of the innings:*
Batting: one point for each 25 runs above 150, ie 175 runs = one point; 200 runs = two points; etc.
Bowling: one point for each two wickets taken.
In a match which began with less than eight hours playing time

remaining, the winning side to score ten points in the one-innings match. In 1969, the number of matches to be played was reduced from 28 to 24, and in 1972, it was reduced to 20.

1973
Bonus points amended to include an additional point for a side scoring 75 runs within the first 25 overs and an additional point for 150 within the first 50 overs.

1974
First innings limited to 100 overs. Bonus points limited to:—
Batting: 150 runs, one point; 200 runs, two points, 250 runs, three points; 300 runs, four points.
Bowling: three wickets, one point; five wickets, two points; seven wickets, three points; nine wickets, four points.

1977
Counties to play 22 matches. Twelve points for a win.

1979
Six points for a tie, plus whatever bonus points scored. If scores equal in a drawn match, side batting second to score six points plus bonus points.

1981
Sixteen points for a win. Eight points each in a tied match plus bonus points. If scores level in a drawn match, side batting second to score eight points plus bonus points.

1983
The counties to play 24 matches each. There is, of course, no longer an over-limit to innings, but bonus points can only be won in the first 100 overs.

Bibliography

Wisden Cricketers' Almanack (various years).

Benson & Hedges Cricket Year (editions 1982 to 1990).

Pelham Cricket Year (editions 1979 to 1981).

The Young Cricketer's Tutor John Nyren.

Alfred Mynn and the Cricketers of His Time Alfred Morrah.

Cricket: A Weekly Record of the Game (various issues).

Recollections and Reminiscences Lord Hawke.

Yorkshire's 22 Championships E.L.Roberts.

The Cricketer, Wisden Cricket Monthly, Playfair Cricket Monthly, Cricket World and various newspapers.